AF598841

UNCOMMON

A STORY WITH A BAND IN IT

THE MAGNIFICENT 7

BY

TONY STALLARD

Acclaim Press
MORLEY, MISSOURI

P.O. Box 238
Morley, MO 63767
(573) 472-9800
www.acclaimpress.com

Book & Cover Design: Rodney Atchley

ISBN: 978-1-948901-72-7 / 1-948901-72-2
Library of Congress Control Number: 2020945669

First Printing 2020
Printed in the United States of America
10 9 8 7 6 5 4 3 2 1

This publication was produced using available information.
The publisher regrets it cannot assume responsibility for errors or omissions.

Contents

"Ability is what you're capable of doing.
Motivation determines what you do.
Attitude determines how well you do it."
–Raymond Chandler

Foreword

The fifties and sixties—what a wonderful time to grow up in Lexington! As with many Boomers, I can still remember hearing early rock and roll on the radio, on a juke box at the drugstore, on the many 45s that the older girl neighbors down the street had, and, of course, on Dick Clark's *American Bandstand.*

Music was undergoing a major transformation—from the swing music and big band sound after WWII to early rock and roll, folk, country, R&B, the British Invasion, Motown, and, later, the sounds of Woodstock, all the way to the end of the sixties.

Elvis, the Beatles, the Stones, Bob Dylan, and Lexington's own Marvin Gaye all filled the airwaves on radio stations, such as Louisville's WAKY and Lexington's WVLK and WLAP. We all knew the local DJs, such as Billy Love, Denny Mitchell, and Artie Kay.

Uncommon: A Story with a Band in It. The Magnificent 7, is a must-read for all those Boomers who grew up in the area listening to their transistor radios in bed, going to sock hops, watching Dick Clark, or experiencing the "Battle of the Bands." I remember going to the old Cabana Club in Lexington's Gardenside in my teens with great anticipation and excitement because my friends and I were going to watch the Magnificent 7 (Mag 7 as we called them) or other local bands perform their own music or versions of the great hits of the sixties. The Magnificent 7 were larger than life! They produced an energy on stage that many of us Lexington Boomers can still remember today. To me, these years were the golden age of music produced and performed in Lexington. One could even argue that this period was the coming-of-age for music nationally or even globally.

Tony Stallard, with his almost poetic style of storytelling, brings this rich golden age of music alive in his book. Not only does he share with us his own personal musical journey, he provides us with an amazing and detailed description of life in Lexington during this period. Through the lens of Tony's own recollections comes a writer's vivid description of life in Lexington, including its cast of colorful and talented characters in the music community.

We can see Lexington's transformation from a sleepy southern college town, dependent on tobacco and cattle, to a city coming of age with the relocation of IBM to Lexington, soon followed by other manufacturing industries. These changes, and an ever-expanding healthcare industry with the rapid growth of UK, all brought in an influx of folks from across the country.

Tony Stallard also shares with us his inner feelings relating to some of the events that defined both Lexington and the nation in the sixties—from JFK's assassination to the Vietnam War to the moon landing. Local color is abundant with his emphasis on the importance of the many unique, locally owned stores of a bygone era. Such gifts, unwrapped, are a kind, nostalgic walk down a once vibrant and bustling Main Street.

He sets us an easy pace with stories of Greek and other life on UK's campus, where the Magnificent 7 played so often, as well as reminisces about musicians of color that played their music at numerous music joints, bars, and clubs that flourished in the sixties. All this storytelling is done through the eyes of an accomplished musician who played for years in one of the most celebrated local bands when Lexington was coming of age. The regional importance of the Mag 7 is told simply and with humility.

After retiring from a long, productive career, Tony Stallard, a graduate of UK's College of Architecture and a largely self-taught musician, has, through this book, given us a precious nostalgic gift. One full of memories of the music we grew up on—all portrayed through the eyes of an original member of the storied Magnificent 7.

—Harvie Wilkinson, Lexington

Prologue

Tired shadows fell on a place in time, staying just past their own to say goodbye. Long ago had been long gone by the time I found the spirit of another at the crossroads of two streets. Yesterday had waited patient, like a player standing after hours alongside a '59 Cadillac. Turquoise, cream, and chrome—drenched in a neon shower, top down, waiting on idle and high on octane. A day dissolves until it's gone, its vapor too often seen in a mirror fading fast away into the night. The cosmic side of someone is not easily understood. Reconnecting with what once was *now* is coming face to face with time.

Tony, where have you been?

I like the scent of fresh-baked bread. Most all my life's a freehand sketch drawn by a fascination with qualities I find in the soul of ordinary objects, time, and place. The essence to be found in the humble strength of a turn-of-the-century wood-sided schoolhouse is priceless. In the sadness of long-forgotten colors peeling, the faint cry of the past screams to be appreciated.

Muted-colored faces, with cupped frail edges, turn like sails to catch the wind of time.

There's an uncommon sense of care living in stories told by creatively placed pieces of brick or stone masonry. Separate pieces held fast in the arms of mortar perfectly struck with a trowel long ago or simply let to softly weep along the edge. You come again, giving some of life's precious time away, an appointment with a tender moment. You touch an object—a sail, a piece of masonry, or a tree—the way you did the day you painted, placed, or planted it.

The note you left behind can be found again beneath the dust of ages past. You sense it in the marrow in the bones of truth that drew you back again. The ivory face of a piano's felt-clad wooden hammer, not having struck a wire and made it sing in far too long ago, is waiting.

It is a joy to play a song in the symphony of time.

The ribbon is blue as a sapphire on yesterday road. I stopped on the way, getting off now and then. Catching up has been delicious. Connecting with the unconditional nature of truth can shape who you are. Writing is a self-liberating experience. Somewhere, in the mystery of things in time is a random harvest called a story.

I have no words to describe inspiration.

After the Blue Moon

In the autumn of 2001, following the Mag 7's February reunion performance in Chevy Chase, I began to jam with Bob McCaw in his studio near Nicholasville. We'd play music for two or more hours, usually on Tuesday nights, two years running. Our mutual effort led to forming an ensemble of players.

I named the band Gratz Park.

The only instrument I had at home was a Hammond M3 organ, no Leslie, and my Fender Strat. from the Temptashuns years. Bobby let me use his studio keyboard. I had been away from music for the better part of thirty years. A family and, before retirement, a career in architecture left little time to get a few chops back.

Some became familiar once again.

Players who expressed interest in Gratz Park were well established in Lexington's music scene: Norman Higgins, drums, and Pat Dice, bass. With Bobby on lead vocals and guitar and me on keys, Gratz Park had its rhythm section. Bob and I had worked up eight ten-song sets. Eighty tunes of good stuff—improvised rhythm, soul, and blues, sprinkled with jazz now and then.

Our music and its influences seemed boundless.

Gary Nelson began occasional rehearsals with Bob and me and asked to put a horn section together, Gary on saxophone and no fewer than two others on baritone sax and trumpet, or trombone. We were having fun, and having Pat Dice and Gary near the end was sunshine on an otherwise trying effort. I got a keyboard, a Hammond B3 with a Leslie, and all was well with our souls and its music.

Sadly, Gratz Park was not to be.

Not long after, Norman Higgins lost his wife. I told Norman to take all the time he needed to grieve. Bobby became terminally ill and passed early in January 2005. Gary conducted Bob's service. We lost Norman

Higgins in 2007 and Gary in 2010, silencing a rhythm and horn section.

Earl Grigsby, an old friend from the house band at the Fireplace in the Chevy Chase days, thought a band with Bobby and Tony in it was a good road taken to mellow out in one's waning years. Earl, who played bass in the Charlie Daniels Band a spell in the seventies, passed away near Branson, Missouri, in 2013.

Such is life. Though sad as it is, the echo of Gratz Park leaves me to wonder what might've been.

I do miss all of them, and others still around.

INTRODUCTION

Yesterday would be a silent movie were not for its echoes. The wind playing the noise of winter's song on its way through a tree outside my window was cold. Naked branches danced with the moon; their leaves long gone. Silhouettes on a happy shade of winter. Stark shadows fast asleep on a bed of snow, shaped by undulations which defined it. Something, still as a memory on a soul, had come to call. February had just begun. I opened an old and tired box and broke the silence of thirty years.

The Magnificent 7 band was born at the sunset of one decade, another's dawn. From here to its end is a story beginning in the fifties. It is about all of us, the times we found ourselves in, and a band on its way to becoming all it could be—Uncommon.

A simple spirit can be found waiting at the crossroads of the ordinary in the quiet reaches of life's portrait. Music is frozen with the times in a black-and-white photograph, cleanly bordered in white ruffled edges. A still life of twenty-one years about to begin itself again at any moment in a single picture. Other bands and personalities memorable to the author during the sixties are celebrated in a mirror of the times in my hometown—Lexington, a place in Kentucky.

Garrison Keillor's live broadcast from the Surf Ballroom met the chill of the night like an unexpected wind on yesterday's face. Morning would not break for some in the fresh hours of February 3, 1959.

A randomly scattered harvest of shattered dreams lay silent, embraced by a cornfield. What might have been tomorrow could be found in the deepest cold of a bleak midwinter darkness all along the fence line. Left behind were echoes in the last room Buddy Holly played. Not wanting ever to escape, the music never died on the last dance by a lake.

Something in it all was saved for me beyond the falling tears of winter.

Things were put aside in my inner tree—the unexpected gifts, photographs, handwritten notes, and artifacts. I began a play a sweet, sweet song named "Once Upon a Time."

I love the fifties. The girls, the women, and fashion. The music, cars, and architecture. Their place in my dreams. All had style. Style seems so far away anymore. Like stars on the sky of a painted dessert, at dusk. Ernest Hemingway was a giant when I was a kid. He wrote of an old man and the sea, of faraway places, Kilimanjaro, and bells tolling, for whom I was never sure. Was Hemmingway a writer on safari or living on a Key, west of somewhere? Was it east of John Steinbeck's *Eden*, or the end of a main street in a Sinclair Lewis novel? How was I to know?

Was it a dark shadow in a shadow at a corner in a Raymond Chandler scene?

I was a little boy sharing the same birth date with Ernest Hemingway. I knew our similarities ended there, even then. I was here. Ernest Hemingway was there, somewhere where I would never be. Hemingway painted pictures with words as epic as the places I had seen in still lifes in black and white in *Life* magazine. Colors were left to be imagined when I was a boy. The mysteries about the people living in unseen colors was beyond measure.

My bicycle carried me to 251 West Second Street on summer days. The park's refreshing fountain near its end at Third Street was a friend in any season. In autumn, it refused to let go the leaves that stopped to say goodbye, at least until November's wind had other plans.

I thought all things should have a setting so kind as Gratz Park. . . . *I'll always be there for you.* You could feel it—you, the boy. Sitting at the feet of tall Corinthian columns, you knew a kindness in its character.

The Lexington Public Library in Gratz Park was a gift to our town from Andrew Carnegie in 1902. Inside was a chance to see the novelists' homes away from home. Their deepest thoughts lived side by side on streets of warm wood, each with a story. A peace separate from any other could be found there. I wondered, do books talk to one another, when no one is around? The intelligent life of words was fascinating.

Time passed; no sound found its way to the next hour. A wandering mind at home on a range in the laziest of hours. Wavy lines in old glass, framed by large windows, painted a surreal landscape, the ever-changing other world beyond. My faithful horse, a bicycle, carried me home.

From now to yesterday is far.

Memories are a way of seeing yesterday as if it were your next-door neighbor. You simply look over the fence of time, and there it is, the past and all the good in it. Opening a box began a celebration. Objects in it let me learn again what each had to say about a time before the echo.

A glance at the past began in a new century. Changes were found since the band's years. Many places we performed are long since gone, their space left to the ages. Space does not forget its place. There is where history lives. Blue highways are rare anymore. They made all the difference. The sense of place lives in a sentimental echo, like a sign along some highway.

—∾—

Club 68.

These would be the most productive years of our lives musically. Frozen in time on a record or still photograph, there's a place of its own. Mystery in the just before and after becomes the life's breath of the moment, alive and cloaked in its veil.

So delicious.

Southern ways and food, southern writers and their stories, are on my menu of interests. The down-home place of double first-names—Bobbie Ann and James Anthony and Ira Joe are mirrored in a clear and elegant frame of simplicity with Scout, Jem, Boo, and Atticus. Simple words are easy to like.

I love you.

There's a separate place to keep an ounce of one's self, where a dialogue of memories can begin. Crayons, a pocket watch, a photograph, two hand-carved soap figures, gifts, and a pencil. A knife and a whistle—a key, wheat pennies, marbles, a ring, and a jack. All are but a snapshot of the story to follow. A marble rolls a lazy path around and in between a treasury of randomly scattered objects in a cigar box. It could be the two of us in a waltz, a glance deep into the heart of a film or play through the stories in its songs, an overture.

I grew up in Lexington. Objects of my affection were often to be found in a cigar box, not so unlike a kid named Finch in Macomb, Alabama. With pictures and colors that fascinated me, names of places on the label of a box told where each began.

"Made in . . . some exotic place I'd never been."

The fragrance of leaf in each was unmistakable. I sensed its presence long after the cigars were gone, like the wake of a ship named *What Was*.

Kept safe away in a Tampa Nugget, my old pocket watch, a Sky King magic decoder ring, compass, a bone-handle pocketknife, and a small harmonica—all one needed to survive. I kept the crystal radio set I built from simple parts in a Prince Albert. Voices from faraway places could be heard. The colors of Cuba were fresh. I could feel it. Music from there was like no other. Havana was a different kind of Latin. I loved it.

Where did we fit in the tapestry of the sixties? And what of the mystery behind faces beyond the edge of a stage or horizon line? I wanted to know. Music mattered deeply to us. Ours was a collective purpose. We could have settled for being simply a band of college players. Rather, our professional approach to entertainment is reflected in what we accomplished and reputation we built throughout the sixties.

The audience was never less than the most important part of what we were about. Given all they could have been doing or other places going, being with us, listening and dancing to our sound of music, was their choice. It was at times neurotic fun, like a scene from a Woody Allen film. The feeling was mutual in the spring of our lives, the flowers of last summer's sun.

Were we seven easy pieces in a puzzle? What shaped each piece, my own in particular? The past became real again. I heard the voices of yesterday, recalling influences on what it all became. I began to see the essence in what once were edges begin to soften. What the band, its members, the audience, and a writer meant to anyone was the voice of an echo becoming free from its place of silence. And, I there to listen.

A one-track path became a two-track road to a superhighway on its way to beyond sound. The unlimited range of possibilities in music is unparalleled. *Les Misérables* and *West Side Story* mirror the collective energy of a symphony orchestra on Broadway. *The Fantasticks* asks one to remember a kind of September they once may have known.

Laura Nero approached a Steinway like a lover, another exquisite performance. She played her heart out. A rose on the piano in its water-filled Waterford Crystal home, listened in silence. Hers was a unique kind of collective energy in the seventies.

A soloist, mirrored in water drops clinging to smooth reflective tiled walls, finds safe haven in a shower. Flaws hidden in the noise of the fog are acceptable. Water is a forgiving instrument to a voice. A shower would never give its secrets up.

Where did we fit in an ever-changing pop culture emerging then?

We were fresh, a little unsure of ourselves in a time between nothing and all. Uncommon is a still life played by a music box to the tune of a faded watercolor time bouquet.

—Anthony Stallard
Summer 2003

1
Gardens in the Rain

We played rhythm & blues, the songs on a soul's landscape. We stopped at Bobby "Blue" Bland, Little Milton, Bill Doggett, Ray Charles, Otis Redding, Phil Upchurch, and James Brown. You could pick up a song here and there, learn a riff or line or the song itself, and play it. We found arrangements hard to find in the *Billboard Top 100*, beside roads less traveled on the map of popular music. I found inspiration in the work of many people. Some things are yours alone to do when the hands of a clock cast no shadow at high noon and Gary Cooper's not around to see it through.

Dissonant chords and lyrics had their way, making you believe you could really cry a river over someone. Frank Sinatra painted a masterpiece. "Autumn in New York" left an unmistakable scent of a season and a sense of place effortlessly. Brook Benton, the Drifters, Ben E. King, the Flamingos, the Platters, Little Anthony, Paul Anka, and Bobby Darin made records lush with strings, chorus, and orchestration. Arrangement signed its name on anything recorded by Sarah Vaughan and Dinah Washington. Arrangement meant something then . . . everything to me. Composers and writers made a difference. I heard Dimitri Tiomkin's genius in film scores for movies set in the West, where the land was big and skies endless. Lerner and Loewe let you taste the wind before you knew its name . . . *Mariah*. Bernard Hermann could make the earth stand still and take you to places by Northwest. *Sunset Boulevard* features a score by Franz Waxman born of a brilliant screenplay co-written by its director, Billy Wilder.

William Faulkner brought a new sensitivity to Hollywood while there. Raymond Chandler left his genius in the lush mystery of words. His were stars on an Art Deco sky, like handprints in the concrete of their times in L.A.

Composers Rogers and Hammerstein, Cole Porter, and Jerome Kern came to Lexington on the silver screen at the Kentucky, Ben Ali, and

Strand theaters. The quality of music and its players in my hometown was commendable then and has never changed.

Rows run long; the corn is tall. The camera's lens breaks free in an Oklahoma field before its harvest, the screen filled to its brim. The landscape leaves one breathless because it is its own. Epic breadth, one horizon to another, was more than I imagined all the sky above could ever hold. It settles on a mind till a life's last breath.

The skyline of a chassis on an old tube radio was the first city I ever saw that never slept. Johnny Mercer was light in glowing tubes. They made my radio sing. He lived in all of them, the crystal palaces with sound-filled paths leading to the place where one's memory begins.

Our golden age was the 1950s. The music was new . . . a little unsure of itself, innocent and unpolished. Such times are often too easily misunderstood. Creative expressions of a generation were planted in music's garden. A shell in Overton Park would never be the same again. Its undiscovered pearl near being found and lifted from the sands of time. Tomorrow held Elvis Presley in its hands.

Leonard Cohen's poetic lyric and carefully crafted melody is a train on its way to the next stop where I am. New Orleans and Muscle Shoals are reminders why music of the Deep South remains important to me.

Styling is a fresh piece of one's self that finds its way to something. A composer leaves space for a stylist to call their own. A song becomes its best. The "Good King Wenceslas" piano countermelody colors Nina Simone's rendering of the sad "Little Girl Blue." What Simone does for "Wild Is the Wind" is beautiful . . . "Don't you know you're life itself."[1]

Gordon Lightfoot wastes little time bringing us to the wreck of the Edmund Fitzgerald. "The legend lives on from the Chippewa on down of the big lake they call Gitche Gumee."[2]

The relentless unchanging melody, endlessly repeated, delivers us to the dwelling place of irony and despair. The lone farewell lies on the bottom. Echoes play a song, of souls and angry waves in the key of goodbye. Superior came swiftly to take a mighty ore boat down on one cold November night. You can't forget the event. Had it been just words perhaps, but the music will not let you.

Ray Charles was an early influence on me, a tether-keeping choice grounded in substance. I was never the same once Ray Charles and his big band arrived with "One Mint Julep," "Sticks and Stones," "Tell Me How do You Feel," "Unchain My Heart," "Tell the Truth," "You Be My Baby," "Mary Ann," and a night in Lexington. I saw Ray Charles in concert at Memorial

Coliseum, 1961. Ray and his band the Raelettes, with Betty Carter, was an artistry-filled gallery. Ray left Lexington for Indianapolis, where he had a little misunderstanding with the local authorities, got over it, and went on with his life.

Frank Sinatra defined impeccable like no other.

A garden in the rain's an ever-gentle notion. Some of us search a lifetime for a garden to define, to find a truth, to enrich, and to tend. Strength lives in the way a garden comes back time and again, so the hope there will be sunshine after the rain. My own was rich in musical delight. I found the soul of its colors in others.

You become the face of the silks you wear, the colors you've chosen.

Music is frozen everything, a still life in a mirror. There's an essence in what is born in a moment of truth. Divine intervention. Humble is a picture living in a Negro spiritual.

Life is the quintessential playground for a child of any age to experience something near spiritual in musical expression, if it is good. "The sweet, sweet kind of spirit that will guide my feet while I run this race."[3] was born in the soul of struggle in a Deep South cotton field, cabin, or church.

Music can be a simple interpretation of beauty. A Curtis JN-3 "Jenny" biplane, a cotton field in the land of. A 1911 Blériot airplane, a John Roebling bridge, and New York City's Flatiron Building are beautiful to me. The style of Art Deco in anything is priceless. Painted scenes by Edward Hopper, a vintage 1930s Lockheed Electra, a Fresnel lens, Catherine Deneuve, and Cincinnati's Union Terminal are beautiful to me. Whimsical English gardens, a Henry Faulkner painting, artist Charlie Harper's playful geometry, the light personality of Spanish moss, and "The Song of Hiawatha" are beautiful to me. A mind is a place where echoes born in other places come to grow. In row upon row in the garden of one's place in time. Their own.

Music can be profound, a positive choice drug for the mind.

I'm a fool for it.

—∿∿—

I met a lot of friends in the 45-rpm and album bins at Barney Miller's, downtown Lexington. Ray Charles, Nina Simone, Wes Montgomery, Chuck Berry, Bill Doggett, Sarah Vaughan, Dave Brubeck, and Nancy Wilson. The Coasters, Fats Domino, and the Shirelles. Little Richard, Elvis, and Patsy Cline.

Some I met for real in my life. Most not. All of them, priceless. Sampling their music in sound booths along a wall in the record department was a hands-on experience. You were alone at post time, in a starting gate at Keeneland about to break loose . . . to run the course in a race to be a winner, someday.

Somewhere.

A platter was one's ticket to time. Much began for me with a wind of voices and saxophones that blew north across Lake Pontchartrain, past Memphis, to put a warm glow on tubes of a radio, falling lightly on my conscious. I was thirsty and it gave me drink. In time, being swept along with it all down a river of dreams to where it is dreams go was the best I could hope for. Some came true.

The ones that really counted.

Dedication

To Nancy

Special Dedication

To the community of students at the University of Kentucky, who somewhere in the decade of the sixties wanted our band to be their band;

My teachers for sharing an unconditional love, without end;

Players in the Band;

To the memory of my late family who heard our music long before the polish was put on any song, enduring the band while we learned.

Part One
Yesterday's Road

2
My Echo, My Shadow, and Me, 1950–1955

1950 to 1955. The fifties were defined by events and the people in them. They are the silhouettes in the harbor of our lives. A day's a raindrop's kiss at the still of water's plane. A week, seven rings of time, borne away from where they all began. Concentric echoes are but years in search of friendly shore and a place to be remembered. They left an indelible reminder of what shaped me, before and since the band.

I like the look of words, alone or with others strung like pearls, expressions on a line. What they all mean is left in the wake you make. I Love You, written with a star on a blackboard the sky becomes at night, is about as good as it gets.

It must begin somewhere-the story in a story.

What happened there?

"Macomb was a tired old town even in 1932 when I first knew it."[4]

I want to know more about the town. "I was born" signs a place in time for David Copperfield in humanity. Charles Dickens defined the times before anything else to begin a story. Longfellow a place: "By the shores of Gitche Gumee, by the shining Big-Sea-Water." Thus, began the story of a spiritual and proud people at a place I dreamed was there. The wind awoke an essence, wrapped in truth, on the branches of my inner tree.

All of it would find its way to the hollow in my soul.

The big band era was on the wane when I began listening to popular music in the early fifties. Radio and music became my fascination. "You Belong to Me," "The Wayward Wind," and "The Wheel of Fortune" were some of the tunes of the day. Bob Wills' "Steel Guitar Rag" was an early lesson on smooth beginnings. Wills and the Texas Playboys band was a near-jazz experience with a touch of blues. Western swing. Johnny Mercer and Hank Williams were stark contrasts in lyric, style, and content. I loved them because of it. Mario Lanza brought a voice of the opera to Top 40's No.1 in the winter of 1950–51 with "Be My Love." A taste of Coca-Cola from a bottle, green was good most any time.

"I Got a Woman" satisfied my thirst for Ray Charles and his music.

An unwanted metal object had landed by some baseball fields in a park near the Washington Monument. Strangers emerged, one with little expression and a powerful light ray, the other with a message of peaceful coexistence. Intelligent life was misunderstood again, and the earth stood still one day.

Times were painted by colors of the matinee. B-movies and stories in music named *Showboat* and *Oklahoma. On the Waterfront* was unforgettable drama. The character you took home with you on a given Saturday afternoon was who you would be the rest of the weekend. It could be William Holden or Montgomery Clift.

Sometimes, it might be you.

You could see yourself in giant mirrors in the Kentucky, State, Strand, Ben Ali theaters or smaller ones at the Ashland on Euclid in Chevy Chase. The Opera House or Ada Meade theaters downtown were a last resort for a movie. They were old and in decline.

Music scores left deep impressions. Bernard Hermann's *The Day the Earth Stood Still*, Franz Waxman's *Sunset Boulevard*, and Jerome Kern's *Show Boat* brought out the best of Hollywood in composers of the day. The masters of lyric and melody signed their names on the face of our soul. One composer and his music, a notion in the mind of a boy. "Purple light in the canyons. That's where I long to be. With my three good companions. Just my rifle, pony and me."—Dimitri Tiomkin

In the darkness of the theater, no one could see you found yourself in the story. It was your secret, yours alone.

Characters in a story's scene were shades of another kind of sensitive. Lawrence Harvey redefined vulnerable in *Room at the Top*. Emotions were shaped in places where pictures moved, leaving one to be swept along in their wake.

All this was at our fingertips in Lexington's theaters. My interests changed over the next two decades from *The Shadow* to "The Shadow of Your Smile."

Its Maker granted us no limit how big we could imagine the sky to be. Clouds in it stayed too little time, before leaving in an airstream, aimlessly away across the sky. The story of a cloud is this. I'll stay with you for a while. Leave you only when the wind wills me to.

The next patch of blue belongs to no one.

Clutter was nowhere to be found on the greatest masterpiece ever begun, the sky.

Space between a cowboy's words echoed the separation of natural features in the scene.

The giant of a composer's music put a notion into the mind of a boy in the dark of a big room. Purple light in the canyons. That's where I long to be.

With my three good companions. Just my rifle, pony and me. – Dimitri Tiomkin

Little could be found on the landscape made by anyone other than God. When there was, it was in some dusty town. Westerns told stories about unexplored places, people looking for their own place in the world, and a coexistence with others and other things. The space between one matinee and the next a week away seemed endless in summer.

Such is the wait for coming attractions.

Who knew the messenger who left it there, the mail order Sky King magic decoder ring in the mailbox, the one a cereal box top and a quarter was sent to get? The soon-to-be-forgotten days of happy trails and no TV were passing. A 50,000 watt clear-channel radio was a bridge to the world beyond. Place can be as gentle as a sigh on a sun-drenched field of Deep South cotton.

The space between those shade trees in your yard is your world when you're a kid, your own Rose Bowl or Ebbets Field. The distance from your front door to the mailbox by the gate is where your world begins. The white picket fence seems far away. It's hard to say goodbye to those kinds of ways you see the world around you. How you saw things, before leaving, are found changed, or long gone since you went away when you return.

"A 'sense of place' implies both firsthand experience gained from living in that place during the formative years as well as the intellectual and historical knowledge of that place. A 'sense of place' further means an awareness of the simple, concrete details of one's life in that place as well as the spiritual qualities that have been emotionally absorbed."[5]

A sense of place is everything. Place is the garden where creativity can begin to flourish, the home address for inspiration. WHAS radio in Louisville, Nashville's WSM and WLAC, and WLW in Cincinnati were clear-channel stations and a sense of place to other places. Clear-channel 50,000-watt stations roamed an uncluttered atmospheric playground, a prairie with no fences. The sun rolled around heaven all day.

Music and radio, were the Lewis and Clark of first half of the twentieth century. The post-war years were ripe for innovation. Those living in them, shaped by it all. Musical influences of the Commonwealth extended far beyond Maysville, Renfro Valley, and US 23, the Dixie, and other blue highways. Clear-channel radio had a starring role. Radio was one garden in a life.

Another tended by two sisters living on Tremont Avenue.

I took piano lessons from Mrs. Augusta Robbins, a widow on Tremont. Piano wasn't baseball or other games in Woodland Park I would've preferred. "Tony, I hope Mr. Bach was kind to you this week." She spoke ever gentle before any unkindness I might bestow on J.S. Bach. I somehow made it through each piece with enough promise to earn a star. Frail hands placed a gold one on the page alongside penciled notes of hope. Mrs. Robbins was too kind to have left any composition without either. Nonetheless, the piano shortened hikes and exploration on Saturdays in the woods and farmland around Idle Hour Country Club. The fence at the end of Carolyn, just past Holiday Road, my gateway to adventure.

Years passed; the lessons ended as lessons do. New ones began about others and me. I wanted to spend time close to the land more often than before; so near should one of us leave, the other might soon die from loneliness.

I asked nothing more than this when I was a kid.

—✻—

Fresh technology and sound effects were shaped by the minds and influences of Les Paul and Leo Fender, Laurens Hammond, and Don Leslie. Audio's range was akin to something in a Western movie scene. Recording engineers found new air to breathe. Electronics development, solid body guitar design, and endless possibility left us breathless. Renewed recognition of traditional instruments and their importance was paramount.

Nothing takes the place of style.

Art Deco, a style found in a design emphasis given much of what was crafted during the thirties, is an immeasurable legacy of good. Art Deco stands as a fossil of completeness. When good design flourishes, it doesn't end abruptly in the creative mind. It is complete, in its fashion, music, architecture, bridges, dams, art, literature, and conscience. It is in the human spirit itself, the unending line and curve in Cincinnati's Union Terminal. In 1931, life and its people weathered times shaped by events my generation could hardly fathom.

America was life in a cash-and-carry kind of world. Mom and pop businesses bloomed in neighborhood settings. Service could be found when you bought gasoline and oil at stations. Banks had names with words Trust, Fidelity, and Security carved in stone.

We looked up to many different kinds of people. Presidents weighed how to end a world war and did so, decisively. Cincinnati's Powell Crosley, Henry Kaiser, Howard Hughes, and Jack Northrop were industrialists with the ability to get things done. Lockheed's Kelley Johnson was mystery to us all at the Burbank airport in Los Angeles. Players of the game named Lou Gehrig, Jackie Robinson, and Joe DiMaggio didn't quit. They were who boys wanted to be like. Aircraft test pilots Glenn Edwards and Chuck Yeager were adventurers with no fear. A simple cardboard box was a Bell X-1.

There were no barriers to one's imagination.

I was touched most deeply by my parents and teachers, my church and radio. Church brought us to the world in an inspirational sense, radio most influential in bringing the world of others to our own. Radio gave us time to think about what we were listening to. Looking back, one could be more interactive than today it seems. I could feel the grass terrace under my feet in Cincinnati's Crosley Field. Grass terraces, a reminder I was too near the outfield fence, chasing an elusive fly ball, an inning-ending catch radio's Waite Hoyt would say had been made. Joe Nuxhall could rest his arm during the top of the next one because of a kid in '53. Nuxhall was one of many I could pretend to be on any given pitcher's mound in a faraway ballpark. Daydreams and twilight double-headers in the playground of my mind were priceless.

Until Sandy Koufax came along.

Once, a writer at Lexington's newspaper visited our class at Kenwick Elementary School. My first six years at Kenwick were filled with life-shaping experiences, one meeting Alfred Bertram Guthrie Jr. Mr. Guthrie had come to Lexington in 1926 to work as a cub reporter for the *Lexington Leader*. He became city editor and editorial writer. A.B. Guthrie Jr. taught at the University of Kentucky until 1952, and in 1953, he and his wife moved to the Big Sky Country of Montana. The big sky was in him and through him. Guthrie had written a Pulitzer Prize-winning book titled *The Way West* in 1950. A movie based on another of his books, *The Big Sky*, was made. He was special to a nine-year-old.

While teaching at the University of Kentucky, he moved to Hollywood to write the screenplay for *Shane*, a film directed by George Stevens. "Starts Today!" read the marquee. *Shane* was first shown in Lexington at Schine's Kentucky Theater: "Prices this engagement only—Adults Matinee 60 Cents, Evening 75 Cents, Children 34 Cents." The ad for the film also read "Screenplay by Lexington's own A.B. 'Bud' Guthrie, Jr."[6] He made quite an impression on each of us. I didn't realize at the time how my life was being shaped.

You put the ribbon you were given in its proper place to wait your time to dance around the maypole with other kids. You made sure you were ready. This was your job on May Day in the sunken garden by the playground at Kenwick School. All the kids looked to each other on the first day in May, ribbons in sunshine, classmates, and loving teachers. It was fun.

Berea, a small piece of peace in a valley, found his mind like a fog since the boy was young; he thought of a time his father, a salesman, took him on a day trip to Foley's Grocery Store in Berea. He sold folks cakes and cookies to folks. Foley's was a customer.

Their first-ever crossing the Kentucky at Valley View together, upriver from the bridge to Madison County on the Clay's Ferry. A father, his son, and a 1951 Chevrolet provided to him by Richmond Baking Company in Indiana. The car's paint was a deep yellow color. The scent of fresh cookies and Simonize Car Wax linger still.

Helping him make it shine on Saturday's under trees in a shaded yard was kind.

Dad talked about Renfro Valley, John Lair, and Red Foley in the afternoon on the way back home. He sang "Peace in the Valley." I believe it to be the only song I ever heard my father sing, except ones from the *Broadman Hymnal* in church. He was a quiet man. Such a day with him is beyond measure. Fathers can paint the world for their children as they see it.

Impressionists' brush strokes of painted faith. My own.

—~—

The Cold War was like a vapor everywhere, mostly unseen. You could sense it, kind of felt it wasn't going to go away. Forever can be such an awful thing to think about when you're a kid. Blue skies were ever around. Cloudy days, few just like "Home on the Range" said they could be. Kind skies were ones you hoped kids in other places in the world in their schools got to experience. Hushed words overheard told me something else.

Korea was cold ground.

The first hydrogen bomb test was November 1952. Eniwetok, an atoll in the Pacific, was on the map of our conscience, joining Bikini and others begun in the 1940s. Hidden in the simultaneous presence of a horrific cloud was an unimaginable presence. We witnessed shock waves in a race beyond sound, one we feared would open heaven's door before its time. I was sometimes scared. All I knew about Korea was the 38th parallel passed almost right through Winchester, Kentucky. I was nine, and we were only five years since 1945. Another war-I hoped not. Carried by the train of one's thoughts, the bomb and polio arrived on parallel tracks. One was meant to get things over with, the other you could get and not get over. The frightening reality of doubts and insecurities were a little darkness in an otherwise happy time.

Place became the crucible where parallel lines of contrasts converged. Music of the first fifty years of the twentieth century passed through a cultural prism, emerging as something new. Lake Popular was a delightful blend of southern gospel, Negro spiritual, country and western swing, blues, jazz, and Latin music. We tasted the lake's good waters. A generation was shaped. It was cool.

Owen Bradley and Chet Atkins had begun to reshape country music's landscape. Decca's Paul Cohen and RCA Victor's Steve Sholes were near a point of entrusting it all to them. Nashville would be a harbor of its own once the ship set sail from New York City to points south.

Billy Vaughn, Jimmy Sacca, Don McGuire, and Seymour Spiegelman were putting Randy Woods's Dot Records in Gallatin, Tennessee, on the map. A musician and three students at Western Kentucky State Teachers College, a little north of Nashville, wore beanies with the trademark W and letter sweaters. The Hilltoppers took what their school was known to be from Bowling Green to the rest of the world. The Beatles' first US appearance on The Ed Sullivan Show mirrored one by the Hilltoppers on *The Perry Como Show* in 1953. One "P.S. I Love You" to another was little more than ten years. Bookends with an in-between.

Mayfield, a rural community west of Bowling Green, was home of Bobbie Ann Mason. Sweet sixteen, Bobbie Ann founded and was national president of *The Hilltoppers National Fan Club*. Don McGuire once introduced me to Bobbie Ann. She re-introduced me to Elvis in her book *Elvis Presley*. Don McGuire, a kind fellow, always with a smile and a story.

Muhlenberg County native guitarist Merle Travis had a part in *From Here to Eternity* with Frank Sinatra and Montgomery Clift. He wrote "Sixteen Tons," a song-story depicting ownership of ordinary people by big coal and big steel. Merle Travis and the Everly Brothers put this part of paradise on the Green River on the map before much of it was captured by Mr. Peabody, only to be hauled away in his coal train.

Kentucky's Bill Monroe was introducing bluegrass music to the world from Rosine in Ohio County. A 1935 8-string Gibson F-5 mandolin held fast in the hands of a master sings sweetly. The all-acoustic goodness of bluegrass is tailor-made for a stylist.

In 1953, "Near You" became the first million-selling single to come out of Nashville. The Crew Cuts hit No.1 with "Sh-Boom," and Buddy Morrow's band was huge with "Night Train." The flavors, dances, and passion of Cuban music were easy to love. Latin was hot music, rhythmic and brassy, sounding great on the new hi-fi players, with lyrics I didn't understand. Edison's invention had taken a giant step in fidelity.

1953. Mrs. Ernestine Ligon was teaching her seventh grade English class the parts of speech at Morton Jr. High School. My classmates and I were learning to diagram every sentence, paragraph, and chapter she could put on a blackboard. Collectively, we would've diagrammed a novel for Mrs. Ligon. We would've done anything she asked. She placed the star in our hands. It would take a lifetime of night skies to write the rest of our own.

I am in a near lifetime taken to appreciate essence in a rare moment, even now.

—ꟺ—

Capitol parted ways with its echoes. "The echoes remained behind in 1954 when Capitol Records moved from 1515 Melrose Ave. to the new Capitol Tower at Hollywood and Vine."[7] Another's sun rose at 706 Union at the Memphis Recording Service the summer of '54. Once a young Elvis Presley recorded "Blue Moon of Kentucky" and "That's Alright Mama" through slapback echo, it was only a matter of time. Sam Phillips, Sun Records, rock and roll, and popular music would never be the same.

Elvis Presley appeared July 30, 1954 at the Overton Park Shell, a 1930s Depression-era make-work project in Memphis. The "Shell, a near-perfect arch," became a gateway from now to forever for a hillbilly cat one night. A hotel's neon "No Vacancy" sign at the end of a lonely street illuminated a bellhop's flowing tears soon after.

Compelling questions slept at a quiet place in my mind. Some would awaken now and then to haunt me.

I embraced *To Catch a Thief* in 1955. Could anyone be more beautiful than Grace Kelly? Ever? Grace Kelly and Cary Grant were charm personified. I wonder even now, what it is to be in the dreams of a woman alone, asleep in Room 623 at the Carlton Hotel, Monte Carlo, France. "Even in this light I can tell where your eyes are looking."[8]

She knew.

Would the lady in the mist survive Joseph Cotton in 1953's *Niagara*? What could I do to save Marilyn Monroe? Would I make it to Niagara Falls in time? I faced a similar dilemma earlier in the fifties. Marilyn had a problem in *The Asphalt Jungle*. Sterling Hayden had come back to Kentucky to die, never to know again the soft nose of a horse on one's face.

There was time enough, though I would need all I could gather in the coming years.

Misfits. Marilyn Monroe and Montgomery Clift needed a friend. Theirs was no way out and little chance to know. I loved her. I sensed the nature of his tragic self. Joe DiMaggio would save the day for me. He was important, and Marilyn needed someone important.

Was I to anyone?

I was to Mrs. Ernestine Ligon and Mrs. Augusta Robbins, but they were older, much older than Marilyn Monroe, and I was only twelve.

3
Written on the Wind, 1955–1959

1955. I was thirteen.

Blues, country and western, gospel, popular, big band, and jazz blended in the postwar years. All came written on the wind, fresh and ready to cook. America's recording kaleidoscope held just three pieces in 1940—Columbia, Victor, and Decca. World War II began. Capitol Records was formed in Los Angeles by Johnny Mercer and company, 1942. Between then and 1955, they were joined by a collection of new record labels born on the coasts, from the Great Lakes to the Gulf and places in between.

What did it all mean in 1955?

Rock and roll began and would flourish in this setting. Kids, growing up in the fifties, harvested from these and other record labels, established or not, to build their first record collections. The homes of Chuck Berry, Ray Charles, Little Richard, Merle Travis, Elvis Presley, Everly Brothers, Hank Williams, Fats Domino, the Hilltoppers, the Four Lads, the Diamonds, the Four Aces, and others were our neighborhood.

Fresh colors and graphics found a visual landscape, ripe for creative expression. The mystique of a label began to be revealed by its graphics. ASCAP, BMI, G2WB 0209-07 were unfamiliar to us. The music brought us to the marketplace.

They defined generations since Edison. Some called them platters, round and seven inches edge to edge. The center opening was larger than the LP records of yesterday. A carved unbroken line uniquely defined a record's grooves.

I'm sitting on the inside of a platter's edge, legs dangling into space. Touching nothing. All's in motion, all around me spinning, 'round . . . the parallel lines, unending, it could be Saturn's rings for all I know. The maker of a universe placed a finger in a groove and played for me the song of life. I listened to the sound. It touched my ears, on its way to what's deep in space.

Slapback echo on Union took a stroll one day, up Poplar Street, past Crown Electric Company, then on to Overton Park. A whisper became a new echo. The beat of a heart was changed. What began in Memphis one summer night had begun to shape me.

I didn't know it then. I do now.

I was hooked on Ray Charles when I first heard the girls backing him and Fathead Newman's sax solo on "Lonely Avenue." Piano, note, chord, and voice are vintage blue. If this was the kind of influence I was under in the fifties, then let it be. His kind of music was delivered— air mail special delivery —to folks or by mail order from music distributors John R. (Richbourg) and Ernie Young. Music raced through nights in an uncluttered atmosphere, swept by 50,000 watts from WLAC-Nashville.

John R's *Ernie's Record Parade* broadcast began at 10:00 p.m. Lexington time for an hour. Ernie's Record Mart, 179 Third in Nashville, could deliver John Lee Hooker, Jimmy Reed, Chuck Berry, Etta James, Bobby "Blue" Bland, and Little Junior Parker to anyplace on the planet.

Gene Nobles followed John R. at 11:00 p.m., sponsored by the World's Largest Mail Order Phonograph Record Shop. Randy's Record Shop and Dot Records, located in nearby Gallatin, were owned by Randy Wood.

Being spoon-fed rhythm and blues by Gene Nobles and John R. on WLAC was different nourishment than found on a *Your Hit Parade* menu from hometown radio.

A song coming out of New Orleans, Nashville, Shreveport, Memphis, or Cincinnati enabled us to know others not found on local radio. Red Prysock's "Hand Clappin'" sounded a different kind of voice in town. "This is Cal, your old platter pal" painted an emerging picture. It began to explain why the paper's white, the notes are black, and why each needs the other in the end. Cal Wallace played rhythm and blues, "race music" on Lexington's WLEX radio. His was unlike music others played in my hometown. Signals broadcast were clear as a block of ice in winter. You moved the dial and were moved by where it landed. The space between the mysteries in it all was unending.

Radio brought us near the place where one's imagination begins.

The veil separating me from things not known was becoming near nothing at all. I sensed how music can free you from bondage, realized or otherwise. Light's soft glow fell on the radio dial like a piece of sunshine, illuminating a world of creative expression still to be explored. Radio was fresh, unblemished in the darkness I sometimes found in the stark uncertainty of growing up.

—⁓—

Owen and Harold Bradley opened Bradley Film and Recording Studios in Nashville in April 1955. Country music, Music Row, and the "Nashville Sound" continued to flourish from Sixteenth Avenue South at Hawkins Street, where it began. Capitol's Ken Nelson began to use Owen Bradley's studio to record Gene Vincent and his Blue Caps. "Rockabilly" was ours to taste, a delicious mix of song and echo. History was made May 4, 1956, in the Quonset hut. Gene Vincent's "Be-Bop-a-Lula" charted No.1. The song was the first million-selling copies of a record made in Bradley's studio. Hits by others would follow. Gene Vincent recorded "Lotta Lovin'" and "Dance to the Bop" in the Quonset hut. Hit records were made in a place where echoes are born. Buddy Holly returned to Bradley's studio on July 22 and November 15, 1956.

Brenda Lee recorded for the first time there between those two dates. "Decca Records wasted no time. They brought me to Nashville's Bradley Studio for my debut recording session on July 30, 1956. Studio Owner Owen Bradley had supervised Buddy Holly's debut sessions there the previous January. In February, the Everly Brothers had staged their disk debut. Elvis had burst on the national scene with 'Heartbreak Hotel' that spring."[9]

Norman Petty's studio in Clovis, New Mexico, richly painted sound distinctly in vivid colors of the Southwest. Place was reshaping popular music. The personality of a region defined its sound and the music born in each.

September 1955 began. I was thirteen. The sign on the door of the house across from the street from Lexington Jr. High on North Limestone read "REM Records." What went on in a room behind closed doors at a place with a simple hand-painted sign on a pane of frosted, near-obscure glass?

A boy on his first day of ninth grade was left to wonder.

The cause of the accident killing the rebel without one was unclear in September. A silver plane brought yesterday's farm boy out of California, back home again in Indiana. James Dean was east of his West Coast Eden, for the last time.

—⁓—

The way from north places to points south passed through Lexington. A paved ribbon between two bodies of water was our welcome to the bluegrass. The Reservoir, our city's water source, was a mirrored image of serenity one finds in a place of scenic beauty. Nearing town, the road became a tree-lined boulevard, featuring some of Lexington's finest homes. A stately portrait framed in wealth.

Ashland, home of Henry Clay, stands on his estate on Lexington's Richmond Road.

Henry Clay, who once said, "I'd rather be right than president," is considered by many the greatest orator the US Senate has ever known. He stands high above all others on a stone column above his tomb in the Lexington Cemetery. Henry Clay faces his beautiful Ashland and his Maker.

Henry Clay High, a city school, took its name from the distinguished senator.

The school was located on East Main Street near the point where Richmond Road, U.S. 25, became East Main Street at Ashland Avenue. Henry Clay's classrooms were arranged around two separate outdoor courtyards. Each court, open to the sky, was an open invitation for birds and rain, for bees and snow. Tall windows could be raised to catch a breeze. One's mind could take a snapshot of forever. The in and out shared a visual connection with each other, enabling one's imagination to wander past the windows to the world beyond. Wondering.

The character of many things appeared subtly altered, seen through waves and imperfections in the panes of clear glass. There was a truth in what each seemed to be saying at the intersections of thought and learning, of dreams and things real.

Establishments across the street from school offered eats and sweets to satisfy young appetites beyond a school's lunch line menu. Clay Restaurant, Jerry's Drive-in Restaurant, Wing's Teahouse, Hughes Ice Cream, Magee's Bakery, and Jake's (a drugstore with a jukebox) were a wellspring.

1924
RUE

The jukebox in Jake's, in the RUE Building 660 East Main, played rhythm and blues: Little Willie John's "Fever," Bill Doggett's "Honky Tonk," Ray Charles's "Drown in My Own Tears," and Ivory Joe Hunter's "Since I Met You Baby." Jake's array of 45s included other hits by the Rays with

"Silhouettes," Sam Cooke's "You Send Me," Ferlin Husky's "Gone," Jim Loew's "Green Door," Sanford Clark's "The Fool," and Coasters' "Young Blood." I fell deep into the never-ending haunting "Endless Sleep" of Jody Reynolds.

You could put your finger on a combination of buttons on a wall-mounted Seeburg at a booth, three rows of happy or sad, A-K, L-V, 1-0. Play a song and dance to a Wurlitzer. A teen could drown a sorrow in a soda from the fountain.

And a memory.

The in-between blended with the rockabilly and rock and roll tunes of Eddie Cochran, Johnny Burnette, Elvis Presley, Jerry Lee Lewis, Little Richard, Gene Vincent, Chuck Berry, Fats Domino, and Buddy Holly. I was listening to something of undeniable substance on first hearing Lefty Frizzell's "The Long Black Veil" in the air outside of Jake's in 1959.

Inspiration at Jake's was priceless. The nature of one's human condition was in its adolescent change. These were the artists who eventually would lead us to a land of fresh creative expression. They took us past doors, once closed, now held open by chains, with links made of blues and country, gospel, jazz, and need itself.

The sidewalk beyond Jake Saloshin's front door was a stage for the antics of rush initiation in the fall. We were sophomores, juniors, seniors, girls and boys thrown together. Pieces in an ever-changing kaleidoscope. A coming of age.

This was ours.

You could sit on the steps near the school's auditorium and look across the front lawn and beyond East Main to the blank page on which your own tomorrow was being written. You could find your place by the words penned in a song. You could find your way through the times and not forget them.

These were ours.

Few things shape the soul like a song when you're in high school. She might be the queen of the hop, real or imagined. Your food for thought was in a song from an open door of Jake's just before the ride began . . . a city bus to Main and Lime, downtown. Woolworth's, Hart's Drugs, Kresge's, and the Schulte-United Store were rendezvous for hundreds of city and parochial school students. A transfer on another bus would bring you and the songs on home.

—∞—

1956. I was fourteen. Destiny had a date with the tenth of January.

At the Methodist TV, Radio and Film Commission at 1525 McGavock Street in Nashville, Chet Atkins put a session together and Elvis Presley recorded 'I Got a Woman' and 'Heartbreak Hotel' with Scottie Moore (guitar), Chet Atkins (guitar), Bill Black (bass), Floyd Cramer (piano), D.J. Fontana (drums) and backup singers Gordon Stoker, Bill Speer and Brock Speer.[10]

"Heartbreak Hotel" shaped a notion. Somewhere beyond the end of Lonely Street, we could chase an echo. Catch it? Who knew?

Capitol Records moved from 5515 Melrose to the corner of Hollywood and Vine. "When the building was completed, an elaborate inaugural was planned, and on February 22, 1956, Frank Sinatra . . . was invited to preside over the very first session in the new studios."[11]

March 21, 1956, Wednesday: "YMCA Arena, Lexington, Kentucky. Elvis, sick with flu, is attended by a physician before the show. He tells reporters his success 'appears to be a dream to me. I hope I can continue to please the public.'"[12]

Author Grace Metalious revealed a truth about misplaced values in a small New England town named *Peyton Place*. Tom T. Hall wrote about Harper Valley and its own values late in the sixties. The Casuals formed Nashville's first rock & roll band in 1956. The thought we would ever meet never crossed my mind at the time.

Fats Domino was ready. A chorus of saxophones the answer to every phrase he sang. He was willing and Dave Bartholomew able to send a piano and saxophone-driven brand of New Orleans rhythm across Lake Pontchartrain, up the Mississippi Delta, to hungry ears. The music of New Orleans was juicy, spicy, rich in flavors of the Easy. The bayou, with its special blend of influences blessing the region, fell in love with Beale Street's blues. The open arms of its lovers embraced the music in Memphis, St. Louis, Chicago, and Kansas City. Sweet, and many saxophones, wrapped in a piano roll was a gift to all of us from the Deep South.

Rock and Roll was cookin'.

Music emerging from the South was a counterpoint to city tunes of writing sanctuaries in New York. A cool jazz presence in West Coast sound was distinct, in part because of other influences near the Pacific.

Billboard's charts mirrored the wide scope of song and spirit. Music was enriched because it drew upon the regional contexts in which it was being shaped. Our local scene found John Jacob Niles, wondering while wandering out by Athens Boonesboro Road, imagining the color of his true love's hair. Out where stars come out at night.

In a way all their own.

—∾—

1957. I was fifteen.

By 1957 teenagers had been under the influence of B-movies and the music of their stories, some of us missing James Dean. We wished on a star, and never dreamed it could happen ever again, to Buddy Holly . . . never.

"Chances Are" was number one. Chances were your chances of getting a date for the weekend, better for some than others. Johnny Mathis was wonderful, wonderful. "A White Sport Coat," Marty Robbins's bid, all dressed up for the dance wearing a pink carnation. Having been taken off the country path to Manhattan's busy streets, "The Story of My Life," "Singing the Blues," and "A White Sport Coat" had become big hits for Marty Robbins. Songs with a definitive pop flavor opened doors for many others in an emerging climate of change.

The Brooklyn Dodgers left Ebbets Field for L.A. Broken hearts were left behind. The twelfth of never had arrived for lovers of the game. Ebbets Field . . . a ball built it; another took it down.

Hollywood brought Elizabeth Taylor and Montgomery Clift to Lexington to film *Raintree County* in and around Danville. The Foleys of Berea were not the only reason Pat Boone returned to the bluegrass for *April Love*. Shirley Jones was a beauty. Having your breath taken away in spring in Kentucky was everything when you're going on sixteen.

Strings, polished arrangements, and orchestration found their way to the music in the mid-fifties. Buck Ram produced the Platters. His arrangements were complete, richly textured for the times of our youth, the hits unforgettable. For a while, I only had eyes for the Flamingos; then Little Anthony and the Imperials put Teddy Randazzo's well-crafted music to a style of their own.

Chet Atkins and Owen Bradley began to use voicing and orchestral arrangements to power the reformation of country music emerging in

Nashville. Dick Clark's *American Bandstand* began in Philadelphia. Music centers far beyond New York City and the West Coast became places where the breath of new winds began to be born.

RCA Victor built its Studio B on Hawkins Street at 17th Avenue south in 1957, one street away from Owen Bradley's Quonset hut. Chet Atkins became head of A&R for RCA Nashville. Atkins began producing hits with Don Gibson and Jim Reeves. Chet Atkins recorded the Everly Brothers when its walls were new. The cadence of sound was well-recorded in Studio B. The beat went on. Elvis Presley began recording at RCA's new studio, not distant from the echoes of McGavock Street. Elvis had gone from driving a truck for Crown Electric Company to wearing a crown.

He had become the King of Rock and Roll.

Bradley and Atkins were taking country music uptown. They and producers for other labels in Nashville were backing their artists with seasoned session players, strings, choruses, and vision. Nashville's session musicians played with restraint. Theirs was style, simple as a Halston gown. Anything less would have been naked truth. Creative audio engineers were master distillers of sound, no matter where records were being made—the coasts and in between.

Country music after Hank Williams was saved, its baptism in the river of popular music.

The Soviet Union launched *Sputnik* in October. Space belonged to us all it seemed, till then. Space became the sole domain of others but only for a moment. We tuned a radio to a 20 MHz frequency and heard the broadcast sound of *Sputnik 1*.

From Outer Space and Russia with Love.

We wondered while it wandered through the mystery of space, uncrowded, dark and deep. Polio, the Cold War, Elvis Presley, Sputnik. . . . What next? What did I aspire to be? Two women may have planned on a porch by the garden on a corner how collectively they might urge their student's interests. What could they do so we might dream to play with words?

—᭙—

1958. I was sixteen. I found myself in Miss Ruth Mathews's literature class. We were given our first taste of Chaucer, Shakespeare, and Frost—music of a different kind, unlike the language of music beyond the world of her class. Miss Mathews knew the language of one's own mind well. She spoke it eloquently to her students.

Student Night was variety entertainment at Henry Clay, a spring tradition. They were the Everly Brothers. Wendell Sams and Fred Anderson gave a memorable acoustic performance on stage in the school auditorium leading us from "Be-Bop-a-Lula" to forever. The memory of a moment cannot be erased by time. This was our chance. Our generation took a bunch of hope and its music down the path of what remained of a decade to its end.

Then, we opened a door to the sixties.

I met up with Wendell Sams and Fred Anderson at the Lion's Bluegrass Fair later in August. The fair was held at the time on the grounds of the Red Mile race course. We left for Fred's house after the fair. Wendell showed me three chords on a guitar. Other than that, I don't remember much about how I got started. I learned in time one can do a lot of blues and rock and roll with three chords. Soon after, I went downtown and bought Mel Bay's *Fun with the Guitar* for $1. I traced the finger positions for each chord on plain paper, taping it reversed to window glass in my attic room. I played left-handed. As long as there was sunlight, there was hope.

I tuned my radio to somewhere and never looked back.

Rock and roll's first No.1 instrumental, "Tequila," put the Champs on music history's billboard. "Manhattan Spiritual," a horn-rich instrumental filled with a spirit, went straight to my soul. Buddy Holly produced the first recording of a friend on September 10 at Norman Petty's studio in Clovis, New Mexico. Waylon Jennings took the stage at the Surf Ballroom to play bass in Holly's band on a cold winter night in '59. Life and its end were there, with chance, on the worn edge of a coin Tommy Allsup had tossed in the air. Richie Valens called "heads," winning the last seat on Beech Bonanza, N3794N. Waylon was close enough to a tragedy to feel a chill passing by his face on its way to midnight.

My Diana was a princess named Grace. Grace Kelly was smooth as the calm reflection of a thought on a silent echo. Could it be she meant all she said in *High Society*? Her voice was like silk. I was easily charmed. Falling in love. True romance . . . forever true.

Part Two
Something Gentle Comes My Way

4
Emily Returns to Grover's Corners, 1959

1959. I was seventeen. Rod Serling's *Twilight Zone* first aired, a dimension of time and space from television to the mind. Tender echoes of a young girl in *The Diary of Anne Frank* were whispers to us all. She believed there was good in everyone, even in a time of human suffering and despair. Lawrence Harvey's sensitive portrayal of a tragic figure in *Room at The Top* was brilliant.

The last veteran of the Civil War was taken to belong to the ages.

Raymond Chandler died. He painted with words stories of postwar Los Angeles. I wouldn't forget a style-filled portrait of a place by the Pacific and its dark corners.

The anti-nuclear message of *On the Beach* went beyond subtlety; few remained in the wake of a nuclear war. The Iron Curtain was an ideological wall in a no-man's-land. The Cold War a near-silent presence yet deafening.

A farmer's comment to Cary Grant, somewhere in the middle of Indiana, was about dusting of a field with no crops by a plane for no reason. N46091 met a Magnum Oil Company tanker on Highway 41, a momentary distraction from dreams of Eva Marie Saint in *North by Northwest.*

Her name was Eve Kendall. I was in love again.

Sensual dialogue between strangers on a train left much to one's imagination. Another kind of intimacy another time on another train down the line in the sixties favored James Bond and the beautiful Tatiana. *From Russia, with Love.*

Daniela Bianchi was stunning in pale blue.

The Guggenheim landed in New York City. Jack Kilby filed Patent #3,138,743, his invention called a microchip. Lockheed was busy at work on a "Black Project" in Burbank and no one knew. Area 51—what was that?

The Winter Dance Party Tour stopped at the Surf Ballroom in Clear Lake, Iowa, on a cold midwinter night. Eternity arrived an hour beyond the midnight, February 3, 1959.

Our senior year began with some uncertainty. Sentimental was written all over it. Bobby Darin's "Beyond the Sea" had a drum break that could tear a soul just enough to get inside you and say, "Listen to me." It's the crack in everything Leonard Cohen wrote about, the one that lets the light come in. Before the spring of '59 ended, the light found me.

The *Life Express* was on its way around a bend in time. This was final. What would become of us? What would we become? Some would come to a crossroads at places where there were echoes, and sound nowhere to be found.

A single note in music is to me a tender moment in the rhythm of its time played in the key of its own life. To me, the note I once passed to a girl in school was more than a dream. I love you. Do you love me?

Emily returned to Grover's Corners.

The band in this story was born.

The Temptashuns, est. 1959.

Lexington was Parkette Drive-In's 'Poor Boy' and fries with slaw in a box, Joyland Amusement Park, Lawrence's Sandwich Shop, Kenny's Frostop Drive-In, Jerry's, *Coke Time*, Frisch's Big Boy, Starlight Drive-In, and doughnuts from Spalding's Bakery. The Lexington Blue Grass Drive-in, Sky-vue, Circle 25, Family, and Southland 68 were rooms with a view and big screens. Pictures moved, carried on a light beam under stars of another kind.

This was my hometown in 1959, on the way to the summer of *A Summer Place.*

I hoped a tree's shade would be there for my heart at seventeen. My classmates and I were on our separate roads to graduation with shared emotions. We could sing "Volare" to ourselves.

Buddy Holly was gone.

Miss Ruth Mathews persuaded me to be in the senior play, Thornton Wilder's *Our Town*. Her light had found its way. The one remaining part was small. I would be a piece of something. Small parts change people.

Young people are small parts in the whole of life. Thornton Wilder, *Our Town*, Emily, and a literature teacher in my junior and senior years at Henry Clay High are significant parts in my own. They keep life from coming apart. I could not have written this story without a recognition of the ordinary and commonplace a kind, caring woman taught me to appreciate.

She tended her students with no less care than the wildflowers in her garden. She loved Robert Frost, birds, and gardens. Teaching and diverging roads in crowded woods. Miss Ruth Mathews painted the things she loved with choices near the heart of life itself. They made all the difference in my own. Since then, I've wondered what might have been in her thoughts those long walks to and from Henry Clay on weekdays and to and from Second Presbyterian Church on Sundays.

Miss Mathews lived by the corner of South Limestone Street and Washington Avenue. Memorial Hall is framed by the place she lived, and the Clarence Wentworth Mathews Building on campus bears her father's name. She lived surrounded by violets and wildflowers, the life in her side yard on a corner. Songbirds were ever-near. Ruth was shaped by nature and the life in it, her students and beloved Vermont. Such is one's own blessing by the local color of another.

Mrs. Ernestine Ligon, my seventh grade English teacher, lived in the house next door. Two women near a garden on a corner long ago, shared how each could inspire kids needing it most. I know this.

Our Town taught me a lot about life and how meaningful one's being in the lives of others can be. Emily's return to Grover's Corners was a glance to how fragile the past is known to be once it arrives again.

I continued learning to play the same acoustic relic, chasing the songs of others with the three basic chords Wendell Sams had shown me one summer night, 1958.

I left an acoustic beginning for another after graduation. My first electric instrument came from Mr. George Hurst at Candioto Piano Company, downtown. George Hurst was a gentleman, a mentor and friend to many in the music community, young people in particular. Mr. Hurst was one of the most honest people I ever met. The lessons he taught me about personal integrity and professional conduct are beyond measure.

He showed me instruments for beginners, an inexpensive Gibson Les Paul Jr. model with a sunburst finish and a Fender Musicmaster. He advised we might more easily adapt the Fender to left-handed play. The neck was friendly to the touch and my inexperience. I bought the inexpensive Musicmaster and Fender's Princeton amplifier. He helped me change the strings around at the store, tuned it to perfection, gave me advice and encouragement, and put a future in its case. Our long and lasting friendship began July 1, 1959.

Before the day had ended, I had plugged it in and changed my life.

I didn't enroll at the university for fall semester. Many of my classmates did. I had no idea what to do with the rest of my life. Not long after graduation from Henry Clay, I bought my first car, a 1960 MGA, and a guitar. Before the summer ended, I was working at a manufacturing plant. The memory of carefree times not long ago still fresh. One, seated on a stool at the lunch counter with friends in Wheeler's Pharmacy on Romany Road after school. Where I placed my fingers lightly on a soda straw and tasted the rich, cool essence of my favorite milkshake.

Hamilton Beach was as near the ocean as I had ever been.

—ᨓ—

A day trip with a friend happened in late August. We left Lexington around 4.00 a.m. for Fairmount, Indiana. The MG's top was down, Indiana flat country like I'd not seen before. The sky was huge, the horizon distant beyond belief. I was young, unaware of my being on the way to becoming a fossil on the bones of time.

The air was fragile coming into Fairmount, a small town. I drove down its Main Street and to Fairmount High School on Vine, before heading to the countryside north of town. The road was two-lane and narrow. We passed Park Cemetery, Carter's Motorcycle Shop, and a Quaker church. I slowed even more on down the road where a white-painted farmhouse stood brilliant in the sun. Placid water of the farm's pond shimmered beyond a barn by a silo. The mailbox read Marcus Winslow. I entered a gravel drive framed by a low wall of native stone at the entrance to turn my car around. Pausing.

The day was near noon.

I knew little about the Winslows or their farm in August 1959. I did know a farm could turn your life around. This one seemed to be at peace with itself, a kindness to know when you're eighteen. We returned to Park Cemetery, which I had passed only minutes before down the road. The MG's wheels stirred gravel under from its bed of rest. Hush was whispered in air owned by the blended fragrance of flowers and fuel. I drove with reverence slowly to a hilltop gravesite to a rose-toned granite stone. It read simply.

James B. Dean
1931–1955

It was but one month shy of four years since a tragedy near a place in California named Cholame. Twenty-six miles east of Paso Robles, two highways, 46 and 41, intersected; two objects collided. Dusk can wear a sad expression on its face, not wanting to leave the day. The air was defined by vulnerability. I wanted life to be forever fresh. Here, east of a place called Eden, I seemed to be on thin ice. We spent a little more time at the gravesite before leaving.

An open road and a 1.5 horsepower Czech-made motorcycle from Carter's Motorcycle Shop represented the kind of freedom to James B. Dean as an MG to James A. Stallard. His had taken him to Gas City at fifteen, my own to Fairmount at eighteen. One-hundred eighty acres of Indiana farmland on Sand Pike Road left me knowing the values of Marcus and Ortense Winslow. It was written all over this place. The Winslows were the caretakers of a human mystery. I wondered how much of this and lessons learned at the Back Creek Friends Church, a Quaker fellowship, remained with him until the end.

Midwest by Greyhound.

Indiana in 1959. I'm in the middle of nowhere, not knowing where tomorrow is. I'm chased by uncertainty, before me, after me, wanting to take a *Now* that was mine for its own. I just got off the bus, a southbound Greyhound. I see it become a mirage in the dust at a place where the road touches the sky. The ever-changing, never-ending line of a planet. I had an appointment with a stranger named Time.

Was this my escape — to a quiet piece of life to think of uncertainty?

Where in it would I find an echo of hope?

They had faces. The signs randomly sprinkled along farm fences on the way back to Lexington. The rusting relics of yesterday, "Funks Hybrids" . . . the corn was tall. Signs were the signatures on the landscape of the mind: "Chew Mail Pouch," "Burma Shave," "EAT," and other neon invitations to find a diner soon. "See Rock City," "See Ruby Falls." "See the *Mirage*;" another sign posted up ahead.

Appearing Tonight! Who would it be? From now till when and where would it be?

Bring Your Own Special Someone. Who would it be?

I wondered what it would be like to be somewhere else, another night. I was at a place in the middle of somewhere, its ever-changing faces on the fence row. I wondered, near the sun's set, would there be an appointment at an intersection of my own ahead? The harmony of four- cylinders and a gearbox precisely brought a tiny polished object and the song of its soundtrack on an open road back home. Chances were a change was about to show up at someone's doorstep.

My own.

—∞—

Jazz on a Summer Evening was showing at the Circle 25 Drive-In. 1959's Newport Jazz Festival featured jazz vocalist Anita O' Day. Along with everyone else George Wein put in the festival that year, she made it one of the best ever. This film found the portal to my being that wasn't there before. Jazz was fresh, unbound by convention, creative notions in music freely expressed. An artform.

Learning about life in less academic ways became the space I needed before enrolling at the University of Kentucky, fall 1963. Intimacy with music can be learned again through a new and different instrument. I had begun on an old acoustic guitar, listening to the work of different players, their personal styles—keeping things simple. I sensed early on where music was made made a difference. Blending instruments, acoustics, studio setting, artist, material, session musicians, producer, and recording engineer make a vision real.

The year 1959 was the best of times to be learning to play guitar. Listening led me to places I could only imagine: center stage, a street corner, or a recording studio somewhere. I just happened to be learning when much was yet to be said in the art of recording. Hours passed . . . days to weeks. Learning became less painful. I seemed we were beginning to sense where we were going, my guitar and me.

James Burton, Chuck Berry, and Buddy Holly were my early influences. Chet Atkins was out of reach though a bunch of good—note selection, chords, and taste were there to borrow. Les Paul was unpredictably delicious. All I could do was listen.

Solos from "School Day," "Johnny B. Goode," "Hello Mary Lou," "Travelin' Man'" and "Susie Q," among others, are a sweet spot to begin.

The solos I learned from Dave Yorko, guitarist in Johnny and the Hurricanes out of Toledo, were tasty. His were clean and well-crafted on a red Gibson ES-355 Series guitar. The intro to Bill Doggett's classic "Honky Tonk (Part I)" was a challenging piece of good to learn.

Buddy Holly's "True Love Ways" suggests what he may have become. Near Paul Desmond-like figures of brilliant saxophone, philharmonic-flavored strings, and a harp's lightness were perfect. The arrangement was near flawless. Maybe I could have a Fender Stratocaster someday like Buddy Holly. I thought I could build a band. All I needed was the parts. Would the need to express myself be enough?

The fifties were about to end. The sixties would shape my generation at a crossroads unlike our own at Main and Lime. Intersections to come would be arrived at down the line of time. Hollywood and Vine, Haight and Ashbury, War and Peace, Right and Not, For and Against, Sixteenth Avenue South at Hawkins Street, our dreams and things real.

Songs were the towns on the road map of music. A band was on its way.

A new group with a new sound was a defining statement by the pushers of music. A recording studio and developing innovations in electronics were instrumental in defining rock and roll music during this time. Buddy Holly may have said to the Crickets, "Hey, guys, let's take the car over to Clovis and make a record. Roy, you and Waylon come along too."

Roy Orbison and Waylon Jennings made their first recordings in Norman Petty's tiny studio at 1313 West Seventh Street in Clovis, New Mexico, west of Lubbock. They took their West Texas music from Wink, Odessa, and Lubbock to Clovis to Memphis and Nashville, swiftly to the hearts of us all. The music of Clovis was Tex-Mex, its flavor distinctive. What happened in Clovis between February 1956 and September 1958 changed my world.

Muted notes shaped by a region's color. The sound was vintage Southwest Tex-Mex.

There was never a question why Buddy Holly didn't sound like anyone else. He was from someplace else. I believe in the fifties, *where* made all the difference. Echo was the sound of a region. Sound became the signature of the place where the music was born.

An echo could begin in a stairwell, in reverberation chambers, in loops on magnetic tape, and slapback effect became the new frontier of recorded sound. In the air, echoes went to play, ever-changing the sound of music. On the air, they changed our lives.

Local color was once important to folks. Broadcast content meant everything in a time of little sameness. A distinct difference between the music on the coasts and music of places in between emerged. It was fresh.

New strings, a vibrato section in his amplifier, and a touch of reverb put Duane Eddy's "twangy" guitar in touch with a generation. The Musitron's synthesized sound in the interlude solo defined Del Shannon's "Runaway," a favorite with people when we played it

Toni Fisher's "The Big Hurt" featured a haunting kind of voicing woven in it. The first time I can recall hearing phasing or phase-shifting effects on a record. Big sounding, brilliantly arranged, with fine chord changes. I still love the song.

Grady Martin's unique sounding solo in Marty Robbins' "Don't Worry" was made possible by a blown tube in the pre-amp of the recording console during a recording session. The take was kept, another hit was born for Owen Bradley in his Quonset hut. Distortion would forever be an overdriven signal, another in an array of choices found on the menu from rock and roll's garden of sound. Grady Martin's dialogue with the narrative in "El Paso" is a master-at-work event in recording history—a session musician inside the story of a song as deeply as the artist and lyricist.

Les Paul experimented with electronic-filled sound with a West Coast style. His ideas shaped the sound of music in our time. Reverberation and the chambers of our mind were a playground for notes and their echoes to play among others. Les Paul's innovations began in a mind's workshop as early as 1950. We all were part of his experiment.

Leo Fender carved his place in music history in 1950 with a blond ash body and a maple neck. One could drive a dream on a long and fretted boulevard. Fender's instrument line added colors of its own to sound. Fresh had only just begun in 1959. Guitars were becoming solid and would forever depend on electronics to bring their sound to the listener. Electronics would do for the guitar what avionics does for the stealth fighter.

Make it fly.

We all have a sense of not forgetting something fresh, often rare. I remember where I was the first time I heard Ray Charles play the first notes of "What'd I Say." The Wurlitzer electric piano was an unfamiliar instrument to me then.

The sweet spot of anything can be found. It is where its essence lives. You've simply got to find it your own way. I'd never heard an echo like "Heartbreak Hotel." An echo—it isn't there, is it? One moment, yes, then it is gone. "Peggy Sue" is music ended. Suddenly.

Heartbreak was a mirage at the end of the lonely street to remembering.

A manufacturer and its instrument line could define the sound of an artist or group. Sound was shaped by place, the artists and characteristics of the instruments and electronic landscape.

A violin or Harley-Davidson- you never forget the first time you hear one.

The mystery of reverberation's timeless quality is this. A heartbeat ago, a note had life then went away. The ink was barely dry on the signature signed by a studio somewhere. Each studio signed their name on a note with ink that was their own. Their distinct presence. Some were that unique. Rudy Van Gelder's studio in Inglewood Cliffs, New Jersey, remains a favorite of mine. Studios in Nashville, Cincinnati, New York, New Orleans, Memphis, Muscle Shoals, Chicago, Atlanta, Clovis, and Hollywood and Vine's Capitol Records on the West Coast signed, sealed, and delivered a kaleidoscope filled with colors to hear.

Something happened to a signal on its way through an electronic circuit in the vapor of a Casablanca-like fog. There was a place sound could live before it said goodbye? The transistor had not completely replaced the glass palaces and their ghosts. Electrons danced with time in the ballroom of a vacuum tube. No one really understood what was going on in there. The mystical quality of sound was given a sense of place when vacuum tubes roamed the electronic range. Before ever leaving its home. The playground where sound recreates with surface and plane, with texture and space is place itself. Sound finds its way to other unique qualities, all held in the palm of where it happens to be. The same can be said for inspiration. One had to be patient in 1959. We gave them time to warm up, to let the dance in vacuum tubes begin, to give romance a chance. We took the time to let a virtue be.

Who did I look to?

Except for a few years of piano lessons, I had no experience in the performing side of music. I know I was drawn to particular artists. Why, I can't explain, other than being left an appreciation of their gift. I've not a single reason, simply the way they blended it all together.

A personality at Lexington's WVLK radio once asked who influenced me most in the beginning.

Ray Charles.

Among the many things I like about Ray Charles is the pace of his music. "I Got a Woman" is in no hurry to get anywhere. Ray put Stella on a pedestal by starlight. He colored leaves on autumn trees. That's good enough for me.

Ray Charles knew his band and how to use its players effectively. All the good ones did: James Brown, Little Milton, Joe Tex, Bobby Bland, Duke Ellington, and others. Great bands have great leaders. The personnel and material you choose are paramount. All that remained in that summer was to get inside myself. I gave an idea some space, enough to build a band. From a summer inside 1959, time would take a band and its music all the way from the sweet corn to hot-buttered soul.

Summer left in its wake the scattered days of easy. Fall became a time to look back on a senior's year, my classmates and teachers and the music. 1959—the songs of my youth were writing the history of our generation. How special would it be to be a part of a single song on someone's favorites list? The name of the band they wanted held fast in ink on a dance or a prom bid seemed far away, a mirage on a dream's horizon.

I was left to find a place on a radio dial and listen. I practiced moves on my guitar and an old upright piano, a Chicago, alone in my room. The Top 40 was a wellspring. Would the rest of life rush away and I be left behind? Winter came suddenly. My inner tree was content with itself, warmed by a sense of purpose. The kaleidoscope turned. A New Year's days fell into place.

Tomorrow's geometry was there to believe in.

5
Popsicles, Icicles, Bright Stars, and Guitars, 1960

1960. I was eighteen. *To Kill a Mockingbird* and *A Separate Peace* were best-selling books. Something went wrong on the way past what should've been a bank deposit. *Psycho*, Alfred Hitchcock's memorable diversion from the Cold War, put minds on a curtain starkly different, more immediate—Soviet iron. A shower's scene, Janet Leigh, summer rain's diversions from reality.

The Magnificent Seven was a Western movie. Elvis got out of the army in March, and "Stuck on You" hit No.1. Percy Faith's lush "Theme from a Summer Place," and Presley's "It's Now or Never" shared the charts with "The Twist" and "El Paso." Ray Charles brilliantly styled "Georgia on My Mind." Tod and Buz put us on the mother road in a Corvette. *Route 66* arrived on television's Friday night.

A Russian SAM took Uncle Sam out of the Soviet sky in mid-May, the U-2 more than incidental in President Eisenhower's second term. A light and warmer side of life was presented in Mayberry when *The Andy Griffith Show* made its debut in October.

The charts were tasty with Ray Bryant Trio's "The Madison Time," Jackie Wilson's "Doggin' Around," Maurice Williams's "Stay," and the Drifters' "Save the Last Dance for Me." Dinah Washington and Brook Benton's duet "Baby You've Got What it Takes" was fine.

Popsicles, icicles, bright stars, guitars, and drive-ins on Friday night were some of the things we loved in 1960. The ordinary—not too much to ask for in a world quite different than now.

You want commonplace to go on forever, but it can't.

Influences, from Buddy Holly and Ray Charles to Bali Hai, knew no bounds. Learning had its frustrations. Alone, not easy at times. A storm and the clouds in it were distant, and then the harvest we inherited from its ever-changing winds would forever change our lives. The dawning of the Age of Aquarius had not begun. An ever faint echo of something in a rehearsal of its own could be sensed. Change was about to come, in Lexington, in America.

Sam Cooke was its historian.

The comfort of the fifties had ended. A decade of commitment and betrayal began. The first years of a new ten were quiet for kids just out of high school, all evolving, all involving. The sixties would change us all forever.

These were the times when soul men tried.

Ours were times between innocence and turbulence—between post-World War II's Iron Curtain forties, Iron Lung fifties, and Iron Butterfly sixties. The times often seemed to be a mirrored collection of misfits. How did we fit into the irony of it all at the ridge of a watershed at the mountaintop of the sixties? People got ready coast to coast, passengers boarded a train. Time for the rights of a civil people was on its way. Before long we all would be California dreaming, our ears tuned to Laurel Canyon and the clubs on Sunset, our eyes to reflections seen in window glass.

Holly Golightly was alone with her doughnuts in the morning at Tiffany's on Fifth Avenue. A catcher wandered, separated by a veil in between the in and out, the right and wrong. A separate peace could be found in The Inn of Indigo Blue. Answers to questions asked lay hidden in between the here and there. They would sadly go yet unanswered. Some would have and others not.

It was a time when you were in college or in country.

Before it all ended, we would have come the distance. From Clear Lake to White Lake, from Buddy Holly to Woodstock, from 1959 to 1969. Ten years. We found our way from the age of innocence into the Age of Aquarius. The times ran deep, for some to sense what other's saw to be a mirage. Together we experienced what it is to be the footprint on a new road leading to a portal of the promise land?

Fifty years and more since I was young, is never far from now.

I first heard "Only the Lonely" on a car radio in Chicago. Roy Orbison recorded his first hit on April 15, 1960, in RCA Victor's Studio B. It was released in June, reaching No. 2 on Billboard's charts. Elvis Presley recorded "It's Now or Never" in Studio B on April 3, twelve days earlier. Destiny can be held in what you feel just touched your senses. Two songs made me think of little else but plans I had made to build a band I had named one summer ago.

The Temptashuns.

"Walk, Don't Run" become the anthem for what remained of the summer of 1960. Other songs I learned to play from the Ventures' first and second albums included "Ghost Riders in the Sky," "Harlem Nocturne," and "Night Train." I wanted to know more about blues music and began visits downtown. Barney Miller's kept bins in their record department, fresh filled with hits to buy, learn, and play. The record department and the support of the late Walter Morris for the band and its members never waned. We harvested most of our material from the garden of that record department long after.

Brian Wilson's creative genius drew upon the distinct sound of The Four Freshmen, who had long been my favorite vocal group. The Beach Boys' harmonies were complimented by a reverb-driven West Coast sound. The Wrecking Crew made them exceptional. Time spent getting around in Southern California was a way of life one could only imagine. The Beach Boys were clean and fresh, straight to me from the echo vaults hidden deep beside the Capitol Records Tower, Gold Star, and other colorful recording rooms in L.A.

My search to find a drummer ended after I heard about a senior-to-be in the concert band at Henry Clay. I contacted George Sadler not long after he returned from Florida that summer. Fall of 1960 and into winter found me in a search to find a third player and fresh ingredients for a tasty recipe and a menu of songs. The downbeat had begun.

The band became a patchwork of different personalities, styles, and strengths in the course of its life. Its colors were personal in the sometimes-colorless world of popular music. We gave each other the space to develop and to be the best we could be. I believe this was instrumental in what we became. Trust became the band's common thread, with respect to its changes in personnel and song. Trust leaves little else of concern. You play off the others and what they do. Instinctively, you don't forget it when it's good.

I was working in a manufacturing plant. Marathon Industries, out of Cortland, New York, had opened a plant here, prompted by the relocation of IBM's Typewriter Division to Lexington. Marathon assembled small components for IBM.

I learned Shelby Lorrison played guitar. Shelby, a 1958 Henry Clay graduate, could be found now and then at a Gulf service station on Winchester Road at Liberty. I believe that's where I first met him. Filling stations and being around them in the fifties was a way of life: car talk, girl talk—guys talking about tomorrow. He was interested when I asked. I began to practice with Shelby at his house two or three nights during the week. We would meet on the weekend on Richmond Road, where George lived. The first months were challenging for the Temptashuns.

I'd thrown myself into the band, learning to play a new instrument. Leadership was new to me at nineteen. The paths of three players were headed to a place of common interest. The positive influence of others in my life gave meaning to the unexpected acceptance we would experience, coming soon. Such is the harvest of determined preparation.

A musical instrument is a door to creative expression. Nothing's quite like an old upright piano. I like their acoustic quality. It's in the wood and wire, remarkably natural when soundboard and enclosure are one with the other. A piano takes its breath of air in air itself. You touch its keys and feel the heartbeat on the soul of its strings. It can change anyone. The relationship between an instrument and its player is unique. Without one, what is the other?

Holding on to one's own years.

Yesterday's highways are mystic connections, blue ribbons graced with relics of place at another time in its history. Driving to towns we played enriched the experience. Two lanes, one to, the other from—the very passages collected during the course of one's life. The lost and found could be found again in the house of time on the landscape of another.

The MG was my way on numerous trips. Radio was the music in the overture of the road. How long would this marriage of hope and unknown last? The thought never entered my mind. The story could be found scattered beside each path, the lessons in it learned. Ours was a landscape enriched by motels for tired and sleepy souls, filling stations for oil and gas, a diner now and then. Kindness was written on ordinary signs sprinkled here and there. The visual spice of yesterday had a tasty presence.

A road on a rural landscape had a ghostly appearance in moonlight. Mailboxes, fences, farm entrances, and lanes to farmhouses, barns, sheds, and small-town main streets were testament. Truth is, the first time we played in some places was my first to have ever been there. Bowling Green, Kentucky, was somewhere way out west.

Sign posted.

"Now Entering the Town of . . . *Somewhere*. Population *Only you and the others*."

The substance was pure as can be. Finding how deep it ran on its way to that place where one finds truth, was ever there. Emily had come back to *Our Town* in 1959. Emily learned how unconditional truth can be by knowing it can be found.

"Walking in The Sand" and "My Boyfriend's Back" played on the car's radio. Hearing them seduced me, the Angels and Shangri-las. "Be My Baby" held my imagination and its echoes captive to the Ronettes. It was liberating, this true romance on my way down a highway on the way to a place I'd never been.

The lyrics of conscience. You could see from here to forever the deeper you looked into polished chrome and paint. Rolled and pleated leather on an ocean of plush carpeting. Glass, clear and sparkling, with no blemish to be found.

The American hot rod and custom automobiles.

Their owners were the sculptors and stylists of American pop culture. This is the way we do it in California. Chopped and channeled, low to the ground, powered by a kaleidoscope of chrome, wire and porcelain, and veins for fuel. All nested in the louvered shade of a polished lacquered hood that opened. Colors on a flawless body born on the palette of a generation, filled to the brim with innovative charm. Appearing live and in person, next weekend, at the Kentucky Fair and Exposition Center, Louisville, Kentucky—The Machines. Stunning.

Another day trip to Cincinnati's Coney Island or the Fairgrounds in Louisville to the next rod and custom Show. There were other nights Dick Clark's Caravan of Stars rolled in to show in Freedom Hall. The notion that a band I know could be on its stage was more than an afterthought on my visits there. Music's sky was filled with the stars and their music, separate pieces pulling on everything else. It happened in time's signatures and gravity held it fast. Young minds wanted only to be entertained.

Another Caravan of Stars, I'm made my way to Louisville to hear "Raindrops."

The feeling's unmistakable, vintage Dee Clark. It's got Spanish moss and magnolia blooms written all over it. The song's got thunder. Tears fall from my eyes, right about the time a Bb chord followed by an A takes me where a D minor lives. Showers are falling in the afternoon on pecan tree groves and fields of thirsty cotton.

Summer snow.

One doesn't easily forget what it's like, caught in the sequined spell of an embrace. The imagined life of a girl group groupie—I never wanted it to end. The message in the voice behind the veiled glow on a radio's dial kept saying, "Baby, it's you."

I left Freedom Hall and put the top down before heading to the Henry Watterson Expressway, taking it to its end at St. Matthews. Shelbyville road led me past Hurstbourne and the City of Belle Meade to Middletown and out of Louisville on my way to Shelbyville, Frankfort, and home. Night was an indigo experience. The old Lexington Road had that kind of hue back then. It was late. I was blessed by the blend of warm summer air and the land. The radio was tuned south, and WLAC took my mind where it willed. AM radio in the a.m., starry nights with little to fence me in. Early times in yet unblemished years that began the sixties were priceless. The MG's lights illuminated the darkness on its path. A late-night film showing on the drive-in movie screen ahead began. I slowed to read the marquee and passed it by.

Louisville had a number of bands that frequently came to Lexington. WAKY radio with nationally known personalities—"Jumping" Jack Sanders, Bill Bailey, and Gary Burbank—enjoyed regional reach and popularity. WAKY offered attractive promotional opportunities for Sanders and the Sambo booking agency he formed with Ray Allen and Hardy Martin in Jeffersontown, a Louisville suburb. Louisville bands, managed by Sambo, recorded on Tilt and Jam record labels. Gene Snyder's Joni Agency managed others.

The Middletown Hop and Louisville's Fontaine Ferry Park were two popular venues to showcase their bands each weekend. Areas around Louisville, southern Indiana, and Lexington were thirsty for live music done well.

WAKY enabled their band's records to be heard. Lexington benefited from the local support they received in Louisville. They brought their vocal style and Echoplex echo chambers, popular with the Sultans, Carnations, and Tren-Dells, to venues in Lexington, one being Joyland Casino. The Sultans' "You Got Me Goin'" with "Cosmo," was the first record I heard by a Louisville group on the radio. A record by a Lexington band was difficult to get played on WAKY. Popular demand on our behalf made it possible in the mid-sixties.

"It'll Be Easy" and "You Can't Get Kissed When You Twist" with singer Tommy "Cosmo" Cosdon were recorded by the Sultans in the early sixties. The band later featured singer Jimmie Orten after Cosmo left the group.

"Toss in My Sleep" showcased the breadth of Orten's voice. The Sultans were an exceptional band.

The Carnations and the Tren-Dells, led by guitarists Hardy Martin (lead), Wayne Young (rhythm), and Ray Allen (bass) was another. The Carnations featured drummer Diane Patton and Eddie Humphries on tenor sax. Theirs was a different look. Combined or separate, the Carnations were a tight band. The Tren-Dells recorded vocals with the Carnations. "Nite Owl" was a favorite. I saw both together numerous times, most memorable in the ballpark at the Kentucky State Fairgrounds when they backed the late Bobby Vee.

"Cosmo" and Wayne Young formed their own band, Cosmo and The Counts, later in the decade. We lost "Cosmo" in 2013. Wayne Young continues to perform with his band, New Legends. He presents well-done tributes to other artists, including Eric Clapton.

Solo artist Paul Penny recorded "Honey," and often appeared with the Carnations and the Tren-Dells. Paul remains active, performing as well as ever in Louisville.

I learned from watching the Sultans and Carnations and Tren-Dells. They let you know how good you had to be to be better than they were. I liked their sound, energy, polish, and the audience response they received. They gave me a confidence early in 1960 we could be as good, even better. Never a doubt in my mind.

The noticeable difference between Louisville bands and Lexington's own seemed to me reflected by the songs in their sets and the personnel. Louisville bands featured a lead singer on vocals, backed by three others and five players. You played an instrument or sang. Nine people made Louisville bands look big. The Temptashuns, like most of the other combos in Lexington, were composed of two guitars (lead and rhythm), bass, sax, piano or organ, and drums. You played an instrument and sang lead or backup. Six players, though not as big a look, could be an expressive combo. It enabled us to present a more complete range of material on our set lists and a bigger sound.

The Temptashuns were not without a piano/organ and brass section for most of the band's life. We featured two horns, sax, and a trumpet or flugelhorn as early as 1962. A trombone now and then a year or so later. Some may have sensed the impact of brass as well. America, its music, the sound of it, and its audience began a change later in the sixties. The fusion of it all would be a bounty without end.

The music of Lexington bands, like Cincinnati, often featured more rhythm-and-blues content than Louisville. People in radio behind the music in Louisville had a lot to do with the rock, pop, and roll music influence on their own bands. Cincinnati, on the other hand, had long been bathed in rhythm and blues. Lexington became the third point of a regional triangle. I can't say enough about the influence of Cincinnati bands and King Records, with artists Hank Ballard and James Brown, on the Temptashuns. The songs of King on Brewster Street and R & B were the day's "Special" on the menu in my hometown. Lexington was rhythm-and-blues rich, with a style of its own. Charlie Bishop's band, the Houserockers, the Pacesetters, and the Temptashuns represented a sharply defined contrast to Louisville's talent or agency managed bands. Most of us in Lexington were not really managed by anyone for a time. Early in the history of the Temptashuns, we did our own booking.

Other Louisville bands arrived. The Epics, with the girls of Sacred Heart H.S., Janie Moss, Lindy Best, and Pam Bertoli. The Mystics, Nightcrawlers, Rugbys, and Oxfords.

The best of the bunch to me were The Monarchs. The boys of St. Xavier High achieved success with their recordings of "This Old Heart" and 1961s "Look Homeward Angel." I liked Paul Penny's fine Wurlitzer electric piano solo on the Monarch's nice version of "This Old Heart." His notes were subtle.

We did James Brown's original arrangement of that song, adding our own horn figures.

The Monarchs recorded "Look Homeward Angel" in Owen Bradley's Nashville studio. The record was released on the Sound Stage 7 label, a subsidiary of Fred Foster's Monument Records, a well-presented piece of music. Later in the sixties, we played now and then on the same night and campus as the Monarchs, a chance to listen to each other. Every chance to learn from more experienced bands like the Monarchs was taken. I thought we could be as good.

It was only a matter of time.

Till then, we looked around, listened to, and learned from what other bands did best. We worked to be as good, to be, in time, the better band. One's ear can be the door to the eyes of the soul. Recalling my father's words, "Tony, who you look to is who you can be." I turned my eyes beyond my hometown, Louisville, and Cincinnati.

My father's words became an anthem for a lifetime.

Branches of old trees line the sides of Ironworks Road. They bend to meet, not touching, a tunnel of a season's leaves. The road's a nave with a farm on either side. The farms define a transept in a sense. It is here, the spiritual nature of nature is personified.

Echoes of Michelangelo were to be found in a pristine chapel. Here in the Bluegrass.

Stone fences are special. Paramount in their making is the care and craft of their builder. Some are built with mortar, a common bond between the stones, others simply dry laid. The integrity of dry laid stone fences begins with how and why each stone is chosen and the care each stone is placed. If it feels right and you care, it will be without end. The builder gave it life; the purpose it was meant have, a part of something meaningful. The Temptashuns had begun with care.

Its scenes once seemed more pastoral then. The Bluegrass was more accessible in another time. Horses ran about, taking time in summer's sun to raise their ears and look at you, as if to say, "Look at me. I am somebody. I was born and raised here." Standing in silence, Thoroughbreds graze till it's time to have their grain. The only thing between you and greatness was a fence of natural stone or four-board painted wood. Brilliant white. They would have their day in the sun, standing near their paddock fence. Sadly, the room isn't big as then, time and its changes. Our day would come, our paddock defined, and once elusive opportunities realized.

I once knew a time to be by myself on May's first Saturday. I'd find no better time than the day of the Derby run to find the tree-lined roads of rural Fayette County. Newtown Road led me to Ironworks, to Paris Pike and Johnson Road—a cleansing experience. In between it all was Castleton Farm, Mt. Horeb Presbyterian Church, Spendthrift, Elmendorf, and C.V. Whitney Farms. Last night's party at the Whitney's was history by then. I passed them once again returning to Russell Cave. It was a time to be apart from the crowd, not a part of it.

A mind can craft a place for memories to play on quiet landscapes like no other. I find favor in time apart from the crowd rather than a part of one. I go there as I did then to find an oft-elusive answer. What it is like to bend one's neck; waiting for the roses, just before the truth is known it was all worth it? Here is the poetry of the Bluegrass.

Knowing this, I am complete. A garland all around my neck, fences in the rose's scent. I am a winner then as now, in a paddock of my own, still in touch with the best a moment has to offer. Ironworks Road is as good a place to be as anywhere, North Elkhorn Creek weaving its magic, meandering through bluegrass-covered limestone fields at a tempo self-defined, on its way to find another.

This was mine in May.

Anonymity can be a priceless gift.

Time measured time by clouds moving on a sky reflected on a little car's windshield. A morning's passage mirrored, moving across itself on red lacquer paint. An MG was a time machine, the timeless beauty of the Bluegrass, breathtaking. Clouds don't stay around long. They've work to do in answer to the call of another place. The wind pushing cotton on its way from here to somewhere can be heard, leaving echoes in a silent wake on the bluest skies I've ever seen.

She bends her neck slowly to let me touch her soft and friendly nose. Chestnut defines her color. She is stunning. She turns, gives her withers a shake, then walks to grass untouched. Until now.

The silence is delicious.

My leaving it all behind an unwanted agony.

North Elkhorn Creek's got a hold on me. What is it about a sense of place and its integrity that finds its way deep inside one's soul? Is it where I was, who I was with, or is it who I am? My eyes have played each movement of a symphony that is this poetic ribbon of water most all my life. The North Elkhorn, a shimmering mirror in the night on the land where horses play. She doesn't seem to favor any one place. North Elkhorn Creek's at home on the land of Whitney, Combs, or Gaines property, or on an acre of the common. Her blend of kindness shapes the way one looks at life.

For the rest of it.

Everywhere Different from Anywhere Else

Open space and objects on it frame a moment as a self-portrait in a piece of time. Neon's glow is everywhere. Somewhere in an unexpected invitation lies mystery in the rendezvous of light and shadow, face to face with strangers and each other. A heart could be captured there, embraced in the arms of sweet voices. The Shirelles, a cascade of charm for the senses. Girl groups filled the summer night in Joyland Park with promises. 1960. She speaks to someone, not me. I could never be that lucky. It could be love for all I know, but love was never meant to be this simple, was it? You will love me tomorrow, won't you?

Hot dogs and French fries and promises, portraits in the gallery of life's delicious tastes, lived on the menu, each and all for sale in Joyland. Promises of other nights long gone, pawned, forgotten, and left behind lay waiting on display in the windows of yesterday for someone. Suddenly a thought is redefined, interrupted by a fragrance. Fresh-popped buttered corn and others. The Penny Arcade at Joyland Amusement Park was life in the "Playground of the Bluegrass." Attractions along its row could be your friend, fresh produce in a garden of fun.

The now and then again sound of cast-metal milk bottles tumbling from their pyramid stack. Someone's won the game and the girl will get the teddy bear she wants—The Prize. Shadows defined this place. It was its own. Mechanical noises from the merry-go-round, Rocket, Tilt-a-Whirl and Ferris wheel were stark contrast to other voices singing in the key of screams. Somewhere in between the space between the song of one and the echoes of another, I held a ticket to ride on the carousel of time.

Background music from the Top 40 made it all bearable.

Garish traits of amusement parks are mere echoes born in the soul of a carnival, light a presence wrapped in darkness. Joyland seemed always best at night, a place one's senses longed to play. You could bathe in the sound of light and know all it is to sense the noise of the neon waterfall, a sound of color on its way from one hue to another, drenched in it all.

Neon's light and delicate touch is seductive, its colors beyond subtlety. Red is rich and raunchy, yellow deeper. Green is more than emerald. Life's breath is made real by neon's intoxicating quality. Its color's all its own, a still life of itself. You can bend it. You can watch it move, quickly like a fox, or light on a once-empty piece of darkness like a butterfly.

What it does to paint color, makes all things come alive at night.

She was to me the colors found in a prism called the night, my true forever splash, nothing subtle in it at all. This was all the way, near every fantasy a boy might know in the coming of his age. All was bright at night at Joyland. When colors such as these meet one another in the night, it is love . . . and I loved it.

Still do.

Light and sound and motion define the essence of pinball. The lost can be found in a gravity-driven game of reflections on the polished face of a stainless-steel ball on the move, as if it were time through a lifetime. A player could not escape the truth with the outcome of a game. All was mirrored on the face of glass, a transparent separation between aspirations and truth. The space between a silence and a noise was no more the moment a coin dropped in the slot and an overture of sound began. You had found a bid and "No Break" card of your own to dance with the night, a tango of light and a delicious noise.

For a nickel, one penny to a ball, you could score enough before the last one disappeared in the abyss of the return slot, a free game earned. A treat for the patient mind, rare any time.

Another run signaled by the sound of wheel on rail. Click. click, click proclaimed the "Wildcat" had begun its slow assent to the top. There, an intimate place of delicate balance was to be found, where one moment and the next are the same. Each wooden timber strained in a futile struggle with silence. I hoped this true romance with time and place would never end.

We could meet at some small café only the lonely know, a place I knew to be my record player and an LP. I was back to where it all began.

Frank Sinatra loomed large in my life.

An amusement park has in its bones a quality like no other. Joyland was bigger than anyone in it yet could make one feel they mattered. Long-ago carefree nights at Joyland were a time when ideas were being shaped and somehow began to make sense. You were somebody.

Empty promises were nowhere to be found.

Joyland was a symphony of light and sound, never at a loss for color, always the same yet never so. Here was a place where a mind could be dazzled by thousands of lights and reflections on glass, polished hand-rubbed paint and chrome on objects waiting, still and silent in the parking lot.

She was there each time I left for tomorrow, the lady in white, a silhouette reclining in the dark window of a summer sky. She was defined by the sensual undulating curves of the roller coaster. Her lace-like pattern of hundreds of white-painted, timber, supports ever-changing as I passed her slowly in my leaving. Joyland was delicious, a good time in my hometown. Some nights a longer way home might be taken, turning left on the road to Paris, all the way to Ironworks.

Ironworks Pike and roads alike were akin to a silk scarf around the neck of prosperity and all that implied. A waltz, with the night in three-quarter time, was easy on the most valuable real estate in Fayette County. The road, lined each side with native loose-laid stone and four-board wooden fences, was a portrait of serenity to her very edges.

Elmendorf's columns strained to touch the moon's light between two lions of sculpted stone. A horse farm defined by a uniqueness of such placid presence, dark and mysterious just before the dawn and dew. Four steps above its lawn, my imagination sketched the lines of a yesterday no longer living behind their welcome. 'Green Hills', a stately mansion long-since gone.

Who will hear their roar? What can the wind say of their silence to the lions of Spendthrift in the yard across the road? Who will know their pride? Elmendorf, a portal in whose outstretched hands the stars can rest, is rare.

Anything that can hold a sky aloft is mystical.

Could anything be more complete? A midnight sky on Ironworks was framed by a leafy canopy of old trees, the quiet peace of Spendthrift and Elmendorf along its sides. An MG engine's four-cylinder rhythm played its duet with Ray Charles on the radio. "Lonely Avenue." Another patch of blue found its place on a quilt of time, destined for a quiet corner in one's mind.

North Elkhorn Creek kept its appointment to meet another somewhere. Two lanes and moonlit, Ironworks was never less than stunning on the way to Russell Cave. The jot em down store was closed for the night at the crossroads of the two where it stands today. The illuminated halo over Lexington's downtown appeared.

Too quickly down the road back home.

A ticket to the next Dick Clark Caravan of Stars concert in Freedom Hall put away in the MG's glove box, mine to see the Shirelles on Saturday night. Joyland, again on Sunday.

Joyland Casino was known for big-name bands that had appeared on its stage in a rich colorful history. The Casino was an impressive room for dancing: a two-level stage at one end opposite a long bar at the other. The Casino's character was defined by tables, seating, palm trees, painted railings, and a sunken wood dance floor between it all. I recall Wurlitzer speakers nested in leaves on palm trees here and there, coconuts of house sound, an essence of Glenn Miller's "Moonlight Serenade" played to a near-empty room. In the near darkness, one could imagine an island of their own in the South Pacific, a beach beside an ocean of wood.

I spent quality time in Joyland listening to Louisville bands. A sweet, sweet rhythm and blues band from Cincinnati, Carl Edmondson and the Driving Winds, blew me away.

The Tikis would come up from Nashville now and then. Bo Diddley, down from Chicago, paid a visit. Lexington's Jimmy Lee Ballard and the Rejects were regulars featured on Sunday nights, their followers loyal. The Rejects were a tight bunch of players, rock and roll blended with some blues and a little country. I learned early in the sixties about performing watching Jimmy Lee, the Rejects, and others at Joyland.

Riding the wave of their hit record "Red River Rock," Johnny and the Hurricanes blew into town, appearing with Bobby Rydell, Jimmy Clanton, and others at Joyland. They were the band that backed vocal performers on this tour. I had learned some of Dave Yorko's solos from songs on their first two albums by then. He played precise, clean, and smooth. I liked his tone, most of all his restraint. I recall seeing Johnny Paris playing sax in the studio band for the popular TV variety show *Hullabaloo* in the late sixties. The Temptashuns were a combo much like his band in our early years.

—∞—

I learned about a gentleman who repaired and made violins by hand, circa October 1960. The unmistakable scent of old varnish, wood stain, and old wood defined the air in his Oldham Avenue instrument shop. "I've not made a guitar before, don't know why I couldn't."

So began a relationship with a real master in the craft of instrument making.

J.R. Miller fashioned a left-handed, somewhat Gibson-looking, guitar. He finished a solid African mahogany body with red transparent stain and edged with narrow bone-white bands inlaid. He faced the hardwood neck with a rosewood fingerboard with pearl inlaid now and then between solid brass frets. Nickel chromium keys and a pair of mail order soap-type pickups from the Carver Company in Covina, California, to go with controls and knobs harvested from my Fender Musicaster completed the instrument.

I took the original serial plate to Miller & Woodward for engraving, an inscription and date, 1-21-61. He attached the neck to the body in the same manner as Fender. Sadly, Miller had no tooling to install a steel rod in the guitar's neck. In time, the instrument's noting wasn't as true and consistent as performance demanded. I was left with no choice but to find another.

We found our place on the songs we learned. The ones we did were done well, some more polished than others. Two guitars and drums at year's end limited our menu and set list. An empty space needed to be filled at the low end of our sound. I looked to find a bass player. Other things needed to be considered. A sound system. We had none. We needed attire to be remembered in a visual sense. More importantly, an answer when someone called to ask "Can you guys be here from when to when on this day for this much to play a four-hour party?"

I wanted to know more about the place of music, how it was made, and where it was made. 1960 ended. Our time was near.

The Temptashuns were there for someone to want. I could taste it.

6
Sunshine, Lollipops, and Rainbows, 1961

1961. I was nineteen. *To Kill a Mockingbird* shared best-selling honors with *The Winter of Our Discontent.* Sandra Dee, William Holden, Elvis Presley, and Elizabeth Taylor were top box-office stars. Audrey Hepburn had breakfast at Tiffany's. Saturday mornings begun on the steps of the Lexington's Public Library in Gratz Park were inspiring. A sack of half a baker's dozen glazed doughnuts that I brought from Spalding's Bakery on North Limestone at Sixth Street was tasty. It wasn't Fifth Avenue, but sitting on those steps presented a long and narrow quiet view in Gratz Park. Sunlight found water drops in the fountain at its end. Historic Old Morrison on Transylvania's lawn beyond was framed by a refreshing study of serenity.

"Moon River," "I Fall to Pieces," "Runaway," and Bobby Lewis's slice of R & B "Tossin' and Turnin'" were hits. The Berlin Wall was completed. Things were going on in Laos and at the Bay of something we'd all rather forget about in mid-April. The Peace Corps was established and the McDonald Brothers sold their restaurants for $2.7 million. The buyer planned a chain of drive-in restaurants.

President Kennedy asked us to do for our country. Dave Garroway was host of the *Today Show* on NBC. People on the street outside Rockefeller Center's RCA building looked through glass windows into an aquarium of meaningful television. "The Twist" was a song and dance craze. The *Andy Griffith Show* made Mayberry a place where I'd sometimes rather be.

Ty Cobb died.

—∾—

George spent much of his time on his senior studies. He lived with his mother on Richmond Road at Owsley, a duplex. We practiced in a large room on the first floor on weekends. I remember wood floors, big windows, and tall ceilings. Three players, learning to walk before we ran, found natural light and openness. It seemed the perfect place to find a way to make it all work out. The sun rose on the Temptashuns near a place where Ashland, home of Henry Clay, stood stately. We were a trio of newbies on the tree-lined boulevard that is Richmond Road, near some of the most unreal estate in Lexington.

I got my handmade guitar from Mr. Miller shortly after January 21.

Midwinter months were slow to find spring. We had thirty or so songs, developing the kind of instincts only repetitive practice can develop. My own expectations were on their way to a place we weren't prepared to go just yet. I was confident the band would be ready. George's classmate and friend Larry Kelley was a drummer in another band, the Torques. Larry would phone George now and then to listen to our practice. Larry was the only person in the outside world getting a sneak preview of coming attractions.

The Temptashuns was a band with purpose.

—~—

March 18, 1961, a Saturday. George called to say a girl from the Pipers of Pan club at Henry Clay had phoned. "Could we play for party they were having that night on Providence Road? Their original band wasn't going to be able to make it." I called her back. "Yes. Eight to twelve." The party was in Chevy Chase.

"Dream Lover" was the first song the Temptashuns played at our first "live" gig. I did the vocals. Shelby and George were solid that night. The Temptashuns Band had arrived.

Our first set list presented all we had come to know, till then.

> "Dream Lover"/Bobby Darin; "Poor Little Fool"/Ricky Nelson; "Peggy Sue"/Buddy Holly; "Walk, Don't Run"/Ventures; "Sleep Walk"/Santo and Johnny; "Johnny B. Goode"/Chuck Berry; "In the Still of the Night"/Five Satins; "Tequila"/Champs; "Splish Splash"/ Bobby Darin; "A Teenager in Love"/Dion and the Belmonts; "Travelin' Man"/Ricky Nelson; "Sweet Little Sixteen"/Chuck Berry; "Since I Don't Have You"/The Skyliners; "It's Raining in My Heart"/ Buddy Holly; "That'll Be the Day"/Buddy Holly; "Come Go With Me"/Del Vikings; "Talk to Me"/Little Willie John; "Stagger Lee"/

Lloyd Price; "School Day"/Chuck Berry; "Oh Boy"/Buddy Holly; "All in the Game"/Tommy Edwards; "True Love Ways"/Buddy Holly.
Our encore: "Night Train"/Ventures.

The Pipers of Pan paid the Temptashuns $15 for four hours. Before the night ended, we had another engagement to play the next weekend. The first set list was a blend of twenty-three vocals and instrumentals. I left believing we had done okay. The essence in a compliment was unexpected: "Where have you guys been?" The measured, determined way things had come into play proved invaluable in the next few months. I could never have imagined how quickly the word would get out.

The second time around was a surprise birthday party the following Saturday for a friend of the host. They wanted to hear the Temptashuns. I asked Wendell Sams to sit in with us. The house, located on Lexington's Windermere Road, had a pine-paneled recreation room downstairs with its own upright piano, an old one. Wendell walked right to it, sat down, and we played "Mother-in-Law." Alan Toussaint would've approved. Everyone had fun.

On my way home, I thought a piano would give the band more chances to perform the broader choice of songs charting in music. I sensed how well Wendell blended with what we were about that spring. We would play some good music on southern nights down the line.

Wendell Sams was singing at the time on weekends at the New Lime House Bar on the corner of Third Street and North Limestone. The bar could be a pretty rough place on a Saturday night. Wendell lived with his parents on South Mill between High and Maxwell, in the heart of Old Lexington's South Hill neighborhood. House owner Jimmy Young played guitar lightning quick through an echo chamber. Young's band played country music regularly at the bar. Wendell sang tunes and played piano in the band. The bar, vacant many years, was saved, became the Atomic Café, and has since closed.

Wendell could sing the Hank Williams and George Jones songs about as well as anyone. His family had a strong influence on who he was, a hard worker before his time. Wendell was genuine; you just loved the guy.

After that night on Windermere, I recalled "Student Night" 1958 and another night after the Bluegrass Fair that summer. Wendell had shown me three chords on an acoustic guitar. Here we were together again, spring 1961. It all seems so long ago. I cannot measure the difference it has made for me in the seasons since.

I asked Wendell to be in the band and loaned him enough money to buy a Wurlitzer electric piano the following week. The Temptashuns, now a quartet, would visit the neighborhoods of Fats Domino and Jerry Lee Lewis. The trunk of Wendell's '55 Buick was just right for the instrument's dimensions. He repaid me in time and many times over; it was a matter of trust. He and I would practice new songs at the house on Mill Street. His family later moved to Alabama Avenue, off North Limestone.

I followed Wendell home to help carry the piano to his room after many nights of music. I recall an hour or so into a winter snow at 2 a.m. Snowflakes may melt on Alabama, but time won't let a memory go away.

They're like a fossil on one's face.

The Temptashuns played our third engagement for The National Convention of Episcopal Youth at Christ Church Episcopal, downtown. Doug Hammonds, drummer in another band, sat in for George that night. I learned Doug could play saxophone as well. We talked about music. Thus began a long and meaningful musical experience for Doug and me.

The fourth was for free. We crossed over the Kentucky River on the bridge to Madison County at Clay's Ferry. Speck's bar in Richmond had a college following, a reputation to uphold, and it did. We played it well. Wendell was going to be just fine as our lead singer.

I met an Eastern student named Gary Edwards that day. Gary was the lead singer in the Maroons, a band based in Richmond. Other bands he formed were Gary Edwards and the Embers and SAGE (Sherry and Gary Edwards). Gary remained in music for many years, performing in Las Vegas. I worked with Gary Edwards once, a memorable evening in Louisville, in the seventies, substituting for his fine keys player Norman Osborne.

Gary is the nephew of Lexington writer Don Edwards; whose creative columns were a breath of fresh air in the Lexington newspaper for many years. I miss Don's wit.

Sadly, Don Edwards passed away in July 2016. I treasure the column he wrote about the Mag 7 Reunion in 2001. We were a part of the whimsy somewhere in the local colors found in his book as well. Don was good to the band, always gracious to me. Those who knew Don well are blessed to have been around him so long, to have caught the essence that must have danced in the air around him, those thoughts and words, the butterflies that somehow never found their way to paper. We corresponded occasionally after he retired, till he became too ill to play the back-and-forth game of a few words now and then, a Christmas poem, or simply a "how are you these days?"

Life . . . it was so good to be young then.

I heard about a band that frequently played Speck's at the time. The Exiles, like some of our own, were in high school. Speck's was as good a place as any in Madison County for J.P. Pennington and the late Jimmy Stokely to find a way to a Church Street soul revival and a Mike Chapman-penned Billboard hit. I happened to be in a Kansas City record store when "Kiss You all Over" hit No. 1, circa 1978. Their record played on the store's sound system. I was Kentucky proud, later seeing the Exiles when they appeared on *Midnight Special* and *The Tonight Show* with Johnny Carson.

They changed their name and direction, in time becoming Exile, a solid country ensemble mixed a little differently than the original Exiles lineup. Today, they represent the bluegrass in a fine way, never sounding better. J.P. Pennington has a nice touch in writing a song and has written many. J.P.'s the son of Renfro Valley's Lily Mae (Ledford) and Ray Pennington. He took the Ledford inheritance, a lineage given him, and its musical gifts to build a life of remarkable achievement. His uncle, Red Foley, is a legend in country music.

—∾—

The Easley Brothers operated a Phillips 66 Service Station on New Circle Road at Meadow Lane. I no sooner finished giving my car a Sunday bath when a friend said I had a phone call. George Sadler told me, "Everybody's here waiting. You've got to come over." Everybody's here? Sunday wasn't on the schedule, the next engagement a few days away. Many of Henry Clay's graduating class had come to George's house after their baccalaureate service. They wanted to hear the Temptashuns. I left to get my guitar and amp for an afternoon in the sun. The Class of '61 was waiting in a backyard of blankets spread randomly on its lawn.

Some hearts liked the way we did "Peggy Sue." Others "Hello Mary Lou." The songs of Buddy Holly and Ricky Nelson blended well with "Walk, Don't Run" and "Night Train." Wendell signed his name with "Mother-In-Law." We ended with "Stagger Lee." The band loaded out to the echoes of Lloyd Price, strangers no more to young faces or chilled punch from a cut glass crystal bowl on white linen.

The sun had begun its set; The Four Freshmen sang about graduation day on the radio, behind the face on my car's dashboard. I would remember always an afternoon in the sun, stopping for a Big Boy platter at Frisch's in Idle Hour and taking the long way home.

Graduation Day turned into night. The faces of the Class of '61, were turned to us again at Spring Valley Country Club. Friends would go their separate ways in four hours. Some forever.

The Temptashuns Band only just begun.

Would a senior class somewhere want the Temptashuns to play their prom next year? Little did I know how many. The American high school gymnasium was no stranger to staging the Great American Teen Drama: the senior prom. Young faces reflected confidence and uncertainty, in near-slow motion across a plane of polished lacquered wood. A timeless image of innocents drifting, as clouds do on the plane of farm pond water. The portrait of a stillness broken in a gallery of still life.

A dance with all it is to be young.

This was theirs; their evening forever. Their evermore. Kids could transform a gym at Anywhere High to Bali Hai in a heartbeat. It was magic to play these places. The imagery is unforgettable.

Rodgers and Hammerstein's *South Pacific* is brilliant. Bali Hai is everyone's *special island*. The sea meets the sky there. Somewhere, we would touch down, often playing songs named below the lines of no-breaks on each card in someone's senior prom. Attendees had written a name to share their place on each, someone for this night only, another for a lifetime.

I fell in love with these nights. It may seem corny now.

Not then. Not on a prom night in May 1961.

We were younger than springtime on our way to older than summer. Autumn was around a bend ahead. The imagery of one's own youth on enchanted evenings comes time and again to a memory.

I heard about a new band at Lafayette High. The Invictas were Doug Hammonds, Earl Morgan, and John Page. A fourth member, John Polk, a student at Henry Clay, played piano. Wendell and I went with Shelby to hear them at a private party. They sounded pretty good. Doug, their drummer, had played a night with us recently at Christ Church Episcopal. I remembered he played sax. The Temptashuns with a sax—a combination like Johnny and the Hurricanes—felt right. A horn section in the band down the line was attainable. Maybe one of the others could play bass.

Not long after that night, the Invictas were no more. We had both Doug and Earl; the reputation the Temptashuns was building around town seemed all the friendly persuasion I needed. This was a defining moment for me because of the musical relationship Doug and I would build together over the next few years. All we had in common musically would turn the Temptashuns and its music in a rhythm-and-blues direction soon. Doug Hammonds and Earl Morgan joined the Temptashuns on drums and bass. We were now five, still young, a rock and roll band with a lot of work to do.

—m—

Harry Dean Stanton was in the drama department, studying acting under Professor Charles Dickens in the Guignol Theater on campus. Bobbie Ann Mason would graduate from the University of Kentucky, head for New York City to begin a job writing for a movie star magazine, and pursue her dream. I enrolled in English 101, an evening class at the university.

Lonely weekends without music would be out of the question for the next seven years.

—m—

We played our first off-campus fraternity party the next night out Newtown Road. Sleepy Hollow Park had a screened pavilion on the banks of North Elkhorn Creek, near the falls of Elkhorn. Time stood still in an almost Paul Sawyier-like setting. Sycamore trees stood stately on the banks of a gentle stream that is Elkhorn Creek. Could anywhere be better to spend a summer evening with the Temptashuns than where moonlight found its way to a sycamore's branches? Great trees always get the best seat at nature's unending live concert it seems. Oh, the mystery in the shadows of a sycamore's bark. We took a ten-minute break on the hour, a chance to listen with my eyes.

That would never change.

We played Lexington Country Club on May 5, a party for a student attending Henry Clay. She danced on her birthday the same day Alan Shepard made his sub-orbital flight over the Atlantic Ocean. Kitty Hawk, Act II, in a play about a journey to outer space had ended that day. Act III would be played out in the theater of the universe by NASA's other players another time.

She was only sixteen.

I daydreamed about playing guitar like Chuck Berry or session players on Elvis Presley records. Doug wanted to play sax like Charlie Bishop and King Curtis. Shelby imagined himself to be the Ventures' rhythm guitarist, George their drummer. Wendell was happy being himself, and that was good enough. I sensed a touch of Don Gibson in him at times. Wendell was anything but lonesome.

Not long into the summer of 1961, George Sadler left the band, having fallen in love. He married the girl of his dreams and moved out of town and on with his life somewhere in Florida. I never saw him again.

Sadly, I learned George passed away December 2016 in North Carolina.

—m—

Doug's older brother, David Hammonds, attended UK and was a member of the Kappa Alpha fraternity. David invited us to play at a backyard cookout, an affair for a few of his college friends and fraternity brothers at their family home. Doug played drums, and we did a couple of R & B songs unrehearsed before that afternoon. It became clear to Doug and me if you're going to play for the college folks around here, you better have a bunch of R & B on your menu. Can't think of anything more important for us to know. We learned most all we needed to know that afternoon to take a show and its music to the fall semester of college about to begin.

Our set lists thereafter were shaped by what the "college" audience preferred. The music felt good. Doug and I went to Barney Miller's for the best rhythm and blues Walter Morris kept in the dark recesses of his 45 rpm record bins. There, we found Freddie King, Phil Upchurch, John Lee Hooker, Bobby "Blue" Bland, Little Willie John, Bill Doggett, Earl Bostic, and other hidden R & B gems.

The band played a private affair at Herrington Lake then spent the rest of the summer at practice, exchanging ideas and crafting expectations. I continued going to see Dick Clark's Caravan of Stars in Freedom Hall or hear Louisville's bands, as I had last summer. Before this summer ended, we played the Middletown Hop for free. September up ahead seemed far away. It would be special for us.

I'll never be lonely anymore or so the Dixie Cups tell me. Now and then I'd head out Georgetown Road, US 25, to the Old Dixie. The place stood just down the road from what once was an old roadhouse known as the Green Dome in Scott County.

I met Earl Grigsby, a member of Kon-Tiki and the Rafters, one Saturday night that summer. I listened at a table to live music outdoors by an old tree. The hour was long past shade. Earl and I shared music and friendship from then on. For many years after the Old Dixie was torn down, the tree stood where I knew it once to be. It was the lone remaining remnant of another time.

It's been gone forever.

Ruby and the Romantics played lightly on the MG's radio. A date was this innocent's dream amid my uncertainties that summer. I needed more than my car and no particular place to go. Seven weeks of summer remained. The thought the Temptashuns might not stay together, or even playing if we did, was on my mind.

In early August, Doug and I asked Larry Kelley, now a senior-to-be at Henry Clay, if a move to another band might be of interest. Larry joined the band. I'd grown to like Doug's relaxed R & B way of drumming. Doug was as good a player as we could've asked for. I hoped Larry wouldn't wonder long if we were right for him. He was for us. Doug could now move to sax full-time, where he really wanted to be. Time remaining that summer gave us space to rehearse with Larry where I lived with my family in Lexington's North End.

The Home of The Temptashuns, a garage band.

It took little time after the band's move to begin drawing a crowd. When the curtain went up, a place for cars and a workshop became a stage. We, the players, carried on, acting out an ever-changing story. Examples of the chart rich playbill of songs made just right for us to learn were "Travelin' Man" and "Hello Mary Lou." Our set list was biscuits made from scratch played with an ever-growing sense of confidence. Such were the times in our lives deep into that summer.

Friday, August 11, 1961. The Temptashuns appeared with our new drummer at Spring Valley Country Club, next to HILLENMEYER NURSERY on Sandersville Road. "The Temps," as local high schoolers had begun to call us, were on the minds of others planning social events to be held in the coming months. As things continued to grow, I asked Larry to handle bookings and contracts, leaving me better able to plan the directions of the band's music and its sound.

Doug was always there for me, too, with good things to contribute, and I listened.

Doug might ask, "Hey, Tones, how about it?"

"Doug, where did you find this record?"

He took me to the answer every time. With a song.

An open weekend allowed me a few days to be away.

August 19, 1961—Nashville, the first time.

My first of five visits to Nashville and the role each played in shaping me musically are beyond compare. The road to Nashville was a Gershwin shade of hue that August, a rhapsody in a roadside-filled collection of the ordinary. To what kind of ocean would this paved two-lane river lead me?

I left Lexington before dawn. A light fog lay like a blanket, dew asleep on the paddock's rich green blades. White fences on Calumet Farm were crisp as starched linen. Silence was never more stunning nor the late summer moon. The watchtower light at Blue Grass Field searched for the lost on the darkest sky, 'round and 'round, finding nothing more than empty there this time of day. I escaped the watchtower's beam, passing ornamental iron gates, now closed, at the stone entrance to Keeneland Race Course, on my way down the hill. I crossed over South Elkhorn Creek on US 60 to the first town, Versailles. All was quiet on Main Street.

We continued west on Main to Rose Hill, leaving Versailles on our way to Lawrenceburg. Soon, the MG and I crossed over the Kentucky River on the car bridge at Tyrone. The span was beside and below another, much taller one. It loomed with a silent presence, a bridge for trains, its rusting steel in daunting silhouette against a thick fog. Unmoving, lace-like and asleep, the Tyrone stood above the river.

She was lovely yet eerie, like the morning itself.

So, it was in these early hours, not so unlike a silent peace up on the hill, where distilled and aging spirits slept in the home of Wild Turkey. The MG ran smooth on its own octane, still life in motion reflected in the face of her polished red bonnet. Such were reflections in the mirror of the world around me. Vapors, borne on the summer air, defined the essence that was that summer and my own.

Bardstown—Stephen Foster, an old home in Kentucky, a place in the sun where spirits Heaven Hill and Old Bardstown were distilled was ahead, anxious to wake.

I slowed on 31E South, a Blue Star Memorial Highway, crossing railroad tracks by the old hardware store at New Haven. One could get a fresh sandwich made for the road to go with a soda and Nabs at the store. The merchant began with, "How thick do you want this bologna, young fellow? Would you like a slice of tomato, some lettuce, and cheese? It's all fresh."

"Yes, sir, and some Miracle Whip and mustard and two Coca-Colas would be fine. Some Planters and Nabs too. I'm in no hurry." He cut a chunk from a block of sharp cheddar and put things on ice. He played the cash register's bell. I paid for it all and thanked him.

He replied, "Come back again."

The narrow metal sign on the door read—Honey Crust Bread. When you opened doors in those days, your hand was on the pulse of a way of life. The sign was weathered, no doubt mirroring the hands of locals having passed this way till then. People were close to the land there and a way of life. I opened the screened-in door and waved. Walking to my car, I imagined many colors of this small piece of Kentucky.

How would they be in October in New Haven in this my natural prime?

Glass bottles were made to last back then, sent from the homes of their bottling plants. The pride of folks to say where each began was embossed in glass of bottle green. The bottom of one read Atlanta, Georgia—the other Montgomery, Alabama. The separate journeys of those two bottles were a momentary thought. The car, the lunch, and I left New Haven, heading down the road to Horse Cave, past the Wigwam Village #2 Motel at Cave City, and on to Park City.

I was in cave country, the place Floyd Collins once called home. The carnival of February 1925 at Sand Cave had long since disappeared, yet the words from *The Washington Post* at that time remained a clear and present truth: "It concentrated in one agonizing individual case the experience of the human race in its struggle for existence."[13]

I drove on to 31W, the Dixie Highway, west to Bowling Green, crossing the bridge at the Barren River. I remember the Bale Tire and Auto Center, once the Quonset Auditorium, a whimsical structure by a bridge near the river's banks. Today was the first of many in, around, or passing through Bowling Green. The road led south to Franklin and the state line of Tennessee.

Soon, I would be in Nashville.

I since learned from a documentary titled *Rovers, Wrestlers, & Stars*, the Quonset Auditorium was a destination for the likes of Ray Charles,

Ernest Tubb, George Jones, B.B. King, Bill Monroe, Fats Domino, Little Richard, James Brown, and the bluegrass and country and western music of local folks—a place for good food, good music, dancing, professional wrestling, and good times.[14]

Since before the Civil War, Nashville had become known as a 'publishing town,' specializing in hymnals, Sunday school literature, religious tracts, and Bibles; however, Nashville would soon become famous also for publishing music.[15]

I had grown up taking songs out of the *Broadman Hymnal* to heart. The hymnal was published in Nashville, hallowed ground I suppose. I do know that "Blessed Assurance" could make you feel something's there to lean on when times seemed too much to bear.

Something spiritual.

I had learned most all I knew about Nashville, Tennessee, from the liner notes of long-playing records, the LPs in the bins at Barney Miller's, and my own records. The sound on records by Brenda Lee and Patsy Cline, the Everly Brothers, Floyd Cramer, Chet Atkins, Don Gibson, Marty Robbins, Roy Orbison, and others had a distinct character. Something made the records what they were beyond an artist and its players. I wanted to find what the essence was. I wanted to be near it as I could. I was there for a few impressionable hours that summer. I had grown to like music made in Owen Bradley's, the sound of Decca, Coral, Capitol, Mercury, and Columbia Records.

I experienced a connection to the golden age of what was is being called "the Nashville Sound" that day in August 1961. The good taste of country was there. A flower had begun to bloom in its garden of sound. Nashville was the bridge between postwar music of the late forties and early fifties, rockabilly, and rock and roll.

I stopped at a service station in Goodlettsville, filled the car with gas, and asked for a phone book—804 16th Avenue South. "It's down off Broadway," the station attendant told me. "Ain't nothin' out there but a bunch of old houses."

Continuing south on 31W, the Dickerson Pike, I drove into Nashville and crossed over the Cumberland River bridge, then turning right passing Municipal Auditorium, I found myself being swept around the Tennessee State Capitol on the hill. The James Robertson Parkway was pulling me in an arc, easy as a swing on an elm tree's branch. To Church Street, past the Hotel Noel and L&C building into the heart of the city.

The signature of L&C, the Life and Casualty building, was its weather-sensitive sign, changing colors depending on weather and its change. The sign, a beacon, lived all by itself on the Nashville skyline. Blue meant "fair" weather. Pink signaled a change was gonna come. Lighting, from bottom to top, meant the temperature was rising; the opposite, top to bottom, true when falling. L&C's sign spoke a language anyone could relate to. I would be changed because of this day.

I would be pink.

Charlotte took me to Printers Alley, a short one-way affair between here and somewhere I wasn't old enough to be. The Carousel, Black Poodle, Voodoo Room, and Skull's Rainbow Room were neon invitations to visit another time. The place was asleep, the day yet early. Turning on Church to Second making my way to Broadway, I passed the Ernest Tubb Record Shop. Its not-so-ordinary sign read, "Ernest Tubb . . . Record Shop . . . Midnight Jamboree . . . 12 to 1."

I planned to listen to this kind of Broadway on my way home.

Broadway on the shores of the Cumberland. . . . Nashville U.S.A. beneath the long shadow of the Ryman auditorium, home of the Grand Ole Opry, everything was happening, played out in a block or two that became a country music mecca to anyone who ever crossed a fiddle with a steel guitar.[16]

The Cumberland was the shining Big-Sea-Water with a place by its shores: Music City.

On Broadway, a right turn on Fifth, a sign on the old church read Grand Ole Opry. The Ryman, once the Union Gospel Tabernacle, was named after a reformed riverboat captain, Thomas G. Ryman. He built the place in downtown Nashville in 1892. Sixty-nine years later, The Ryman stood stately; being near her made one humble. I drove by the mother church and joined an unbroken circle. Drawn to something I couldn't explain, felt like an abstract awakening. Spiritual matters can make one feel at peace with many things. They need no explanation.

Saturday morning. The place had been awakened by sunshine falling warm on its large stained glass Gothic windows. Inside on the Ryman stage, colors must've danced like the children of light on its playground of hallowed wood in an unbroken silence. Tonight, the Ryman would hold weekly services for the lovers of country music. Heaven, Martha White Flour, Royal Crown Cola, and Prince Albert Tobacco were always down-to-earth at the Ryman.

Tootsie Bess's Orchid Lounge waited for its next customer across an alley behind the Ryman. I made my way again to Broadway, passing Union Station, a natural stone icon with its signature clock tower. It nearly touched the sky, my train of thought left to one of arrival, departure, and time.

Finding Sixteenth Avenue South, I had arrived.

It was different then; a turn-of-the-century neighborhood, an ordinary place that felt right to be around. Old curtains in tall windows opened were the kind of cloth that moves effortlessly with the breeze on its way through. Lace moved with the wind, its song near silent. Old glass, beveled and imperfect, defined the way light is shaped, passing through it. Near human, it was that tangible. Sixteenth South was front-porch-swing, with a cat and hound and alley now and then. I witnessed the face of a place with a kind character. I felt a welcome, as if it were an invitation to a table and Sunday dinner.

About the only thing out there in 1961 was Decca Records, a house with a Quonset building directly behind it. The Owen Bradley Recording Studios.

I was hungry, an old tree's shade near Owen Bradley's all I needed to begin. Cotton-white, breeze-driven clouds drifted on their way to an appointment somewhere. I was spellbound, a setting so unlike the sad inheritance of tumbleweed blown about on a dusty street in a Texas town the day after the last picture show.

Butcher paper peeled back, signaled a lunch beginning a whisper shy of the Deep South. Nearer than I had ever been. A priceless moment had arrived. Silence was broken by the sound only a sandwich can make when ham and cheese and lettuce begin their noisy dance in the bread ballroom. Time was still. Sharp cheddar cheese and Nabs shared their moment with my drink. I fed Planters salted to the remaining half of a cold Coca-Cola. Lunch ended with a last swallow. An empty pale green bottle from Atlanta, Georgia, told me lunch would do till dinner.

What was the history of this place?

What brought friends and a piece of land together around Christmas in 1954?

Bradley and Cohen [Paul] stood in an alley-way behind an old, wooden-frame, two-story house on 16th Avenue South, which was then a run-down residential neighborhood, now the heart of present-day Music Row. Cohen had threatened to take his business to another town unless there was another recording studio. Bradley's roots were in Nashville and he had no desire to move. Cohen offered to go in on the $7,500 purchase price of the wooden-frame house. He guaranteed Bradley 100 Decca sessions a year if Bradley would turn the place into a state-of-the-art recording facility.

Bradley Film and Recording Studios was born. Owen Bradley installed a little studio in the basement, knocked out the first floor so it had a high ceiling and set up an office on the second floor. He stocked the studio with Ampex 350 tape machines plugged into an Ampex MX-10 mono-mixing board. But Bradley wanted more sound, which meant more bodies and the studio was too small. So shortly after opening, he created a second studio by adding a military-style Quonset hut and installed a second control room and mixing board. Word spread that the new studio had the greatest acoustics in the world. Right away, 'the Quonset Hut' as it was thereafter dubbed—became the headquarters of the nascent recording scene in Nashville.[17]

I walked to Capitol's Nashville office, an old, white frame house nearby, and returned to my car. I drove around the block to 1610 Hawkins Street on the corner of Seventeenth South, my first-ever glimpse of RCA Victor's Studio B. Two places near one another, where stars were born, where legends played. The studios were the homes of Owen Bradley and Chet Atkins.

Ever-present signs, freshly painted and made straight, stood in the yards of some old houses. Panes of clear glass with waves, clean and sparkling, old and kind . . . not perfect, lived unbroken in windows framed in wood. I saw reflected in their faces an old neighborhood, one which seemed to have been given a reprise in the early years of a transformation. Music Row it wasn't quite yet; the scale was human.

The only things taller than old trees in August that summer were aspirations.

Sixteenth Avenue South was a neighborhood texture defined by old residential homes on the wane, with others in 1961. The houses of music publishing. Most could be found living in old houses, tastefully restored, behind a random collection of signs. They didn't mean a lot to me on my first visit that day. All of it simply stated and well-blended, so new to me. These places with given names.

Cedarwood and Pamper, Acuff-Rose Publishing, having moved here from their place on Melrose. They were the homes of William Denny, Roy Acuff, Wesley Rose, and thousands of hit songs. Tree International, then located elsewhere, would move to 905 Sixteenth Avenue South in 1964. There, Buddy Killen would build an empire on Music Row to go with an array of mixed emotions he would be a part of in the next few years.

I sensed BMI and ASCAP were important, one or the other always beside the name of the publisher on all my record's labels. Here were the gardens of music, where ideas were planted in the rows of Music Row. Nothing I had written had been published.

The neighborhood around Hawkins Street at Sixteenth and Seventeenth South was a place where you could still hear someone's hound dog bark or see one listening to his master's voice-over at RCA Victor. "Nipper" had been listening since October 3, 1901.

Buildings can acquire an unforgettable personality over time. I get sentimental over some when their given time is passed. To those, for whom it mattered then and matters even now, there's sadness in things that get lost or never the same as they were, before the storm of new arrived.

The personality of this place, this neighborhood and its garden, remained strong until a change in the corporate culture of the music industry, less than a decade hence into a new century. How music was being inspired, written, made, bought, and sold changed, leaving what once was meaningful content helpless to survive.

In the coming years, the light in an analog room would be going out, the warmth of tubes no longer relevant, becoming a chill on sound. The heart and soul of anything can be sold, lost in the wind of unfriendly change. It's sad.

That day was a near spiritual time to be in Nashville. Owen Bradley and Chet Atkins were the Meriwether Lewis and William Clark of new directions in music. Two stylists of the Nashville Sound were part of the new movement, one they continued to compose, a symphony the recording center it was becoming. "It was the greatest time to be making records in Nashville. It was just magical how it all came together."[18]

The modest humility of Owen Bradley and Chet Atkins mirrored the spirit of a place where restraint was the hallmark of session musicians who left a lasting impression on me.

The echoes in my mind were ones of wildflowers on a music landscape like no other. I miss the neighborhood of 1961, one of open windows, of glass with its turn-of-the-century flaws. Breezes and cotton curtains, like sails moving a room through time.

It wasn't perfect. It was priceless.

Late afternoon came quickly. No one else was around. I made my last trip around the block before heading back to the bright lights of another kind of Broadway, dinner on the Gallatin Road, and a long drive back home. The hour was on its way to sunset. Nashville made itself ready for the night as I crossed the Cumberland on my way to Madison. Bright lights were showing in the MG's mirror. Farther on up the road, I remember seeing a bus parked by a building. Letters in its destination window read "Ray Price." Hendersonville was up ahead.

Monument Records—passing 530 West Main Street in Hendersonville, I wondered, could Roy Orbison be nearby? He and his wife Claudette had a beautiful piece of land and a home next door to Johnny Cash overlooking Old Hickory Lake. The radio was fine-tuned to WSM by the time I got to Gallatin, Ernest Tubb broadcast live from Broadway after the Opry. Sometime in the night, I moved the dial to WLAC for music of a different color. The world was a simple place and so the spirit, or so it seemed. I crossed the state line near Westmoreland, Tennessee, into Kentucky on my way to August 21, Scottsville, and Glasgow. I followed US 31E back home, thinking how quickly my life and its moments seemed to be passing by.

It may have been the first time.

The next day, August 21, 1961, a Monday, between 7:15 p.m. and 11:15 p.m., in Bradley's Film and Recording Studio, forever was laid on tracks one and three of Owen Bradley's three-track board. Owen reserved track two for a songbird wounded in a recent car accident in nearby Madison. Patsy Cline put a voice on the echoes of "Crazy" in one take, mere days after my rendezvous with history. There, I had my own picnic with destiny, a dreamer's lunch, just hours before. Owen Bradley produced the session and the players on the record some of Nashville's finest.

Knowing this makes events that would come to pass near Camden, Tennessee, all the more poignant today. Something was mystical in it all, at this crossroads where two strangers would never meet. My first time in Nashville that weekend had a profound influence on the way I would look at music and many other things for the rest of my life.

—∾—

It was good to be home. The Temptashuns played Tates Creek Country Club and a ballroom in the Lafayette Hotel, now Lexington's Government Center, on Main. We returned to Sleepy Hollow on the thirty-first to entertain members of social clubs from each of Lexington's high schools. I reflected on the film *Picnic* and Kansas near summer's end and Labor Day. The camera pulls back. William Holden's long train ride is taking him away from it all in the end, overtaken by a patchwork of Kansas farmland. The scene plays on in my memory, this last dance near the banks of my beloved North Elkhorn Creek on a band's first summer.

Fences are edges of richly patterned landscapes, suddenly softened by a separation as vast as then and now. Someday I would pull back from it all, like the film's Hal Carter, and see a patchwork of my experiences in the life of a band and things I've since left undone. I may have felt a separation at Sleepy Hollow overtaken by it all, perhaps. September was about to begin.

The Temptashuns Band, Fall Semester 1961, in order of appearance:

Tony Stallard, lead guitar, vocals; Shelby Lorrison, rhythm guitar; Wendell Sams, organ, lead vocals; Doug Hammonds, tenor sax, backing vocals; Earl Morgan, bass, backing vocals; Larry Kelley, drums; Mickey Levy, girl lead and backing vocals.

Phi Delta Theta and their dates danced to the Temptashuns on the first in Frankfort at the Reservoir Clubhouse, near Juniper Hill. The Apple Pis of Henry Clay, another night at a house on Fincastle.

—∾—

Session guitarist Hank Garland was in an automobile accident on the eighth around 5.00 p.m., north of Springfield, Tennessee, on Highway 41N. The brilliance of *Jazz Winds* became a sudden calm leaving yet another empty space in music. I had been in Nashville twenty days earlier. I would never hear him jam at Jimmy Hyde's Carousel Club after an Elvis session in Studio B.

Grady Martin produced a jazz masterpiece in the Quonset hut, *Jazz Winds from a New Direction*. Columbia JCS 8372, ever still on my mind, is honey for one's ear. The guitar artistry of a session musician on August 23, 1960, became an echo, one to sustain a memory long after tracks of tears on the face of his music went dry. As long as there's a wind, no matter how wayward, there'll be a song. In the breath of itself on strings.

With or without lyric, something will be felt.

Four of Doug's classmates at Lafayette made guest appearances with the Temptashuns on a number of occasions. The girls—Mickey Levy, Pam Nallinger, Bettye Jo Betz, and Susan Farmer—were members of the Charmettes, a select girl's chorus at Lafayette. We named them the Tempettes. They looked great and sounded terrific. Lafayette's Charmettes director learned about their band appearances. They were given a choice: Temptashuns or Charmettes.

Mickey took a chance on the Temptashuns. We asked her to sing with us. The others declined. We featured Mickey as lead vocalist on her own songs and with Wendell. She joined Doug and me, backing Wendell's vocals. The three of us, our voices and personalities, fit together well, with each other and the times.

Mickey was petite, cute, and full of personality, only a junior at Lafayette. She was right for us at the right time. We were the only white band in town with a girl singer that I recall. The popular Dave Perry Orchestra and other such bands performed big band instrumentals and featured women singing standards for social functions around the Bluegrass. Bands of color featured women of color who sang most anything, blue the most memorable.

I gave Mickey a ride to any place any time we played, then home. I was often less nervous about our show or performance because of her enthusiasm and energy. She made things light. Her parents were confident of my word.

Mickey gave the Temptashuns another dimension. Songs by girls and girl groups were abundant on the charts early in the sixties. We were having fun in an innocent age. The Temptashuns were becoming better, more confident, and in demand.

Louisville's Epics featured Janie Moss, a girl of their own, later on. Janie was a strong performer. The Epics were good. Collectively, the Temptashuns delivered a broader set list and, with our horn section, a bigger sound. We had voices too.

Mickey sang with us during her senior year at Lafayette, staying early into her freshman year at Kentucky. She then left the band, joining a sorority and Angel Flight, young women representing UK's Air Force ROTC on campus.

Mickey taught English at Lafayette Senior High after college. Things had come full circle for Mickey and me. She was back at Lafayette. The personality of Mickey (Levy) Settle and her positive manner looking at all things remains to this day.

Mickey's set list with the Temptashuns mirrors our magic moments together.

"A Thousand Stars"/Kathy Young and the Innocents; "All Alone Am I"/ Brenda Lee; "Baby It's You"/Shirelles; "Hey Paul" with Stan Tucker/Paul and Paula; "It's My Party"/Lesley Gore; "The End of the World"/Skeeter Davis; "Loco-Motion"/Little Eva; "Remember (Walking in the Sand)"/ Shangri-Las; Others; "C.C. Rider," "I Don't Know Why," and Linda Scott's "Yessiree."

I saw Mickey on February 17, 2001, A Magnificent Seven/Temptashuns reunion at the Blue Moon in Chevy Chase. Time was frozen with sunshine, lollipops, and rainbows all over again. "I'll pick you up at 6:30 on Friday night. We're playing for the Chi Os, and, Mickey, don't forget, we'll be at Joyland next Saturday night."

"Good night, Tony. Thanks for the ride."

—⁂—

Fall rush signaled the beginning of a new year at the university. The Temptashuns played our first college affair for Kappa Alpha fraternity at their house on Kalmia. Their first party after rush. The South's northernmost chapter of the fraternal order was at Kentucky, a distinction shared with the KA chapter at Transylvania College across town.

The Temptashuns were not the first to play the basement room of the KA house at Kalmia and Rose, preceded by the likes of the Ike and Tina Turner Revue, Parliaments, Royal Knights, and others. We began the evening with the Mar-Keys' "Last Night," Phillip Upchurch's "You Can't Sit Down (Parts I and II)," and a garden of other R & B delights. Mickey sang "Loco-motion." A shuffle led Doug into and beyond "Honky Tonk." Bruce Chanel's "Hey Baby" was my chance on harmonica and vocal, not knowing who Delbert McClinton was at the time. Mickey's vocals added spice to our menu to go with cute. The KAs and their dates danced to the Temptashuns, a band playing their first-ever college house party. That moment, a party for the KAs to end fall rush, opened a door that would remain open for us for many fine years at UK.

What can I say? They loved us. We never forgot each other after that night. Guys and coeds wanted more rhythm and blues. Doug and I spent nights we didn't play learning from other bands performing at Danceland. The nightspot stood on the banks of a stream named Town Branch, just down Manchester Street from the James E. Pepper Distillery. Danceland and its Friday nights shaped our development profoundly.

—∿—

Doug and I began going ever more often to Danceland. Not yet twenty-one, we listened outside the club to the style of its music. Because of it, classics like Bill Doggett's "Honky Tonk (Part II)" and anything by James Brown would, in time, become our own hallmark in the Temptashuns band and its sound. Some of the best rhythm and blues I've heard was played right here in Lexington at Danceland.

Paris, Kentucky's own Charlie Bishop played the sweetest sax this side of King Curtis. The Charlie Bishop Band was the first I heard play "Honky Tonk" live. Willie Barns played organ and was fine on vocals. Lexington had its own Bill Doggett songs done like no other. We learned "The Continental," a popular R & B-style instrumental, by listening to Charlie Bishop. The tune and its dance were popular in our town, tailor-made for group dancing.

The Houserockers, another band, formed 1950 in Georgetown, played fine on other nights at Danceland. Their various lineups over the years are more than I remember. Players I do recall are Sonny Williams, singer; "Little Orbit," singer/organist; and Alonzo "Snooks" Robinson, George Gentry, and Leslie Todd Bailey, saxophonists. Little Orbit could do "Tossin' and Turnin'" as if Bobby Lewis, who belonged to the hit, was in the room. I heard the Houserockers do Freddie King's "Hide Away" for the first time. We played it for years.

A soul of color defined Johnny Ballard, bass player in the Houserockers. He was white. The mixed-race lineup of the Houserockers spoke to me about the interdependence of music and race. Though blind, he felt music like few I've ever met; Johnny Ballard was genuine, a natural musician and friend. His late brother, singer-guitarist Jimmy Lee Ballard, had local success on Lexington's REM records label.

The Pacesetters, formed by Bill Pace, was another popular bunch of good R & B players. I got to see organist Winston Walls on rare occasion. Winston played a Hammond C3. It was "Star Time" when he got behind a Hammond organ, I do know that.

The late Angie Dee was a featured singer with other Lexington bands. Angie sang with the Temptashuns on one occasion. We were lucky. Her set list was rich in the best ladies of early rhythm and blues, from LaVern Baker to Carla Thomas to Etta James. I wonder today what happened to these people—the ones in my hometown, mostly of color, who signed their names on my soul. I hoped the Temptashuns would play Danceland someday for college guys and coeds,

We could be the band for any age in this place.

Friday nights, on the outside looking in with Doug Hammonds made us better players and the Temptashuns a better band. It was never long before we learned to play the songs we heard on Manchester Street. Warm summer and late September distilled into cool October nights in my hometown—The Charlie Bishop Band, Houserockers, and Pacesetters. I believed early in a long-ago decade—it doesn't get any better than this.

I wonder even now if it ever did.

I heard Duke Madison for the first time in the Rebel Room at Southland Bowling Lanes. Duke was most things sax players and other jazz musicians around here aspired to be. Duke Madison had played everywhere, from venues with the big bands to the Spider Web Tea Room on Georgetown Street. Unforgettable, Duke never stopped getting better, and we never stopped being better because of his gift to each of us.

The first year or so we carried our gear individually, arriving places we played in separate cars. I had bought a Fender Showman amp from George Hurst Music. The Showman was one of a two-piece line of amplifiers Fender introduced in their line. The Beach Boys and Ventures were using them, and they looked great. Shelby got the same when he bought a Fender Jazzmaster guitar and John Page a Fender's Precision bass. The band had a Beach Boys look in its front line, Hawthorne, California, east. The times were casual for us then. Weekends were becoming less lonely.

Lasting are the echoes in a long-ago snow.

A night of play ended, the Toddle House, a diner on Euclid in Chevy

Chase, was the next to last stop for Doug and me. Pecan waffles, with an ocean of maple syrup, to go with hash brown potatoes, sausage, and coffee. We could see another group of young and older patrons beyond the glass. Out for an evening, leaving the Buffalo Tavern across the street. Town folk or students heading back to campus and tomorrow's football game on Stoll Field.

Doug and me in the Toddle House in the a.m., two players just stepped into the scene of an Edward Hopper painting. We were nighthawks, bathed in the neon of the Ashland Theater's marquee light.

Light began to dim on leaving to drop him off on Cochran Road, where he lived.

The Temptashuns played next weekend for the Newman Club on Rose Lane. The Catholic Newman Center was an inflatable structure, a natural echo chamber with a wooden floor. Place can confuse sound enough to make it little more than sameness. No sooner after hearing what you've played, it's back to want itself again. "Runaway" sounded fine that evening in that echo, "Harlem Nocturne" and "Soul Serenade" full of blue. We played our first sorority party at Kappa Delta on the twenty-ninth at their house on sorority row. The next night found us at Delta Tau Delta fraternity on Audubon.

New faces were seen in the crowd each weekend. We learned something new from each other. We learned about us from them. We became a better band quickly, and the word around campus about our music fell on many ears favorably.

Fall racing at Keeneland was on its way.

—ꟿ—

Horses ran down an avenue of hope at Keeneland Race Course. Jockeys and their rides wore silks of pretty colors. Women, with yet undiscovered moods, could be found there, in silks of their own and wearing smiles. The fillies of the Bluegrass, young ladies, had come to see a drama played out on a stage of richly colored earth. Thoroughbred racing at its best, a game played between the rails and the roar of a crowd. The freedom to frolic untethered in a paddock of one's own was waiting. Everyone a winner; tomorrow's grain was good if you willed it to be.

Folks would be coming to Lexington from Athens, Tuscaloosa, Oxford, Baton Rouge and Nashville to follow their teams, do a little wagering on the horses, have their share of bourbon in the afternoon, and attend Southeastern

Conference football that night. Before the lights turned bright on Saturday night in autumn, the party began around high noon at Keeneland and its afternoon post times in my hometown.

The University of Kentucky was considered by many at the time to own the best college football weekend anywhere. Music in Lexington was about as good as could be found on a college campus in 1961. The KAs might even be having Ike and Tina Turner at their house to entertain for a party after the game. The Ike and Tina Turner Revue could stay the night in the basement of the house before heading down to Lebanon to play the Club 68, after James Brown or Mary Wells the night before. It would define our college weekends and other nights for the Temptashuns down the road for many years.

—~—

Much of radio's programming was live broadcast; the stations were well equipped to serve as recording studios. A 50,000-watt clear-channel radio voice such as WLW in Cincinnati fell like stardust on our lives with a rich quality. Some of Ray Charles' early recordings on Atlantic were made in studios on Georgia Tech's campus radio station WGST in Atlanta. He also recorded in Miami and New Orleans. These field recordings are vintage sessions, some of his best.

Local radio personality Denny Mitchell had a popular call-in program, *Denny's Den*, weeknights on WLAP. The station was in the Carpenter-Warren Insurance Building on Upper, between Church and Second, downtown.

Denny had heard about the Temptashuns through the grapevine. I believe he contacted Larry Kelley, wanting to meet us. We took our show to WLAP's studios and did some taping. Hearing our music on tape for the first time was a glimpse into the band and our weaknesses. We were new to the music business, his advice valuable. Denny shared thoughts about a band's responsibilities; most importantly to an audience, as entertainers, to themselves as performers, and to furthering the fine art of being professional. We took his wisdom seriously.

Denny had a good friend at Columbia Records in New York. Denny planned to send demo tapes we recorded at WLAP to Columbia and other record labels, with a personal letter of introduction. A business card I received from a gentleman in Camden, New Jersey, in charge of Promotion and Production leads me to believe he may have been someone at RCA Victor Records in Camden.

Before Denny Mitchell came along, we were playing quite frequently. Bookings were steadily coming our way, effortlessly. His words on airwaves to waiting ears. . . "The Temptashuns will be appearing with me this Saturday night at someplace for someone who wanted him to bring us along to appear with him." Thousands of his listeners would hear the message on the radio each weeknight. We first appeared with Denny Mitchell at Meadowthorpe on Saturday, September 30, 1961. We played for free. My notes indicate the Temptashuns appeared with Denny about a dozen times over the next eighteen months. The word "free" appears more than we deserved. Denny was never our manager. He listened and gave advice. We listened and were grateful. The band worked it all out collectively, continuing to handle our own bookings. We wanted to shape who we were and where we were headed, taking whatever time necessary.

—ɱ—

A bright new Corvette, top down, pulled into Easley Brothers' Phillips 66 Service Station on New Circle at Meadow Lane. A man, a woman, and an infant, the family was out for a nice summer afternoon drive in the Bluegrass. The face was familiar, a nice-looking guy. I left polishing my car to fill their tank with gas, check the oil, and clean the windows. Soon they were on their way down the road and I to my own, a sparkling iron horse, its leather and lacquer, waiting.

My life was an unbridled calm.

Nick Clooney was a popular personality on Lexington's WLAP AM radio. His afternoon program was broadcast live from a small shop facing South Ashland in Chevy Chase.

Nick hosted a Saturday afternoon dance program for teens, *Coke Time*. The broadcast originated in the studios of WKYT Television. The site later became home for WKQQ Radio.

The consummate host, Nick asked the Temptashuns to appear live on *Coke Time* on three occasions I can recall. We played, teens danced, and that great Clooney smile gave us a confidence beyond measure. We heard from people we didn't know: "I saw you on television yesterday."

Nick Clooney is the brother of the late Rosemary Clooney. Nick and Nina Clooney named their baby George. That summer afternoon is pretty special for me. I'm reminded of a time we were once young, four people passing in a moment.

The baby, George Clooney, was born May 6, 1961, in Lexington.

This would not be the last time to see the Clooney family and their car around town. Our appearances on Nick Clooney's program were good exposure for the Temptashuns. His regional audience was large; his advice on performing for a live studio, or any audience, invaluable. The Temptashuns had an ever-growing teen following. Opportunities were ripe, and the band ready to perform at school dances, sock hops, and parties.

Nick Clooney remains as personable and confident today as then.

—∞—

A dramatic turn of events in September 1961 would shape the Temptashuns in ways which, at the time, posed concern to what lay ahead for us all. The Cold War appeared destined for a long winter in a deep chill when, in late summer, President Kennedy countered with a blockade designed to end the affair. The Berlin Crisis prompted the president to call the 100th Division of the Army Reserve to active duty for one year at Fort Chaffee, Arkansas.

The Temptashuns suddenly lost two of its own in the wake of the incident.

Wendell and Shelby reported for duty to Ft. Chaffee, Arkansas, where Elvis Presley had reported in 1957. Doug's brother, other students, and friends we knew at the university were also called to report. I took over for Wendell, sharing lead vocals with Mickey. We asked John Page to join the band to replace Shelby on rhythm guitar. The band didn't miss a beat, despite facing new challenges. The opportunity gave us new wind and renewed creative energy. Every time we said goodbye, the newest member brought a new dimension to the band. The good of it was reflected in fresh set lists.

Newness is refreshing, like a warm loaf of fresh-baked bread . . . heaven's scent.

Larry Kelley, our drummer, assumed the role of business manager, coordinating our bookings and financial matters. I continued music duties: song selection and arranging. Doug was never far away to help with the music. John Page kept our sound system together. My new Showman amp had begun developing some problems. Mr. Hurst returned it to Fender for a replacement.

The Temptashuns were fast becoming a popular band in Lexington, and the word was about. The American Federation of Musicians expressed interest. AFM Local 554 paid us a visit; Welcome to the Music Business, and all that implies. We are your tomorrow; our bylaws and newsletter are yours. Dues are your ticket to any work you ever care to get.

I don't recall their cost.

—ᴧᴧᴧ—

I visited George Hurst on October 9 in his store, the house where he lived on North Ashland Avenue. My new guitar had arrived, Fender's Stratocaster, a left-handed blond beauty. The replacement for the two-piece Showman returned to Fender arrived in the same shipment with their blessing: "From Fullerton, California. With Love, Fender." The Vibrasonic was Fender's newest model and top-of-the-line amp at the time. The Vibrasonic, with its fifteen-inch Lansing speaker and integral four-inch tweeter, never disappointed me. Its life was many years.

The middle of autumn began at Sigma Alpha Epsilon house on South Limestone at Bassett Court. We were at the Carnahan House the following weekend out in the country on Newtown, a Friday night. Saturday began with three hours of show at Joyland Clubhouse, known to most as the Little Casino. The clubhouse was located directly behind Joyland's big room.

We did a show at Meadowthorpe Hop with WLAP's Denny Mitchell, ending the evening at the SAE house. The Temptashuns had arrived at three venues and played five hours of the best that we were, a taste of weekends to come.

The Stratocaster was a dream to play. The amp was a voice of fine tone with a bunch of depth. I was on a path between the two. Where would it lead?

October ended sounding great at Franklin County High in Frankfort on the twenty-ninth after a football game. We headed westward the next day to Bardstown's St. Joseph Prep School. The leaves had turned a collection of bright and muted colors. I held the poetry of this autumn close to my soul. My mind was on New Haven, a sandwich, cold drinks, and other tastes. Lunch made in a hardware store by the railroad's tracks to be shared with a neighborhood out on Sixteenth Avenue South. August was not so long ago.

The leaves, they must be stunning there, all blown about.

November began a month of fraternity and sorority affairs. Delta Kappa Epsilon was our first at Centre College in Danville. We would play the DEKE house numerous times over the years, all memorable.

The bounty of Thanksgiving was beyond measure in 1961. Autumn's leaves and the first months of a band named the Temptashuns were yesterday. I spent what remained of the afternoon after Thanksgiving dinner at home with family. Alone, my mind wondered how things might turn out down the road. I was at the portal of a moment with little idea how busy December would be.

—ꟺ—

We began December at Henry Clay, a sock hop on the first, sounding our best since the band's first gig in March. We introduced the band's new sound system in the gym at Lafayette Senior High after a basketball game. Before that night, we had been playing on rented sound on borrowed time from Lexington sound designer Paul Shaw.

Paul put a nice system together for us. Components consisted of Altec Lansing amplification and speakers, with Shure and Electro-Voice microphones and chrome round-base stands. We later added a reverb unit and a three-channel mixer to complement the different moods of places we played and their rooms. Paul's advice was invaluable, free and appreciated. Our sound had a nice new flavor. John Page kept it all finely tuned and always ready.

December played out with nights in Paris, Elizabethtown, and two consecutive evenings with the Lexington Country Club just before Christmas. Following three days' rest, the band ended our first year at Spring Valley Country Club on the twenty-ninth.

—ꟺ—

A year like this was quite a new experience, a different play on a much different kind of stage than another in 1959's *Our Town*. Being a part of what was becoming as meaningful to others as to us had a lasting appeal. Looking over notes I had written on the way, photographs, and lists of songs we had played together since just before spring, I was satisfied.

The Temptashuns Band had played fifty-seven engagements since its beginning in March.

The last thing on my mind before sleep arrived was a quiet drive I would make in a few hours. The year was new, and Shakertown was waiting.

For me.

7
Clear Elegant Simplicity, 1962

1962. I was twenty. Frank Sinatra, Janet Leigh, and Lawrence Harvey appeared in *The Manchurian Candidate*, a disturbing-yet-so-possible-it-could-happen film. *Dr. No* was a low budget beginning for a fellow named Bond—M, Q, and Moneypenny ready to save the world and the Crown from SMERSH and SPECTRE. *The Tonight Show*, starring Johnny Carson, premiered; Walter Cronkite replaced Douglas Edwards at CBS; and the golden age of radio, which began on NBC in 1920, ended.

Marilyn Monroe died.

"The Days of Wine and Roses" was a hit for Henry Mancini, "Walk on By" for Burt Bacharach and Dionne Warwick. President Kennedy announced a trade embargo against Cuba to be followed in October by an air and sea blockade. Khrushchev took his toys and went home.

Game over.

The first American orbited earth; John Glenn parked his Mercury in the Atlantic. "The Twist" was a national dance craze and the Peppermint Lounge "the place" to be in New York City. I went there three years hence only to find the Peppermint Lounge about to close its doors. Joey Dee had gone away.

We began the year with a sock hop after basketball on the fifth and a Valentine's dance on the twelfth, both in Lafayette's gym. The Temptashuns ran their patterns well, not so unlike those of Florence, Peck, Lickert, Shively, Duvall, Mullins, Jaracz, and others in this place of championship basketball.

The Valentine's dance began with "Last Night" and "You Can't Sit Down." There was no question rhythm and the blues was the road the band was taking. Mickey was doing popular girl group tunes for her classmates, a nice way to keep our music on the pulse of anywhere.

Doug and I sang backup for Mickey's vocals, she and Doug for my own. The sessions taped at WLAP persuaded us to be cautious, with little time between songs. We knew what our next would be most times.

We ended the dance with "Walk, Don't Run," sounding about as West Coast as anyone east of Sunset Boulevard. The Rocket Boys taped some of the night's play. Their recording of "Walk, Don't Run" that night survived all the years since then. Hearing today how we sounded in 1962 leaves no uncertainty at all. We were having fun.

—⁓—

The Rocket Boys were four Lafayette students who helped the Temptashuns for a time. They were the only sound crew our band ever had that I can remember. Mike Marsh, John Bell, Charles Holdaway, and their friend John Chaplin followed the band in the early days. Equipped with a reel-to-reel tape deck, a bunch of electronics know-how, and a try anything wit, they recorded the Temptashuns before we ever made records. Sound effects of their personal interests made it to our own.

Charles Holdaway, an honors student, was headed to MIT after his graduation from Lafayette. This was not simply another big experiment to him. Mike Marsh asked Doug one day at school if it would be all right to run our sound through their taping equipment. Doug's nice and easy "Whatever you guys want to do's okay with us" echoed my own feelings. What the Rocket Boys had in mind remained a mystery.

I remember the band had a touch more depth in Joyland's Casino. The inherent acoustic qualities of the room were instrumental in enhancing the quality of our sound at Joyland. The room was good to us. Other reasons for the essence were evident. The Rocket Boys let their collective imaginations roam those nights in Joyland. They did their work, most in attendance little aware what it was. Neither were we.

Charlie devised a continuous loop of magnetic tape, such that record and playback was near simultaneous. Homemade Les Paul and Sam Phillips were at their fingertips. Charlie took a Roberts tape deck and crafted an echo chamber. "Heartbreak Hotel" wasn't on our set list; had Elvis been in the building, he would have felt right at home using our sound system. It was pure, as pure as slapback echo from Memphis straight to the heart of Joyland could be.

The Rocket Boys pre-recorded slices of other sounds on their own, surf being one we used on "Ebbtide." They recorded a friend's car, speeding away from a standing start on the street in front of Charlie's house on Chinoe. The Sunset Strip had come to the neighborhood, the language of the hot rod loudly spoken by Hollywood mufflers. They recorded a Harley-

Davidson and fed it through our sound when Mickey sang "Leader of the Pack." Mickey was exciting on "Walking in the Sand," an inviting smile on the bandstand. The sweet, sweet blush of surf on its way to embrace a Malibu beach to go with a song could've been their signature.

Background scenery courtesy of the Rocket Boys was fun.

They shaped our sound in the moment we played. They mixed these and others in our sound with the band's vocal and instrumental music with impeccable care and ingenuity. It was never easy to hear the band distinctly at the time a song was done live. We heard our music and their assorted effects on its way back to the bandstand.

Truth is we had no clear idea what the boys had done till the night ended. Usually the next day, a Sunday afternoon at Charlie's house in Rocket City, is where we found the truth. What they had blended a few hours before was exceptional.

Mike and John built their own radio station, operating out of Mike's house on Cooper. WEAK Radio wasn't a 50,000-watt giant threatening to take the air away from the likes of WLW or WHAS. You could tune to their frequency, though weak, and with its five-mile range listen to WEAK radio in your car while out and about in town. I remember hearing our first record "Autumn Love"/"The Big B" at Jerry's and Parkette Drive-ins or cruising around Romany and other roads.

It was anything but weak. To me it was everything.

The late John Chaplin was best known in the Bluegrass as Herb Oscar Kent, a respected radio personality and producer at stations WLAP and WVLK. John enriched my life. I've thought of John Chaplin often while writing this story. He was humble. The Rocket Boys are four of many reasons why these times in the band's life had such meaning. We were blessed in clear, elegant, and simple ways. John always spoke highly of the band. My fortune was in letting him know how much I appreciated what he had done for us over the years. He passed away shortly thereafter.

Mike Marsh was on the line in August 2003.

Mike called to say he had copied a tape of the Temptashuns "live" at Lafayette Senior High School gym, February 1962, and our live performance in concert, spring 1966.

"Would you like a copy?"

"Yes, Mike. Thank you."

—ɯ—

The Temptashuns entertained 800 in the convention hall at the Phoenix Hotel for a Chamber of Commerce banquet on the seventeenth. We played for a polio benefit hosted by Denny Mitchell in Carlisle. The event, held in in the old Western Auto Store, was for the March of Dimes. Local folks asked us for autographs, wanting to know when we were going to make a record. Attention we were getting that night in a small town was special, the first time for us to be something to someone in a brand-new way. An autograph.

We backed "Cosmo" at Christ the King School the first week in March. The Temptashuns, with organ and trumpet, presented a different composition than Louisville's bands. Our full instrument voice was unlike the voice-based sound he was accustomed to in the Sultans.

Cosmo seemed pleased with the night and the band. He eventually left the Sultans to form Cosmo and the Counts with Wayne Young, guitarist in the Carnations. The Counts, featuring a horn section like our own, were a fine bunch of musicians.

I visited Carl's Music Center on West Main early one Saturday afternoon. Carl wanted to loan me the Fender reverb unit I was considering, the same model I was using for my guitar's amp.

"If it doesn't work out for you, just bring it back to the store."

The band reached another place on its road that night at Centre College in Danville. The Temptashuns opened with "Bo Diddley is a Gunslinger" and the Thurston Harris tune "Little Bitty Pretty One." These and others mirrored a band playing with confidence, sounding impressive that evening; March 24, 1962, the first night a new, fresh, and bigger sound would take us to tomorrow.

The Monarchs, from Louisville, were on campus. Our Fender tube reverb met their Echoplex. Each band came by to hear the other. We never missed a night to learn. I returned to Carl's on Monday with cash and a "thank you," a promise kept on a handshake.

Reverb remained the only effect the band would use to complement our sound, replacing the homemade slapback echo the Rocket Boys had built for other nights at Joyland. We ran our microphones through a three-channel mixer. The rest was natural.

March ended with a week of self-restoration during spring break. We returned to campus beginning with a dance for the freshmen football team at Wildcat Manor on Fraternity Row, another at Sigma Phi Epsilon fraternity.

—ꟺ—

Spring break had given me a chance to visit Nashville a second time on the seventeenth and eighteenth, a Sunday. The drive down mirrored my first the previous August. I checked into the Allen Hotel on West End Avenue, planning to stay the night. Nashville wasn't Spanish moss and magnolia blooms yet as close as I had ever been to the Deep South.

A portal to a way of life I wanted to know more about.

The closer one gets to the South, the less you feel like a stranger. Nashville was southern—grits and red-eye gravy, so at home with country ham, currant jelly, and biscuits, eggs, juice, and coffee. Here was a portal to my being.

I headed out to the neighborhood again where I'd been last August, slowing on Sixteenth Avenue, passing the Belmont Church of Christ. What began with a tent revival in 1911 became a Greek Revival style piece of history built in 1915. Turning right at Grand Avenue and another right a block down, I made my way on Seventeenth Avenue South to RCA Victor's Studio B at Hawkins Street. I parked the MG. It was spring and Nashville beautiful in full bloom.

Leaving Music Row, I drove farther on out West End Avenue for a glimpse of the campus, Memorial Gym, and other points of interest around Vanderbilt and George Peabody College. Further on down West End, stopping a while to experience the charm of the City of Belle Meade for the first time, I had dinner there. By the time I returned to my car, parked near the Belle Meade Theater, her marquee had become a chorus of bright lights. She was vintage May 1940.

Filled with the spirit of Belle Meade's mansions and well fed, I returned to my room at the Allen. I let go of the night to fall asleep with Sunday on my mind.

The sound of sterling on china was the song played by fork, knife, and spoon in concert, my way to start the morning deliciously. Breakfast was over with the last buttered biscuit dipped in what remained of red-eye gravy in my plate, a lasting bite of country ham, and draining a white china cup of the coffee in it. The *Nashville-Tennessean* paper bought in the hotel's lobby after breakfast provided casual reading in my room.

The day before had seemed rather quiet. Today was Sunday. Nashville was on its way to church. The paper's magazine entertainment section noted Patti Page had spent the last few days recording songs for a new album at Owen Bradley Studios. Soon, after checking out of the hotel, I left to see who might be there.

Since my first visit in August 1961, Owen and Harold Bradley had sold their Quonset hut studio to Columbia Records, February 1962. Owen moved his work to the new Decca Records building nearby on Sixteenth South. He later converted an old barn into a new studio, located on about sixty-five acres of beautiful Mt. Juliet land, across the Cumberland just east of Nashville. He named the studio Bradley's Barn.

The Quonset hut was quiet. About the only thing going on in the neighborhood was at the Belmont Church of Christ down the street. People were celebrating the Lord's Day, making a joyful noise, all things made better by it, and so the collective spirits gathered there.

I parked my MG on Hawkins at Studio B to begin a walk around the block. It was just past noon. Soon, the congregation was descending Belmont's steps, all dressed in their Sunday best, filled with the Holy Spirit.

The character of this neighborhood was heavy, its people and its age. I felt its bones, the texture of front porches and echo chambers, its flowers and stardust. I was spellbound once again, here in a garden of common sense. Looking back at Studio B before leaving, I wondered, would the Temptashuns ever get a chance to make a record?

What was it about this neighborhood and a crossroads in a life, one where the paths of what I am and what I really want to be intersect? What was the secret of sound beyond the veil of another time? After Hank Williams, country music had come to crossroads of its own by the mid-fifties. I was standing in the middle of an intersection of my own. The way out of town was unclear. A mind has many roads to serve. Which would it be and where would it take the Temptashuns?

Where would it take me?

Nashville's A-Team players in the best of their years, the ones between 1957 and 1964, represented prime time there. A select bunch of "first-call" session players was not so unlike the way music was creatively recorded elsewhere then. Recording sessions using the Wrecking Crew in Hollywood, others in New Orleans and New York City, are examples. The early sixties was an important time for me to be in Nashville.

I bought Chet Atkins' *Teensville* at Barney Miller's. A vinyl showcase, the album was a taste of Nashville and what its players could produce. *Teensville* and I wore each other down, me learning the parts of its songs, the album putting up with it all. I learned restraint from Chet Atkins. Restraint to me was an aspiration, whether for playing music or how I wanted to live the rest of my life. I put my mind on the space between the notes, between the words, between the pages.

That is the place where creativity finds its wings.

Country music may have been going uptown, but the place of recorded sound at this place where I stood was pure front porch swing.

Owen Bradley and Chet Atkins, Bradley's counterpart at RCA Victor had been experimenting with a number of new ideas, including the use of vocal choruses, overlaying country singers and country songs with the full lush sounds more typical of pop music. The idea was to create a vocal cushion under the singer.[19]

In March 1959, Bradley hired a string section consisting of musicians from the Nashville Symphony to work on a Brenda Lee date—the first time Bradley had ever used strings on a Nashville session. The song 'I'm Sorry,' set Brenda's sound, a crying style against a full orchestral backdrop, that he would subsequently use with even greater effect with Patsy. Overnight Brenda became an international singing star. Not long afterward, the term 'Nashville Sound' started cropping up in the lexicon of the popular media. By the end of 1960, 45 percent of all hit records were cut in Nashville.

Key to the creation of the Nashville Sound was the A Team. Bradley claimed the mythic 'sound' was just 'a way of doing things.' Musicians like Hank Garland, Grady Martin, Harold Bradley, Bob Moore, Buddy Harman, Floyd Cramer, Ray Edenton and Hargis 'Pig' Robbins played on virtually every session in Nashville because they worked together efficiently and thus helped keep studio costs down. The result was a spontaneous, loose, jazzy feeling to the sessions in Nashville. . . . Recalled Jordanaire Ray Walker, 'They all knew each other and they all had that wonderful nonintrusive way of playing. It was great.'[20]

Often the most emotion a song will be given is the moment it's put on tape. The lasting impression is surpassed only in the emotion of doing something for the last time and putting it forever to rest. Then is what your history becomes.

The silent song flows over its brim; its echo is the most profound. You must touch the earth where the clay came from to understand the vessel you want to shape. It's in your hands and yours alone.

The Quonset hut and Studio B were laboratories giving life to sound. The two had contrasting shapes and sound characteristics. A quality of music was defined by experiment in these places where sound is born.

Sunday, March 18, 1962.

I reluctantly left Nashville that evening after dinner on West End. Elsewhere, cars began arriving at 17th Avenue South, and Hawkins St. Bill Porter was carefully placing an assortment of microphones in Studio B and working the four-track recording console in the control room. Session musicians loaded in their instruments and amps. Singers arrived to begin two days of session work with Elvis Presley in RCA Victor's Studio B. The session, to last the night, ran from 7:30 p.m. till 10:30 p.m., 11 p.m. till 2 a.m., and 2:30 p.m. to 6:30 a.m. The cast was stellar:

A&R/Producer: *Steve Sholes*, Engineer: *Bill Porter*, Players: *Scottie Moore*, guitar; *Harold Bradley*, guitar; *Grady Martin*, guitar and vibes; *Bob Moore*, bass; *D.J. Fontana*, drums; *Buddy Harman*, drums; *Floyd Cramer*, piano; *Boots Randolph*, sax and vibes; *The Jordanaires*, vocals; *Mille Kirkham*, vocals; and *Elvis Presley*, singer.

The session continued March 19, lasting from 7:30 p.m. till 10 p.m. and from 11 p.m. till 2 a.m. These sessions produced the Doc Pomus/ Mort Schuman song "Suspicion," Pomus/Stoller/ Leiber's "She's Not You," "(Such an) Easy Question," and other tracks for Presley's *Pot Luck* album, LSP 2523/1962. After a photograph taken outside Studio B in the early morning hours of March 20, Elvis slipped out of Nashville in a silver bus, his night train back to Memphis.

I crossed the Cumberland River on the Gallatin Pike heading for Madison, Hendersonville, Gallatin, and home. The MG slipped through the night; the radio played to voices of four cylinders with a sweet, sweet-sounding accent. I'd get about five hours' sleep before Elvis finished the first of two days of sessions booked at RCA Victor. My mind was on looking back at Studio B before leaving three or so hours before, not knowing until now what had begun since that glance.

—ɯ—

The front-page photograph in the Thursday, April 12, 1962, *Nicholas County Star* newspaper describes the appearance of the Temptashuns for the Carlisle Teenage 4-H Club at the Armory Saturday on the seventh. Proceeds for the benefit went to the 4-H Club Camp Fund. This was our first time to make the front-page news, not the last time we would play for the benefit of a need.

Shown in the photograph are Larry Kelley, drums; Doug Hammonds, sax; Earl Morgan, bass; John Page, rhythm guitar; and Tony Stallard, vocals and lead guitar. Wendell, not pictured, was there on organ. Making a guest appearance with us that evening was a singer, a protégé of Denny Mitchell. The same singer and Denny appeared with us the following weekend. On a clear day, one could see far enough to know the singer needed a band and Denny Mitchell thought we were the one.

We had other notions.

April 14, 1962. We asked Johnny Burrows, attending Henry Clay, to be a guest on trumpet. We also invited a vibrant quartet of teen girls from Lafayette to come along for the evening. The Temptashuns had a chorus of cute, the ones we had named the Tempettes. There would be other times for them and us. Girl group songs and brass was fun.

The Sadie Hawkins Dance brought us to Danville on the twenty-seventh. We played the Jackson High School prom the following night in Breathitt County. Johnny Burrows was our guest on trumpet. May began with the Bryan Station Prom on the fourth, with the Tempettes. We finished out the month with proms at Bourbon County in Paris, Mt. Sterling, and Paintsville High schools.

The assent from the old Brooklyn Bridge and Kentucky River coming home from points south on US 27 led me past Camp Nelson National Cemetery and the Austin Nichols Distillery. I climbed toward the crest of a blue highway between two hills. Kentucky bourbon was kept in an eight-year sleep on one, souls in eternal rest on the other.

The distillery, moonlit and bathed in the personality of its own lights, stood stark on its grounds. Shadows revealed little about what slept in those buildings or its age. Faces of empty expression on the faces of shadows seen on corrugated metal siding, left little clue. If the moon was just right, the buildings and all around them would appear in silhouette. The imagery and its noise defy description. Nicholasville wasn't far from this place of spirits and souls and, soon, my home.

Camp Nelson, the original site of a Civil War-era camp, 1863–1866, remains. The 525-acre Camp Nelson Heritage Park is a glimpse of life in a Union army depot and refugee camp. I listened to the echoes along the palisades . . . the voices of the vineyards in the mist. The cries of vintage silence–surely, they must be the hushed dreams of a people, too bound to find their own way or a river to make its way to reach the sea. Theirs was a cruel time, a time not so long ago.

—∞—

July 1962. "I Can't Stop Loving You" was a hit for Ray Charles. Wendell and I spent the weekend of July 7 and 8 in Nashville. I gave him the grand tour of where I'd been before and the others had not. We checked into the Noel Hotel downtown, then ventured out the Franklin Pike to find the homes of folks in the business, down, or on their way out of country and its music.

We spent some time getting to know downtown and the spirit of Nashville's lower Broadway before a visit to Printers Alley and dinner. "Visit Famous Printers Alley" . . . "Finest Food" . . . "Sparkling Entertainment" were signs of the times; others—Carousel, Black Poodle, Rainbow Room, Voodoo Room, and Jolly Roger. The Carousel Club was a known venue featuring some of Nashville's finest players. Since we were not yet twenty-one, the girl at the Carousel's door politely told us no. Neon invitations were not to be.

"I'll see you on my next birthday" may well have been on my mind.

To keep their chops, musicians like Garland, Cramer, Moore, Harmon, Chet Atkins and saxophonist Boots Randolph jammed at the Carousel Club in Printer's Alley and what they played, more often than not, was jazz. Producer George Wein was blown away by what he heard and booked some of the Carousel Club musicians for the 1960 Newport Jazz Festival . . . then in 1960 Hank Garland recorded a straight jazz album.[21]

An exceptional jazz recording featuring Hank Garland was made without leaving Nashville. Hank Garland was joined by the young vibraphonist, Gary Burton, from Princeton, Indiana, Joe Morello, drummer with the Dave Brubeck Quartet, and fine-mellow bassist Joe Benjamin. The session, recorded August 24, 1960, at Owen Bradley's Quonset hut studio, was produced by Grady Martin.

Jazz Winds from a New Direction is a brilliant piece of work, a timeless recording.

We left the neon fog of Printers Alley behind, heading for Broadway's bright lights and the Ernest Tubb Record Store. Saturday night, arrangements were being made for the weekly live radio show in the store once the Grand Ole Opry's show had ended. A radio in the store was tuned to WSM. The night was still young in Music City when we left to see what else could be found on and around the lights of Broadway.

Our walk around the block ended on Fifth Avenue, near the corner of Broadway, on the steps of the Ryman Auditorium. The doors were open, the Opry well under way. We had no tickets. The usher politely let us enter. We walked in and sat in a pew under the Confederate Gallery above, ate popcorn, drank soda pop, and listened to Marty Robbins, Minnie Pearl, Faron Young, and others perform.

This was their dream, played out on hallowed pieces of varnished wood.

Nonstop entertainment was flavored with live commercials selling Martha White Flour and Coca-Cola on the radio power of WSM (We Shield Millions) all around the world from this place. The Ryman remains a near-perfect sound stage. Spiritual it may have once been, this once-upon-a-time church. Anyone who heard Hank Williams or Patsy Cline sing anything in the Ryman must surely be a fossil in search of life that once was and is no more. The words of Lester Flatt and Earl Scruggs were like a vapor adrift, lightly chasing one another beyond stained glass windows, open to the summer night.

"Goodness gracious, good and light, Martha White."

It's Saturday night in Music City USA. There's no better biscuit to be found anywhere. Pass the butter and honey.

Sunday began with breakfast, goodbye to the Noel, and a drive around downtown and through Printers Alley before heading over to Sixteenth and Seventeenth Avenues. The neighborhood was its quiet self on a Sunday afternoon. No one was making a record today. The fifty-five-gallon drum in Columbia's parking lot was filled to the brim with used recording tape and other reminders of the business of music: notes and such, stained by a stream of coffee and soda from now empty cups left behind.

Someone had been putting down hit record tracks in Owen Bradley's Quonset hut.

Music had been made here. Who and what tour bus or fancy cars had stopped there? RCA's Studio B was empty, too—all may have stayed too long at the fair and gone home. We were on the outside looking in. It was lonely. The place of the sun in the sky told me it was time to leave, not knowing how long the drive this time would be.

We left Nashville on Highway 31E, the Gallatin Road, through Madison, past Old Hickory Lake, through Hendersonville, passing Randy's Record

Shop in Gallatin. Wendell suggested we stay in Tennessee a while longer. I turned south on US 231 to Lebanon, Carthage, and Cookeville, then north on Tennessee 42 to Livingston.

Wendell held the map. I drove the MG. The sun began its set; the mountain air became a little cooler. Acker Bilk's "Stranger on the Shore" played on the radio. I put my thoughts on what remained of the summer of '62. The car was quiet; a silence broken only by the dialogue of four cylinders with my hands on the wheel.

We ate dinner at a roadside diner somewhere and then sang songs—country songs—the rest of the way home: Don Gibson songs, Hank Williams songs, and Johnny Cash songs. I had stolen the Opry, and it happened to be a friend in an MG on my right. I never wanted to give it back. Once you've got the Ryman in you, it's forever yours to keep.

We crossed the state line near Dale Hollow Lake and Albany, Kentucky, continuing north on US 127 past Lake Cumberland to Russell Springs and State Highway 80 to Somerset. US 27 took us the rest of the way: Stanford, Lancaster, Nicholasville, and Lexington. I took Wendell to Alabama Avenue to his family and me to my own. The hour was late.

—ɱ—

Highway 68 revisited

A blue highway had quietly turned to white in the first hours of an early January day. My mind was on a new semester in college and its spring. The snowy landscape along an empty US Highway 68 silenced the conversation I had begun with the road. A lady in a beautiful state of mood just before becoming frozen in the still of itself. Night felt as if it were alone, not strange that I should notice near 2:00 a.m. coming home from places west of Lexington. The band had left folks in Lebanon, Danville, or Harrodsburg happy. Forgetting how tired I may have been, came easy simply in how a road I was on presented itself. 68 wrapped a coming attraction appearing in silhouette with care. The MG's headlight beams distilled all but the spirits of the village up ahead.

The silent empty that was Shakertown.

The road turned left at an old Shell Oil filling station, closed at this hour, then right again, up a way on the road to yesterday. I was a stranger on my way somewhere going down Main Street, an awe-inspiring avenue of long-forgotten buildings in random scatter, each side of lonely.

Stone and picket fences followed an undulating lay of land to the heart of the spirit of a place in time. It all represented to me an expression of simple in uncommon ways; God willed there be no end to their number. Here were thirty-four nineteenth-century buildings and the endless space between them.

Space. Born in nothing, living to be something, becoming everything.

Stark shadows and emptiness defined the once vital part of this rural community near Harrodsburg in 1962. I thought to pass it by as on many times before, a witness to the rarest essence of simplicity anyone could know. Slowing before leaving, I brought the car to rest, stopping at once was the Trustees' house. Today, The Trustees Table, a fine restaurant.

Snow had fallen in the night while on my way to the middle of somewhere beside Highway 68. Leaving the warmth of an MG on the main road in Shakertown, I stood among a random collection of simple gifts between the bookends of time and place humbled by the wonder of it all. In the company of white silhouettes dancing on the darkest sky and a Fender Stratocaster, I found no greater peace.

"My Lord what a morning when the stars begin to fall."[22]

The soul living in the architecture of Shakertown was kind, its use of natural materials and God's light the kindest to be found in Kentucky. A moonlight serenade under the stars at Shakertown then was to experience calm, like a pecan grove in southwest Georgia on a Sunday afternoon or late summer snow on fields deep of south. Here was the sound of slow steady rain on a piece of thirsty southern ground. Shakertown was my peace, a sensitive, common sense simplicity of an architecture designed by a unique people.

Its buildings and the night were spiritual with a near-divine essence.

I saw them alone in their silence, where the children of yesterday once played, saw history mirrored in the moments after leaving close its eyes to my own to sleep until I came this way again.

The Shell Oil filling station would be gone in a few years, the turns replaced with a gently bending curve as US 68 continued in a new arc. Shakertown became an island of memories.

I continued on, on my way to see night shadows play on the tiered and textured faces of the palisades, limestone that held of the history of a river's written past to its breast.

—∾—

Moonlight fell on the palisades along the river on the road past Shakertown. Night shadows played on their tiered and textured faces. Limestone held the history of a river's written past in a story to its breast. Palisades, the frozen parallels of nature's stone, then and now ever-changing places, ever-changing me. The road descended to the new Kentucky River Bridge, winding upward once again on the way to Wilmore and home.

A river shimmered. I heard its silence then left it all behind.

The landscape of yesterday was a lady clothed in patches, wonder-filled and tied in tender ribbons. She held my hand all the way through and beyond Shakertown more than many nights. In the summer of 1962, destiny stirred itself a bit. An echo was reborn to become the beautifully preserved Shaker Village of Pleasant Hill, Kentucky, 2,800 acres of simplicity carefully restored.

One's inner tree holds precious memories in its arms with the blessed assurance of never leaving. Such are those I put away of a night on the blue highway of a long ago. They live in me as much today as then.

The Temptashuns would build on the experience of this night's work.

—∞—

My twenty-first birthday.

"Welcome to the Carousel." A pretty one with a smile at the door. I was twenty-one; she the same girl, wearing a black cocktail dress, who just two weeks before had told me no. I had come again to hear the featured band. Boots Randolph was appearing with his combo.

The first set was broadcast live on radio. Boots was kind enough to give me an autograph on a napkin during a break. Soft-spoken, he played standards mostly and some nice jazz. I stayed for most of his second set before leaving the Carousel for another nightspot in the alley, the Black Poodle.

Charlie McCoy and The Escorts were appearing that night—The Candy Men, Roy Orbison's tour band. I met Charlie McCoy during their intermission. We talked briefly at the bar. He was rearranging order of songs in the band's next set. Charlie took what remained of his time to show an interest before heading back to the stage and the band.

Bobby Goldsboro, who had become Roy Orbison's guitarist in 1962, was also a member of the Escorts at the time. Others in the band were Ken Moss (guitar), the late Kenny Buttrey (drums), Mac Gayden (guitar), and John Sturdivant on sax. The Escorts were a fine band.

Wayne Moss and Kenny Buttrey along with Charlie McCoy later formed the first Nashville super group 'Area Code 615,' circa 1969. Others in Area Code 615 were David Briggs (keyboards), Mac Gayden (guitar, French horn), Weldon Myrick (steel guitar), Norman Putnam (bass, cello), Buddy Spicher (fiddle, viola, cello) and Bobby Thompson (banjo, guitar).[23]

Charlie McCoy had only been in Nashville about two years, becoming a highly sought-after session musician. He sang vocals, played bass and harmonica that night. Charlie McCoy signed his name with a harmonica on Roy Orbison's "Candy Man," his first Nashville session. The day after Valentine's in 1962, he played harmonica on Patsy Cline's session that produced "Anytime." McCoy's harmonica is a brush that painted "He Stopped Loving Her Today" like a single teardrop making its way slowly from the soul of George Jones, to one's own mind, becoming still in the instant of a silent, shattered mournful splash.

Record discographies of Chet Atkins, Elvis Presley, Roy Orbison, Boots Randolph, and other artists reveal Charlie McCoy was a session musician on other instruments: bass, guitar, organ, and vibraphone on their sessions. He recorded as a solo artist on Fred Foster's Monument Records label.

Charlie McCoy became musical director for *Hee Haw*, popular in the seventies and eighties. A founding member of Area Code 615, McCoy was named CMA Instrumentalist of the Year in 1972 and '73. He was inducted into both The Country Music Hall of Fame and Nashville's Musicians Hall of Fame.

Music knows no strangers. I stayed another set before leaving and the lights of the alley.

I learned this because of that night.

The Temptashuns needed a trumpet player who had been sitting in with us since mid-April. The sax and trumpet combination of The Escorts was a bright touch of brass, and we were ripe. I knew Doug would want it too. A change about to come would one day paint us to be an uncommon ensemble of driven players.

Rhythm and blues were standing on the corner waiting for our long unforgettable ride the next few years. When the train from Muscle Shoals and Memphis arrived, it stopped right here. Our emphasis on music—horn-based, southern-made—distinguished us from other bands around here. I don't believe there was anyone quite like the Temptashuns band at that time.

It would happen only once in my life, my golden birthday. I was twenty-one on the twenty-first. A day trip to Nashville, a walk around downtown, some fine food, and a memory. I heard Boots Randolph play music in the Carousel.

Long after the neon's glow and southern charm of a young woman in a black dress had dimmed, I had a souvenir of it all. I put a cocktail napkin, its autograph, "Sincerely Boots Randolph," away. I still have it.

—~—

The Temptashuns first played in Joyland Casino on July 28, 1962. It wouldn't be the last. Joyland's large room was a giver of fine acoustics. A stage projected onto the dance floor in a half circle, its second level well equipped with concealed show lighting near the back wall. With Joyland, you got a baby grand piano and acoustics that made you sound big. Every band I ever saw at Joyland looked good on that stage. You looked bigger and sounded great in that room. Tables and chairs were arranged on either side of its spacious wood dance floor, sunken one step down. The opposite end of the casino featured a long bar.

The floor was separated from the tables by palm trees and pipe railings. Joyland's railings felt thick, like Tupelo honey. With so many coats of paint, like rings on a tree, you could've peeled the layers back to a time when Harry James, Tommy Dorsey, Count Basie, Duke Ellington, or the Billy May Orchestra brought excitement to the place with high performance swing music.

You could sense the passion of this dance hall in its fragrance. Scents of perfume, bourbon, loneliness, and stolen moments were everywhere. They lived in the dance floor's wood long after everyone had gone. Passion and perfume lingering long after the dance to write their own chapter in the history of Joyland Casino and its secrets.

July 28, 1962. The Temptashuns put on a show, playing our best, beginning a chapter of our own in this place. We would get much better than that night. The penny arcade, hot dogs, and French fries they sold were on my mind. I thought about the sounds, the lights, and the nights in the summers of 1959–1961.

We had come so far.

—~—

Ours was a new look—Post time had arrived. Red Lacoste tops, with a small white **T** on a black diamond-shaped patch. Khaki slacks, black belts, and our black-and-white saddle Oxford shoes and white socks were our signature for a time. Mickey in her red top with a khaki skirt and saddle Oxfords, looked terrific. The Temptashuns were a sharp-looking band in 1962. We complimented each other well, sounding great that night.

Mickey, Doug, and I backed Wendell's vocals with confidence, my guitar solos coming along better than expected. I wanted to play the piano in this place another time in this band. The opportunity, not known to me, wasn't that far away.

The *Lexington Leader* ad, August 2, 1962, read "Happy Wants to Meet You at the Fair." We played the following Friday night at the Lion's Bluegrass Fair. He stayed till our show ended. Albert B. "Happy" Chandler was out mingling with folks. His compliments on our performance were encouraging. I believe having Mickey with us had something to do with the former governor's pause before he found another hand to shake. He could always find a way to be "Happy" and make most anyone feel the same.

We were in Joyland Casino five more times through September. We were having fun. I bought myself a Model-140 Wurlitzer electric piano, pretending to be Ray Charles after hours in my room.

In time I traded the Wurlitzer in for my first organ, a Thomas, continuing the practice of winding down quietly in the middle of the night in the middle of music in my room at home.

Though weary, I sometimes played till the feeling of tired was gone.

My car was small. I had been taking the passenger seat out to make room for my gear. The amp and my guitar fit fine on the passenger's side. All was well. An MG, its fenders, and me with ones of my own, Stratocaster and Vibrasonic.

I had bought a Fender tube reverb. It seemed a rather small piece of gear. I was about to learn letting go of one's first car isn't easy. The MG and me had a history written in lots of quality miles together since the summer of '59. I needed a place in the car for the reverb. It wasn't to be.

Bye, bye, love.

I reluctantly traded my MG for a Corvair Monza that summer at L.R. Cooke Chevrolet on East High. The parents of a young and pretty girl bought my MG for their daughter, a UK cheerleader. An MG deserved a cheerleader. She was a coed whose family once engaged The Temptashuns

Band to play music for her birthday, a party at Lexington Country Club. I saw her in the car many times around town and campus after that. The girl and the car looked great together.

—ꟺ—

Johnny Burrows had come to Lexington with his family. Johnny, now a senior at Henry Clay, was the band's most trained and accomplished musician. Originally from Chicago, Johnny had contracted polio while a youngster there. He had been visited in a Chicago hospital often by a famous musician. The man gave Johnny encouragement and a few early trumpet lessons. This friendship resulted with a photograph in *Look* magazine and a relationship that continued well into the sixties and seventies. The musician's name was Jonah Jones.

Any time he appeared in the area, Jonah would ask Johnny to make a guest appearance with him. The late Robert Elliot (Jonah) Jones, born 1909 in Louisville, an extraordinary role model, won a Grammy in 1958 for best jazz group performance.

Johnny began appearing with us often, beginning May 4, 1962, at Bryan Station High prom. We asked him to join the Temptashuns some months later, September 21, 1963. We were at the crest of something, about to see how high the next would be. I was Johnny's transportation to and from gigs for the next few years. We shared countless miles and experiences and opinions together.

We played out by the pool at the Lansdowne Club one night that summer with a new drummer. "Last Night" was our signature tune at the time. The Temptashuns shared the same instrument combination as the Mar-Keys. Doug, now on tenor sax, and a kid named Johnny Burrows alternating between his trumpet and flugelhorn.

The Temptashuns could've lived that summer on "Last Night," "You Can't Sit Down (Parts I and II)," "Honky Tonk," "Harlem Nocturne," and "Tossin' and Turnin.'" These and others presented on a night the Temps and rhythm and blues came to Lansdowne. Once we played "Last Night," we all knew where we were headed. The green light turned on at the crossroads where rhythm met blues—Soul Street.

I spoke with Johnny in the eighties. He was living in Carmel, near Big Sur, in California. He later called Salinas home and never left. It was there he passed away.

Doug Hammonds and Johnny Burrows were a great fit. Personalities and musical interests differed enough to make our horn section nice to be around. The band became more interesting because of our collective differences. I grew musically; my record collection began to acquire a different look.

Johnny graduated from Henry Clay and began working in the record department at Barney Miller's downtown. The store's content and influence had grown since the fifties. We grew musically because of the late Walter Morris, a friend. The vinyl universe of our own collections was becoming enriched, harvesting a bounty from a garden of good, and delights of the rows in it. I began buying albums of Nancy Wilson, Wes Montgomery, Dave Brubeck, and Jimmy Smith, listening ever-intently to arrangements and their arrangers—Verve's Oliver Nelson in particular. The bluest of notes danced with improvisation in Rudy Van Gelder's studio in Inglewood Cliffs, New Jersey.

I was blown away.

The Temptashuns might offer a piece of "Take Five," "Peter Gunn," or "Blues for J" in a solo from one of its players. Selected horn figures might feature a taste of Jimmy Smith's "Slaughter on Tenth Avenue" or "Who's Afraid of Virginia Wolf." "Walk on the Wild Side" might find its way to an organ solo in another song.

A slice of expression from jazz artists into a solo or improvising another was a sweet surprise. A passage from Nancy Wilson might be just the color we needed to paint a popular hit on our set list differently. The band found a way to hang a portrait of others on the wall of our sound. Our version of Stevie Wonder's "Uptight" played heavily off Nancy Wilson's arrangement of the song on her album. Some whispers were heard. Where do they come up with it all?

Nancy Wilson was that good, and we knew it.

—∾—

Nashville, the fourth time.

My Corvair was two weeks old and could seat four. I took Doug, Wendell, and Shelby to Nashville in August. We checked into the Downtowner Motel, at Seventh and Union, where we planned to stay the night. We left for a drive out to Hendersonville, Old Hickory Lake, and Gallatin that afternoon before dinner. I planned a Sunday visit to some of the places Wendell and I had already been and others yet unseen the next day.

We spent time after dinner in and around Printers Alley, Church Street, Broadway, and the Ryman. We didn't go in. Windows were open. Voices of Marty Robbins, Bill Monroe, Minnie Pearl, and Faron Young were on and in the air. Fifth Street near Broadway was the planetary center of country music. You don't forget the sense of the Ryman's place in the universe.

Sunday morning breakfast was familiar, tasty as before.

The band had a ton of miles to go in our young years. Breakfast ended too quickly. We checked out of the Downtowner, leaving Seventh and Union for Broadway and Sixteenth Avenue. I parked on the street at the Decca Records building, Decca's new home.

Columbia had purchased Owen Bradley's recording studio early in February.

Wendell took a photograph of me, Doug, and Shelby by my car, parked in front of Decca. The building stands today. Little has changed at this place Owen Bradley, Brenda Lee, Patsy Cline, and others once called home. I look at the photograph and others now and then, recalling the walk around the neighborhood that day with friends. We saw a place on its way to being redefined before it was. It's nice to remember a place of another time.

Knowing today what it became.

Friendly things that define the ordinary character of life itself had not been lost. In between, the music and the rest of life, porches—some with swings, old trees, and human scale—defined the quiet there. One could be at peace in its simplicity.

We stood on sidewalks where stars had walked, saw doors through they had passed. One could look through glass into places where secrets were kept. Until a song was heard on a radio, played on a jukebox or listened to and bought in a record store, secrets were there.

Capitol Records and Cedarwood Publishing were nearby. We walked up Sixteenth across the small parking lot at Columbia to take a closer look of its Studio A, the Quonset hut. I touched brick on its side wall, felt vibrations of its yesterday. The rhythm of the wall's buttress-like stone-capped piers were fingers on the hand of its length. The wall held aloft the Quonset hut, a corrugated metal barrel vault. I sensed the tempo of a waltz, the aspirations and expectations of many. On the outside looking in, again.

We walked down Sixteenth Avenue to Grand around the block on Seventeenth to RCA Victor Records. The front walk on Hawkins Street led to the door where Chet Atkins came to work. RCA Studio B was built in a way the folks in New York City couldn't have done.

The Methodists believed Chet was bringing 'bad people' into their McGavock Street building. So on the back of a napkin at the Nashville airport, RCA's chief engineer Bill Miltentong, drew a picture of what was needed. The napkin drawing became Studio B, where Porter (Wagoner) and everyone else cut so many hits. They moved into the new studio on 800 Seventeenth Avenue South in November 1957. Songwriter and journalist Walter Carter described Studio B for Country Sounds: The new building took four months to build and cost $39,515. Through the next 20 years, revenue from records cut there would easily top $100 million. Much of the equipment was fashioned by engineers Bill Porter and Al Pachucki. Studio B had natural echo, a live sound and no one used earphones. Al Pachucki was engineer on countless Porter Wagoner records, and he said, "The beauty of the room was that everyone could hear everyone the way they should."[24]

Chet's *Teensville* album had been a door for me. In reality, I was fresh paint on canvas. Liner notes on another of his albums, *Chet Atkins' Workshop*, told of a place at his house equipped to record. He could experiment with sound and his music there. A player and his instrument away from distractions was familiar.

They surely would be finished with their Sunday meal. Maybe we could go find where he lived. It was too soon to leave for Lexington. We left Decca, headed over to Broadway, past Vanderbilt, and out West End Avenue to the City of Belle Meade. West End became Harding Pike. Belle Meade was a portal to deep front yards with a southern-sounding name. She was old, southern, and all that that implied. Exclusive and lush, an old money wonderland defined this piece of Nashville.

I don't recall how we found clues to where he lived, driving down a quiet street in Forest Hills. Seemingly lost in another fashionable neighborhood in Nashville's West End, four hopefuls looked to find a name and number on a mailbox or a front door. Better still, a street-side billboard with a message, "Here is the home of Chet Atkins." I stopped to ask a kid on a bicycle riding with friends if he knew where Chet Atkins lived. "Sure. It's there, the white one." Green leaves on old trees filtered the light and shade. Neighborhood folks may have wondered. Who is this? You don't see too many Chevrolets in this part of the West End. The street was quiet and kind, a Chet Atkins version of serenity.

It was a nice brick home, a well-landscaped yard in a fresh-in-the-trees landscape of a neighborhood of fine finish. I pulled into a driveway; the solemn promise others would go with me to the front door.

If this was where he lived, what would I say— "I really like your records"?

I stopped my car behind the Cadillac parked in his driveway. What if I had no voice? Having come this far, not knowing the truth about who lived there was out of the question. I put concerns aside, walked to the brick front entrance step, and rang the house chime.

She came to the door. "He does live here. I am Mrs. Atkins. He's taking a nap." I figured Chet had probably played Jimmy Hyde's Carousel Club in Printers Alley the night before and was tired. She spoke softly, "You can make an appointment with his office at RCA Victor if you wish to see him." Pausing to continue, "He'll be there on Monday." Hearing his master's voice, this or any Sunday, was not to be. She was kind, may have sensed a hint of disappointment on my face.

Inside, I was shattered or so it seemed. Mrs. Leona Atkins was polite, a charming lady with a warm smile. One of the guys took a photograph with my camera, a large negative bellows-type Kodak. I'm standing by an open door with an understanding woman at the entrance to the home of Chet Atkins, August 1962. I took another of the house from my car from the street before leaving.

The photograph is black and white, with white ruffled edges. I still have it.

Mrs. Leona Atkins passed away October 2009 at home.

We drove away. I had brought something to leave at RCA Victor before we left Nashville. The promotional playbill I left under the mat at the entrance to RCA's offices told of our upcoming appearances at Joyland's Casino.

JOYLAND CASINO. The Temptashuns Live Saturday August 18th and 25th 8 till 12.

JOYLAND CASINO
The Temptashuns Live
Saturday August 18th and 25th
8 till 12

The only taste a thin transparent veil of separation would give us at this home of Atkins, Elvis, and Orbison that day would be looking through the door's glass into another world. I returned to the car, where Doug, Wendell, and Shelby waited, and drove to the alley behind the studio to take a picture of the building.

He came out the back door of the studio, walking over to ask. "What are you boys doing here?" Was this our end? The Temptashuns would never be a part of RCA. Chet Atkins would hear about this on Monday, the poster found. I told him I just wanted to take a picture. He thought a moment, then asked if we'd like to come inside. "I'll show you around. I work here now and then." He led us to the studio door at the back wall and introduced us to the room.

"Welcome to RCA's 'Nashville Sound' Studio B."

A frozen ballet of Neumann's, a Telefunken now and then, were suspended midair. A Calder rhapsody of still life, waiting for its next voice, hit, record-setting, chart-smashing No. 1 record. Microphones are silent partners of artists and players, the sophisticated ladies of recorded sound. These ones had been mere inches from Elvis Presley, Don and Phil, and Roy Orbison, and the lips of others. He was kind in a way you don't forget. I didn't know then how many other times he and I had met in the past.

I do now.

I learned by a note posted by his son commenting on a photograph I had taken while we were there that day that the man was Grady Martin. I had met him before, on a bunch of favored records I owned. Grady Martin was a session leader, guitarist, or producer on many of them, the heart of Nashville's creative A-team.

He let us roam the room for a while, touch things with care, like the polished ebony Steinway piano and its keys. Floyd Cramer signed his name, with crystal clear notes, on the echoes of "Heartbreak Hotel." I didn't know that the piano was this Steinway. I did know they had been played by the same who touched these keys. A satisfied mind was the connection to a notion. My own.

He told us, "They call this room Studio B. The studio's control rooms are beyond those windows, where Bill Porter and Tommy Strong, the engineers on most all sessions here, come to work." Our faces were reflected in the glass of the studio's control room. We had so much to learn. A Vibraphone sat nearby, mallets ready for a player of good. He described the echo chamber for Studio B, a separate room up above with tile on all its surface planes.

Follow the echo was the name of the game in that room.

He explained the front door, reception and offices up the hall were for Mr. Atkins and Mr. Sholes, when he comes down from New York . . . "Can't take you too close." We returned to the studio.

Hank Garland's guitar expressions on Presley's "Little Sister," "A Big Hunk of Love" and "I Got Stung" mirrored a "bright" expression in Presley's sound. Were the echoes of Elvis born in a stairwell on McGavock Street living in an empty room above or reflected in faces on a control room's glass that day? I had left our aspirations at the doorstep.

Standing in the relative silence of the studio, I wondered if anything remained of "Heartbreak Hotel" in the room above. He gave us enough time in Studio B for Doug, Wendell, and Shelby to get their last look. I visited a Hammond C3 organ there. I've seen it in a photograph picturing Elvis seated, the Jordanaires gathered around him singing a hymn. They had recorded twelve sides of gospel songs. The album titled *His Hands in Mine*. My own had touched the same Steinway and a Hammond. I had taken some photographs inside Studio B of Doug and Shelby and Wendell. Sadly, the one behind the lens is anonymous—seldom seen. The one photograph of me pictured with Grady Martin that day in Studio B taken by Wendell is priceless. We thanked him for taking a chance on us. Fifty-four years since, the events of that day are fresh, almost as if vine ripe.

I sense calm in the air even now, the genuine southern hospitality of Leona Atkins on a doorstep in Forest Hills. RCA Victor Studio B, Hawkins Street at Seventeenth South, in the heart of what was becoming Music Row, a distinction shared with a Quonset hut, one block away.

A custodian might find the poster another time while sweeping autumn and its leaves away at the front door there in October.

It was now or never. We had to leave it all behind.

My second visit to Nashville had been on March 17 and 18. A discography of Elvis Presley's recording sessions indicates the last time he recorded in Studio B prior to our being there was March 18 and 19. Elvis recorded "Suspicion;" Grady Martin was guitarist on the session. Elvis returned again, May 26–27, 1963.

We were there on a Sunday, in between the two.

Roy Orbison would be in this studio in two days, Tuesday, August 14, recording his hits, "Working for the Man," "Leah," and "I Get So Sentimental." I wonder where Roy Orbison might've been that day. Was he in Hendersonville? It was Sunday afternoon; maybe he was out on Old Hickory fishing with his sons. He may have been with his neighbor next door, Johnny Cash, discussing the music of America. He was happy then.

Studio B became a museum dedicated to studio musicians, the anonymous unsung heroes of recorded music. The studio was purchased by Mike Curb and has been restored and giving itself back to us today. Studio B is a working laboratory for the Mike Curb School of Music Business, Belmont University. This room was never destined not to be an analog fossil of yesterday. All recording done in the studio was planned to be done using original analog equipment. I knew this would be my last visit for some time; a day trip would be a rare opportunity. We were playing most every weekend.

September began with two consecutive Saturday nights at Joyland, the room filled with teens and college students. Another summer was on its way to over, fall semester about to begin at UK. The band's share of two open weeks was spent putting together enough new material for a new show. We were immersed in tightly knit rehearsal sessions working up fresh arrangements.

The Temptashuns emerged more polished than ever, a bunch of driven players.

We finished September's last weekend at Lambda Chi Alpha and Sigma Alpha Epsilon fraternities. October began, busy with two engagements at Transylvania College. We were down on the banks of the Kentucky River at Clay's Ferry, bringing our kind of rhythm and blues to an ever-growing audience. Afternoons at the Circle H with a fraternity or sorority and their guests was special any time. We entertained Delta Tau Delta fraternity and their friends for three hours under the bridge to Madison County the third weekend of October. Autumn along the Kentucky River is stunning.

The serenity of this one was about to change.

My full-time day job continued. The band's ever-increasing time demands became difficult to keep separate from responsibilities at the manufacturing plant.

In late October, the U-2 spy plane produced aerial surveillance over Cuba showing a Soviet ballistic missile base and other installations on the island. President Kennedy countered with a blockade designed to end the affair. An unsettling strangeness about things was present, an ominous light through a prism that seemed unclear.

Unclear, nuclear. What was the world coming to?

There was more to this than a simple rearrangement of letters in a word. It remained a situation nonetheless that wasn't clear at all. We later learned it to be "The Cuban Missile Crisis," October 22, 1962.

James Brown appeared two days hence, October 24, on 125th Street in Harlem. His history-making *Live at the Apollo* album was recorded at the Apollo Theater. People came to Harlem on the A-train. They took the night train home. King Records brought the taping back to Brewster Street in Cincinnati. A fine piece of watercolor art was done there, liner notes written, the performance made its way to vinyl—an album was born.

November began with a hayride at Vernon Hatton's camp in Versailles. We were at Danceland for Alpha Delta Pi sorority on Friday night and for a Saturday afternoon jam session with Kappa Kappa Gamma sorority and Sigma Alpha Epsilon fraternity. Having sounded our rhythm and blues best at Danceland, we delivered four solid hours of R & B entertainment, from Manchester Street to the KA house on Rose that evening.

The following Friday night, we played at Lafayette for a sock hop in the gym after the football game. Appearances at the Phoenix Hotel and Sigma Alpha Epsilon, were followed by a road trip to Bowling Green for Western's Sadie Hawkins Dance. The band returned to Joyland for Delta Tau Delta and November's end at Tates Creek Country Club for the Lambda Chi's.

December was fully booked with appearances in Carlisle and Corbin, Kentucky, Spring Valley and Tates Creek Country Clubs in Lexington. Spindletop Hall provided an elegant setting for two engagements in its intimate dancing room downstairs. The Louisiana Courtyard, with its beautifully designed floating wooden dance floor and a gently curved star-filled ceiling, featured a night sky: deep blue, illuminated softly.

You could lose yourself, charmed by the one you were with in that room. Dancing in it was poetic. Couples in motion in the night dancing to something blue, a nocturne played under a dark and tender sky. Hushed sighs played with the whispers of tiny stars; Spindletop was light and easy, with an intimate bayou kind of pace. Delicious.

We played here several times over the years for the cotillion and other private affairs. I loved this space with its serenity and fragile acoustics. Extravagant—yet in its elegance, this little room seemed all by itself and shy. All that oil money, printed with the ink an East Texas oil field represented, was reflected in the mirror of depressed times in the early thirties in the Bluegrass. It was for some a reason to resent the Younts of Beaumont and their famous oil strike they called Spindletop.

The mansion and 1,051 acres of grounds on Ironworks Road were donated to the University of Kentucky by Mrs. Miles Frank Yount of Beaumont, Texas. Spindletop became a place alumnus could play and dine, in the soon-to-be diminishing bluegrass countryside.

"Are you as oblivious to the song as I at this moment or did we get lucky this time around and there's a distinct possibility I'll fall in love with you? Why is it so important for you and me to be holding each other? This feeling that I have . . . I never knew uncertainty could be so wonderful."—T.S., from Cotillion, *a poem looking back on happy uncertainties of another winter. From the winter of 2003.*

The cotillion gives girls and boys dance cards, handheld pieces of society holding hands with names put there by someone else. Who will be paired with whom, is not their choice. A question, with no easy answer, seemed to escape from the fog of it all.

Once the dances begin, is the other the one you really want to be with?

The year ended with performances in Bowling Green on the twenty-eighth at the Armory and at the Phoenix Hotel for New Year's on the thirty-first. I played something nice and easy to the silence in my room in the newest hours of 1963. Looking back on what had quickly become another yesterday, the clear, elegant simplicity of it all felt warm. The city limits of another Top 40 town were down the road somewhere. Little did we know how defining the days and months ahead would be, how the band and ourselves once again would be shaped by the times.

Good tastes are seldom anything less than special. I began a rite of winter on the year's first day as simple as I knew. I spent the afternoon of a New Year's Day at Doug's house on Cochran, in a pine-paneled basement room in Chevy Chase. His dad (Mr. Conrad Hammonds) and Doug shared with me Connie's annual tradition of bowls: ones of bean soup, with diced onions and cornbread.

Orange, Sugar, Cotton, and Rose.

Part Three

A Day's Beginning, Seen in a Mirror, Fading Fast Away Into the Night

8
The Road to Uncommon

1963. I was twenty-one. Echoes of Nelson Riddle's "Route 66" were fresh from a twelve-week run, having charted 30 in *Billboard* magazine. The hit parade was blended by The Beatles' first hit for The Beatles in America, "I Want to Hold Your Hand," Peter, Paul, and Mary's "If I Had a Hammer," Frank Sinatra's "Call Me Irresponsible," and Crystal's "Da Do Run Run" were hit records. Gregory Peck won Best Actor for his performance as Atticus Finch in *To Kill a Mockingbird* the previous year.

President Kennedy went to Berlin and told a million people, "I am a Berliner." The wall never moved. Martin Luther King Jr. told us he had a dream. Sandy Koufax had a great year. In late November, the eyes of everyone were upon Texas.

The year would be defining for the band.

I stood reflected on storefront glass, a cold January day on Main. The array on display in Shackleton's window made me wish for a bag of six glazed doughnuts from Spalding's. I needed something more than furs kept out of reach in Lowenthal's vault next door to deliver me from the chill. And a choice.

The store opened for business. I was shown to the second-floor showroom, promptly given a product booklet. The complete line of Hammond organs was on display. I had a choice to make. The difference it would mean and for how long was uncertain. I needed to put some space between me and tomorrow.

Winter's air was cold returning to Shackleton's the following morning. The salesman let me roam an endless range of possibilities: one of tone wheels and wire, of vacuum tubes and polished wood and metal, and style. The M3, Hammond's companion to the B3 model, was a fine instrument. The Hammond L-100, new to Hammond's line, featured reverb the M3 didn't have. The Leslie speaker gave the Hammond its signature expression. It stands alone in sound. A Hammond organ with one, or two, is unsurpassed. My choice that day was Hammond's L-100 and a Leslie model 51-C speaker to go with it. I acquired a Hammond M3 in the seventies. Thirty years beyond in a new century, a B3 and a Leslie found me.

A Hammond organ, famous for patented tone wheels and drawbars, is the DNA from the mind of Laurens Hammond, Laurens was the inventor of a silent spring-driven clock and other mechanical objects. From a silence, he created a priceless presence for sound itself. His creative genius gave us spinning wheels to generate tone. The Hammond organ's rich, endless flavors offered an unlimited range of creative possibilities. The Hammond was an electric instrument. Other makers—Wurlitzer, Thomas, Conn, and Baldwin—offered electronic instruments.

Anyone who passionately played a Hammond organ could find their own favorite settings hidden somewhere in the mystic. You could park each of nine drawbars, at one of eight places. One's signature can be shaped beginning with 00 0000 000, a code in waiting. A player's own drawbar registrations were sacred back then. A Hammond organ can express itself in countless combinations. A player can keep it in a hushed whisper or make it scream.

It was like having an Enigma machine at my fingertips.

Shackleton's delivered the organ and Leslie to my room the next day. I began to learn.

We played our first gig in 1963 on January 4 for Delta Tau Delta fraternity at the Delt house, four hours, $110.00, and then Lambda Chi Alpha fraternity at their own the next night after Kentucky's basketball game. We were in Carlisle, near Paris, on the twelfth, featuring the band's newest members, a chorus of three UK students from Louisville.

We numbered ten.

The Temptashuns—January 1963, by order of appearance:

Tony Stallard, lead guitar; Shelby Lorrison, rhythm guitar; Wendell Sams, organ and lead vocals; Doug Hammonds, tenor sax; Larry Kelley, drums; John Page, bass; Mickey Levy, girl lead and backing vocals; Stan Tucker, lead vocals; Allen Purdy and Ed Wardle, backing vocals.

At ten members in 1963, we had become one of the largest rhythm & blues bands in Kentucky. We had a lineup good enough to present most any material the Billboard Hot 100 could list and more. The Temptashuns were a versatile, confident collection of players and singers. The set list, taped to my amp, was testament to how good we were becoming.

—ꟽ—

Patsy Cline died on March 5 near Camden, Tennessee, returning from a benefit performance in Kansas City, Kansas. We were reminded again how suddenly it all can be over, a life, anything. I saw hurt in lines on the face of a woman where I worked the next day. She was plain and simple, a humble soul who loved country music and the Grand Ole Opry. Her days were hard, the product of repetitive work, all of it to send her son to Vanderbilt to study, where he would, in time, become a doctor.

She cried. Something had been taken from her. Her Patsy.

I searched for a meaning in it, unsure of any comfort I could give. Sad, I was aware for how close one can get to another they've never really known, the artists of song and creative expression itself. It may have been the first time. Then again, a long-ago chill, an Iowa cornfield in 1959 was a reminder. I ask, "Can snowflakes be the tears of winter?" To this day, I wonder. There's something written on each of them.

It speaks to me. There is no doubt.

—ꟽ—

We were introduced to a guy working at Kent Men's Wear, located at 120 South Upper near the corner of Main. Gary Bloom had come to Lexington from Louisiana. He and Johnny Rivers had been high school classmates. Gary had a bayou kind of manner, his pace unhurried. You're the most important thing in my world; "now let me show you guys some sharp-looking suits and shoes."

He fitted us with new attire of the entertainment kind—striped coats with black slacks, white shirts, and black ties. We returned to be fitted for more formal "in concert" style suits: burgundy jackets and slacks to go with crisp white-pleated shirts, with French cuffs, black Continental-style ties, and black boots. Gary knew high fashion, with a sharp eye on how a group should look. He remained a source of sound advice for several years after.

—∞—

They had graduated from Hollywood High in '55. The Four Preps, a popular vocal group from Los Angeles, appeared in March in concert at Memorial Hall on the UK's campus. The Four Preps began to record for Capitol in 1957, the youngest vocal group on a major label at the time. A *Cashbox* magazine poll voted the Four Preps "Most Promising Group of 1958." Their best-selling album, *The Four Preps on Campus*, sold a million copies. The college campus was where they seemed most at home.

Tonight, they were appearing at the home of Kentucky.

I attended their concert, rushing to SAE fraternity immediately after it ended. The band had loaded in earlier that day and promotion photographs had been taken. One, in the house, featured The Temptashuns, with a new look. Mickey wasn't with us that day. The SAEs were having an after-concert party. We were their band again, in the basement of an old house, one with big rooms, an upstairs and a downstairs, a fine house for a fraternity. Not long after beginning our first set, two of the four Preps joined us for some unplanned fun.

Bruce Belland, leader of the Preps, and another member were appearing live with the Temptashuns at the SAE house. The fraternity was then located on the corner of South Limestone at Bassett Court (now Chrysalis). The other two Preps were just up the street at the Plantation, a popular bar on Lime at Maxwell for some after-concert spirits of their own.

Together, we did two of their own hit songs. They joined our three backup singers on some fifties standards, featuring Stan Tucker with Alan and Ed. They joined us on "Sherry," "Walk like a Man," and "Big Girls Don't Cry," three popular hits by the Four Seasons.

The band sounded super that evening.

The Four Preps were the first nationally recognized recording artists to appear with the Temptashuns Band. There would be others. They left us and the party to join the other two Preps at the Plantation. We finished the night, taking a few days off for spring break and what remained of April.

—∞—

We made a positive choice and changed our direction in a span of seven days in May 1963. We practiced at my house on the first, a Thursday, with a new lead singer, and I made the move from lead guitar to organ. From a Stratocaster to a Hammond was like changing coasts. Two nights from then, Pi Kappa Alpha fraternity and their dates experienced a band with a new look and sound at Lexington's Holiday Inn North. We were a new train with a new freight headed from a different station to tomorrow. Such change in any creative endeavor often becomes, to those who appreciate your art, your signature.

We signed our name on those seven days.

I met two people named Larry on the same Saturday night before then. One was Larry Elgart, a musician and big band leader of renown. He and his brother Les Elgart once formed the Les and Larry Elgart Band. The other was Larry Orr.

Larry was singing with the Torques, another local band. Two bands were playing in separate ballrooms in the same venue that night, the Lafayette Hotel, today Lexington's Government Center on Main. Doug and I drifted over to hear them in during one of our breaks.

One look was all it took.

I dropped by Doug's house the next day after church. Doug and I went to Starlite Drive-In Restaurant on Stone Road for our customary Starlite Sunday lunch. We talked about the band and all Larry could be in it. We left the Starlite looking to find stardust. Soon after, we walked up the steps of Sigma Nu fraternity. The house was on Euclid at Harrison, just down from Memorial Coliseum and Stoll Field. Sigma Nu was an attractive corner to be in 1963. We knocked, the door opened, and a brother led us to the kitchen. Larry, standing at the sink, turned with a smile. We took little time to ask if he would be interested in joining the Temptashuns. Larry was enthusiastic.

There was no doubt in our minds that with Larry Orr as our lead singer and the instrumental complement we could give him, what we could become was unlimited. Larry was no stranger to the arts of communication and entertainment, having been given professional dance instruction as a kid. He knew the moves well, a pure showman. Larry said, "Yes." I left Sigma Nu with Doug that afternoon.

We never looked back.

All we could think about was going with Larry to Barney Miller's and finding the kind of material he preferred. It was to be a never-ending dream ever-ending happily. The Temptashuns fit together well. We now had a certain sparkle that was nice that summer, having begun to polish our material, our choreography, and ourselves musically.

Walter Morris would pull a record out of his dusty bin of 45s long past fresh. "Have you guys heard this?" One listen to an R & B horn-filled blues shuffle in one of Barney Miller's record booths left little to say. "Walter, this one's a keeper." They were relics left over from the fifties, music for lovers of music to make difficult choices: two-sides, 98¢.

45 rpms, the best of times.

—ʍ—

James Brown and a Maceo Parker-led JB Orchestra with the Famous Flames had arrived at the Apollo Theater in Harlem in 1963. The Temptashuns Band arrived at a station of its own on the R & B Line. "A-train," "Night Train." Our Train. Next stop—up-tempo music, a new voice, a Hammond organ, a soul-based horn section, and well-blended rhythm and blues. These and more waited just around the corner. Our claim ticket couldn't arrive soon enough.

The likes of artists James Brown and Mary Wells appearing at the Ballroom in the Holiday Lanes on Georgetown Road and the Lyric Theater on Third, had an undeniable influence on The Temptashuns.

Rhythm and blues had style we understood, and folks around town knew it.

The influence of Muscle Shoals, the Swampers, and Wilson Pickett was becoming self-evident on us. "Last Night" and "Green Onions" brought Memphis to our doorstep. Stax had Rufus and Carla Thomas, the Mar-Keys and Booker T, the MGs and the Bar-Kays and Otis Redding.

The Memphis horns and Muscle Shoals rhythm section brought flavors, added over time to our menu of soul. The band had a lot of work to do. Finals and the end of spring semester were near, a promising summer up ahead. The Temptashuns were becoming a better band, moving on because of Arthur Alexander and Solomon Burke.

We played Henry Clay senior prom on the eighteenth and an event for Albert B. "Happy" Chandler on the twenty-fourth.

Linville Puckett, pride of Clark County High basketball, left Coach Rupp's Kentucky basketball team and opened a bar at the entrance road to the Circle 25 Drive-in Theater on New Circle. He named it the Palms. The Palms featured a small wooden dance floor with a basketball floor theme, some painted lines and imagined goal at each end. Game lines and social lines, all blended in a subtle, nonexistent separation of social and cultural classes.

The Palms was a place where some of Lexington's young horse set could spend an evening sprinkled among ordinary folks, commonplace meets discrete elite. When the featured house band Little Enis and the Fabulous Table Toppers put on their show of good old rock 'n' roll, the appetite of patrons for a good time at the Palms was satisfied.

The band was a four-piece combo: Little Enis (guitar), the Trimble brothers—John on drums and Frank on organ—and Bucky Sallee (tenor sax). Pure rock and roll, they were exceptionally good. The Palms was their home. Friday and Saturday nights at the Palms were the talk of the town. The story of Little Enis, The All-American Left-Handed Upside-Down Guitar Player was well written by the fine local author Ed McClanahan and published in *Playboy* magazine in the seventies and a book.

The Temptashuns played the Palms mostly for fraternity and sorority parties. The scent of bourbon and beer was in the wood and air, as if in a game waiting an evening's last dance. The scent of similar night places rests lightly in a memory for as long as you will it to stay. Illuminated by the presence of socialites, you could read a lot between the lines in a place like that. The games people played and the secrets they kept lived somewhere in the mystery in its shadows.

The eagle would fly on Friday. Some of those I worked with in the factory would cash their checks and head down the road to begin the evening at Eastland Lanes for bowling. They might spend some time in the Terrace Room Lounge before finishing the evening at the Palms. The band appearing in the Terrace Room, the Jaguars, featured a guy getting his licks together for an appointment down in Georgia. He helped Bob Dylan paint the Nashville skyline in a Quonset hut. Charlie Daniels, passing through Lexington, had decided to stay for a while. He liked it here. Charlie was around for a couple of years in the sixties before becoming an uneasy rider and moving on. The music scene in those days was pretty exciting in my hometown, and the Temptashuns were a part of it.

Charlie Daniels originated the Volunteer Jam, an annual music event in Nashville. He settled on a farm in Mt. Juliet, near Nashville, after he outplayed a devil to rest in between engagements on the road the rest of his years.

The Temptashuns played the Palms for the first time on June 1, 1963. We played at the Holiday Inn for the Georgetown Club on the seventh

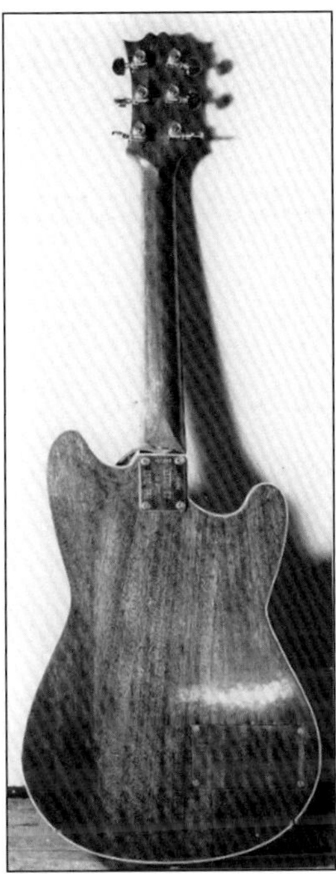

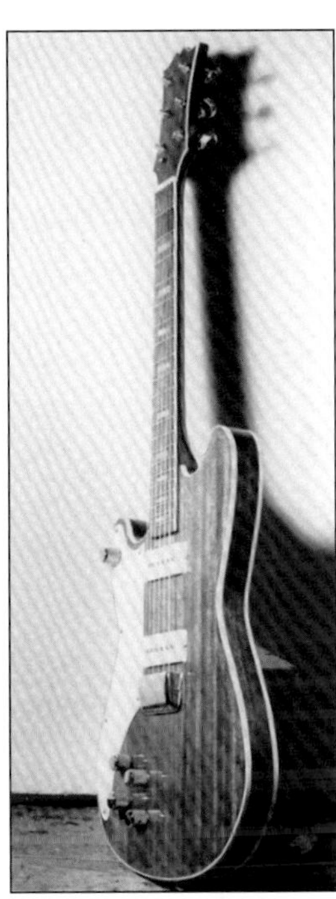

Club 68 Sign, Lebanon, Ky. *J.B. Miller, made guitar. Design by T.S., early 1960s*

Pine Mountain State Park Amphitheater, early 1960s

Wendell Sams (foreground) Left to Right; John Page, Shelby Lorrison, & Tony Stallard - Tony's garage, early 1960s

Mickey Levy, Larry & Doug - Tony's garage early 1960s

Fraternity Row, 1961

"The Tempettes" at Lafayette Senior High - L-R; Bette Jo Betts, Pam Nallinger, Susan Farmer, and Mickey Levy, Feb. 1962

Fender Instruments, 1961

Doug, Mickey, & Tony ... the Del-Vikings of Joyland, "Come Go with Me" 1962

The Temptashuns & "Tempettes" at Lafayette Senior High, Feb. 1962

Elmendorf Farm, Lexington. Courtesy of the author

The Temptashuns at Lafayette Senior High, Feb. 1962

The Temptashuns at Sigma Alpha Epsilon house, 1963 – Photo believed to be by John Zeh.

"Take Five" ... Quiet time at a Baldwin just before it all begins. Joyland, 1961

Temptashuns Band trailer

L-R; Doug Hammonds, John Page, & Tony Stallard - The Temptashuns at Meadowthorpe, 1962

The Temptashuns with Denny Mitchell at the Meadowthorpe Hop

The Temptashuns at 10 members ... Mardi Gras Dance at Eastern, Richmond, Ky. 1962

Left to Right; Allen Purdy, Ed Wardell, & Stan Tucker, ca. 1963

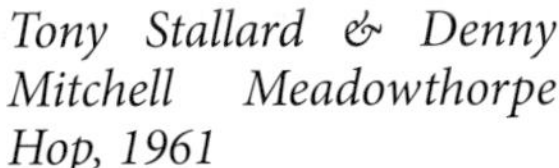

Tony Stallard & Denny Mitchell Meadowthorpe Hop, 1961

Five-cent Day at Joyland -Lexington Herald-Leader advertisement.

Postcard - Danceland on Manchester St. — Courtesy of Lexington history group page, Facebook.

The Temptashuns in-concert at Memorial Hall. The band changed its name to the Magnificent Seven a few short weeks later. Photo believed to be by John Zeh.

University of Kentucky campus setting, ca. 1961 – Photo from U of K Alumni Booklet

Mirage ... a coed dream in an ad from a distant page in The Kentucky Kernel student newspaper

Changes, July 1965

It's a Motown thing. The Temptashuns, R-L; John Burrows, Doug Hammonds, Carter Hackney, John Page

"One Fine Day" Magnificent 7 with the Chiffons at the Gold Digger's Ball, 1966

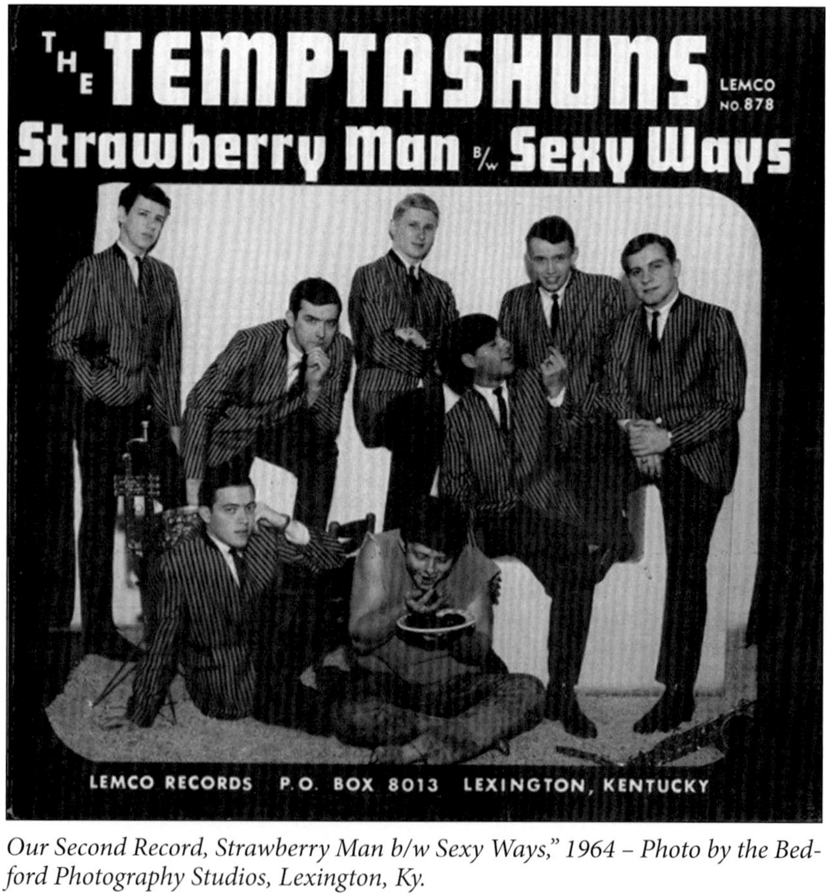

Our Second Record, Strawberry Man b/w Sexy Ways," 1964 – Photo by the Bedford Photography Studios, Lexington, Ky.

Temptashuns- Strawberry man (Federal) **Version:** 2005/3/6

: Great manic soul/garage (in the 60's sense) by the Temptashuns who also went on the record this for Lexington based Lemco records
and later changed their names to the Magnificent Seven, recording 'Stubborn kinda fellow' for Lemco.

Killer drumming, and absolutely classic organ work make this a breath of fresh air for hammond organ lovers IMO.
(By the way, nothing in the hammond section is supposed to be NORTHERN SOUL, but I like hammond stuff, and just though some others might as well!)

Strawberry Man Review - Northern Soul, England

Stubborn Kind of Fellow

WVLK

HITS OF THE WEEK

RADIO 590

Lexington's only Authentic Survey

WEEK ENDING MARCH 3, 1965

THIS WEEK			LAST WEEK
1.	Stubborn Kind of Fellow	Magnificent Seven	11
2.	My Girl	Temptations	2
3.	This Diamond Ring	Gary Lewis and the Playboys	3
4.	College Life	Avo and Ray	8
5.	Hurts So Bad	Little Anthony	7
6.	Twine Time	Alvin Cash and the Crawlers	6
7. **	Downtown	Petula Clark	1
8.	The Birds and the Bees	Jewel Akens	16
9.	Ferry Across The Mersey	Gerry and the Pacemakers	14
10. *	You'd Better Get It	Joe Tex	..
11.	Eight Days A Week	Beatles	18
12. **	Goodnight	Roy Orbison	10
13.	Yeh, Yeh	Georgie Fame	..
14.	Midnight Special	Johnny Rivers	40
15.	Little Things	Bobby Goldsboro	37
16.	Goldfinger	Shirley Bassey	17
17.	King of the Road	Roger Miller	12
18.	Red Roses For A Blue Lady	Bert Kaempfert	21
19. **	Shake	Sam Cooke	9
20.	The Boy From New York City	Ad Libs	19
21.	For Lovin' Me	Peter, Paul and Mary	23
22. **	Lemon Tree	Trini Lopez	29
23.	Come Home	Dave Clark Five	..
24.	Don't Let Me Be Misunderstood	Animals	..
25. **	Can't You Hear My Heartbeat	Herman's Hermits	26
26.	New York's A Lonely Town	Trade Winds	..
27.	Laugh, Laugh	Beau Brummels	25
28.	Tell Her No	Zombies	20
29.	What Have They Done To The Rain	Searchers	27
30. **	Apache '65	The Arrows	28
31. **	I've Got A Crazy Feeling	Classics	31
32. **	Somebody Told Mary	Kenny Price	36
33. **	For Mama	Connie Francis	..
34.	I've Got A Tiger By The Tail	Buck Owens	35
35.	Ask The Lonely	Four Tops	38
36. **	Stop In The Name of Love	Supremes	..
37.	Shotgun	Jr. Walker and the All Stars	..
38.	People Get Ready	Impressions	..
39.	If I Loved You	Chad and Jeremy	..
40.	Send Me The Pillow You Dream On	Dean Martin	..

* WVLK GIANT x EXTRA ** WVLK PIC HITS

WVLK Pic Hit of the Week – THE RACE IS ON – Jack Jones

This survey is compiled each week by Radio Station WVLK Lexington, Kentucky, from reports of all record sales gathered from all leading retail record outlets in the Lexington area. This survey is a true, accurate and unbiased account.

ARTY KAY ★ ★ ★ ★

5:30 A.M. - 12 NOON

MONDAY THRU SATURDAY

WVLK Hits of the Week, On Top of the Top 40. March 3, 1965

She's Called a Woman, The Soul of Sue Records, New York City 1966

. . . on Abbey Rd., London

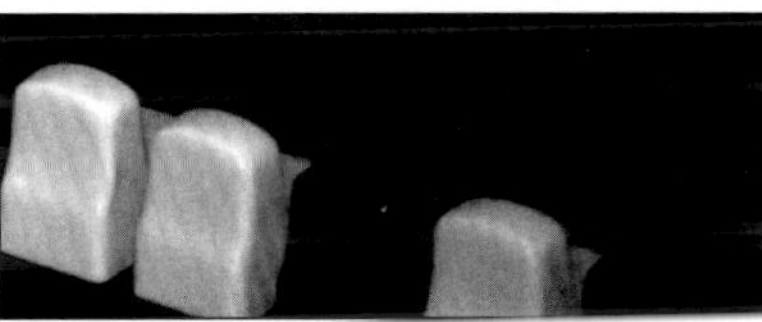

Drawbars . . . windows to the soul of sound

The Soul of Sue Records, New York City 1966

Ooh, Baby Baby, Dial Records 1968

Strawberry Man - Federal Records

Pretty Ways - Federal Records

"Love Gone, Love Return;" an unreleased track recorded at King Records Cincinnati, 1964

King Records 45 rpm record sleeve

Mag 7 promotional photo session at King Records, Cincinnati, 1964 – unused proof from King Records Art Dept., Cincinnati

King Records 1540 Brewster St., in Cincinnati's Evanston neighborhood, 2017

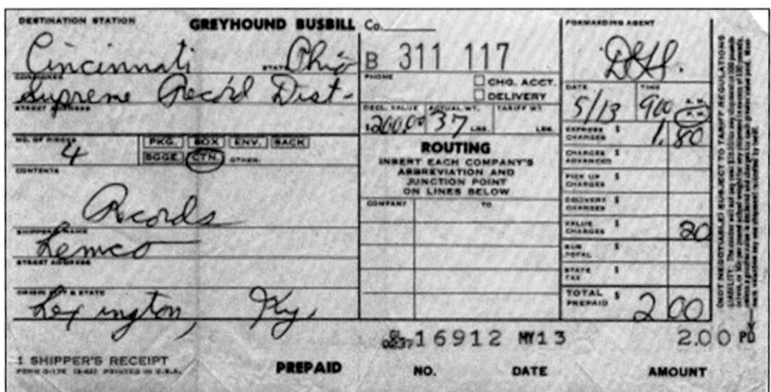

DESTINATION STATION GREYHOUND BUSBILL Co.
Cincinnati, Ohio
B 311 117
Supreme Record Dist.
CHG. ACCT.
DELIVERY
DECL. VALUE $200.00 ACTUAL WT. 37 LBS. TARIFF WT. LBS.
NO. OF PIECES 4
PKG. BOX ENV. SACK BGGE. CTN. OTHER
CONTENTS Records
ROUTING
INSERT EACH COMPANY'S ABBREVIATION AND JUNCTION POINT ON LINES BELOW
COMPANY TO
SHIPPER'S NAME Lemco
STREET ADDRESS
ORIGIN CITY & STATE Lexington, Ky.
FORWARDING AGENT
DATE 5/13 TIME 9:00 P.M.
EXPRESS CHARGES $ 1.80
CHARGES ADVANCED $
PICK UP CHARGES $
DELIVERY CHARGES $
VALUE CHARGES $ .20
SUB TOTAL $
STATE TAX $
TOTAL PREPAID $ 2.00
16912 MY13 2.00 PD
1 SHIPPER'S RECEIPT
PREPAID NO. DATE AMOUNT

Special Delivery

Once when winter signed her name. The palisades along the Kentucky River. – Courtesy of the author

York St. neon

Flamingo Club card

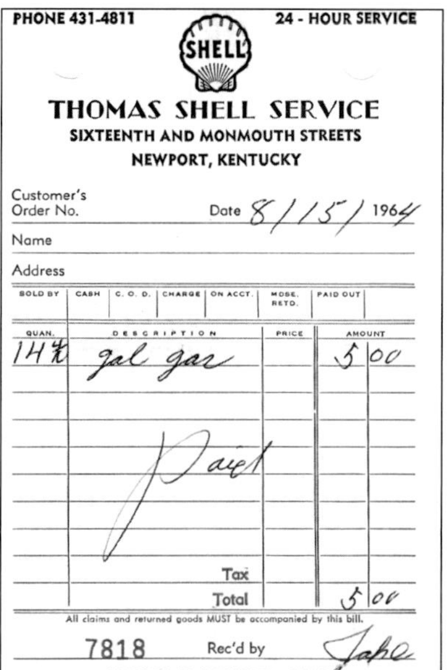

PHONE 431-4811 SHELL 24 - HOUR SERVICE

THOMAS SHELL SERVICE
SIXTEENTH AND MONMOUTH STREETS
NEWPORT, KENTUCKY

Customer's Order No. Date 8/15/1964

Name

Address

SOLD BY	CASH	C. O. D.	CHARGE	ON ACCT.	MDSE. RETD.	PAID OUT

QUAN.	DESCRIPTION	PRICE	AMOUNT
14½	gal gas		5 00
	Paid		
	Tax		
	Total		5 00

All claims and returned goods MUST be accompanied by this bill.

7818 Rec'd by Jake

Newport fuel

Sound Check in the middle of a neon dream ... Flamingo Club, Newport ca. 1964

The Temptashuns ... Sound Check at the Flamingo Club, 633 York St., Newport, Ky. 1965

Shelby Lorrison; rhythm guitar (Temptashuns)

Earl Morgan; bass (Temptashuns)

Wendell Sams; organ-vocals (Temptashuns)

Tony Stallard; lead guitar-vocals (Temptashuns)

Larry Kelley; drums (Temptashuns)

Doug Hammonds; tenor-baritone sax

John Page; bass

John Burrows; trumpet-flugelhorn

Meade Brown; drums

Carter Hackney; lead guitar

Larry Orr; lead vocals

Tony Stallard; Hammond organ-vocals

The University of Kentucky

presents

Little Kentucky Derby

1966

Program of Events:

Friday, April 15 TWIRP NIGHT

7:30 Debutante Stakes
Queen Contest
Presentation of Talent Finalists
Honda Door Prize
Memorial Coliseum
Admission: $1.00

Saturday, April 16

10:30 Turtle Derby on lawn in front of Student Center
1:00 Little KentuckyDerby Preliminary Heats
3:00 Entertainment: U. K. Troupers
3:30 Little Kentucky Derby Final Race
Sports Center
Admission: $1.00

8:00 Concert at Memorial Coliseum featuring:
Chuck Berry • The Shirelles • The Coasters
and The Magnificent Seven
Admission: $2.00 advance
$3.00 at the door

LKD Program of Events

LITTLE KENTUCKY DERBY

April 15 - 16

FRIDAY, APRIL 15

7:30 P.M. Debutante Stakes, Miss Little Kentucky Derby Queen Contest in the Memorial Coliseum —Tickets will be $1.00 at the door — A Honda from Nickens' Honda Sales will be given away — The U.K. Wildcat Basketball Players will be cheerleaders

SATURDAY, APRIL 16

10:30 A.M. Student Center Board Turtle Derby on the lawn in front of the Alumni Gym

2:00 P.M. Bicycle and Faculty Races at the Sports Center — Tickets $1.00 at the door.

8:00 P.M. The Coasters, Chuck Berry, The Shirelles, with Magnificent Seven as the back up band at Memorial Coliseum. The tickets will be $2.00 in advance and $3.00 at the door. They are on sale at Barney Miller's, Dawahare's, Kennedy's and Palmer Drugs. Proceeds go to the University of Kentucky Scholarship Fund.

Ad in Kentucky Kernel Student Newspaper

THE MAGNIFICENT "7"
Lemco 882
STUBBORN KIND OF FELLOW
Jobete, BMI) (2:16) — Gay, Stephenson, Gordy
Flip is "In Mist and Rain," (Lemco, BMI) (1:55)—Stallard
A new group on a label out of Lexington, Ky. Side was published by Tamla-Motown's firm, Jobete Music, and it bears a Detroit quality.

Music Business Magazine - Review

2 – THE KENTUCKY KERNEL, Monday, April 18, 1966

Songs From Past Offered In Show

By JOHN ZEH

As the show started, most of the 3,500 in Memorial Coliseum Saturday night probably expected little more than the Magnificent Seven in concert. But the big name attractions at the LKD concert scored heavily with most, but provided little more than refreshing, nearly nostaligic, relief from today's Beatle-type music.

From Chuck Berry's "School Days" to the Coasters' "Along Came Jones," collegians present were no doubt reminded of their own earlier school days when those tunes were popular.

The audience reception of the Shirelles' "Soldier Boy," probably the prettiest song in the show, was colored by the girls' humorous, and unappreciated, dedication to all the draft-conscious fellows in the crowd.

The Magnificent Seven, certainly not unknown to the jam session set, opened the show with

A Review

Wilson Pickett and Otis Redding rhythm and blues soultunes in a style that lived up to the adjective in the group's name.

The expert showmanship of Larry Orr, a UK English major, coupled with the Mag Seven instrumental sound made some listeners remark, "The rest of the show will have to be pretty good to top this." The guys didn't close the show with "Stubborn Kinda Fella," but if they had, the lead "Here's the one you've been waitin' for all night long" would have been appropriate.

After "Respect," "Don't Fight It," "Midnight Hour," and "Satisfaction," the Mag Seven yielded to Chuck Berry, who squeezed that unique sound out of his magical guitar throughout his old hits. Playing an instrumental lead-in for "Memphis," he danced and cavorted into nearly every position possible, except wrapping himself and his guitar into a Centennial device.

Most vigorous applause came during a bawdy version of "Reelin' And Rockin'," a big seller on 45 rpm, without the suggestive humor. Move over Hot Nuts.

The Shirelles, shaking like lime Jello on Meade Brown's drum heads, entertained with more old rock, sock, and roll favorites, including "This Is Dedicated," "Mama Said" "Tonight's The Night," and "Baby It's You." Their version of "Satisfaction" would make the Stones roll over in their graves. The girls are good, but their's is not the Motown Sound and show of the Supremes.

Enter the Coasters, and more humor. They started out typically, performing (if that's the word) "Yakety Yak," "Searchin'," and "Charlie Brown," but the finale sent the audience home discussing semantics. Crude, gross, and obscene were the words in question.

The concert could have head-

Kernel Photo by Rick Bell

The Magnificent Seven's Larry Orr sways to the soul music of Wilson Pickett's "In The Midnight Hour," in the Lexington group's part in the LKD show, held in Memorial Coliseum.

Chuck Berry rides his electric guitar across the stage while playing "Memphis" at Saturday's concert.

READ THE KERNEL CLASSIFIED COLUMN DAILY

After the Concert Review in The Kentucky Kernel student newspaper. – Photo by John Zeh

The Magnificent 7 1965 – Ed Weddle, Photographer

The Magnificent 7 1965 – Ed Weddle, Photographer

The beat went on . . . Late 1960s, L-R from the top: Richard Peck, Earl Grigsby, Bob McCaw, Charlie Shuck, John Burrows, Meade Brown, & Doug Hammonds

COLLEGE CIRCUIT

ARTIST(S), Label	SCHOOL (Correspondent)	DATE	ATTEND-ANCE	REVIEW	DEALER REACTION
MODERN JAZZ QUARTET Atlantic (Monte Kay Artists)	Oberlin Oberlin, Ohio (Paul Eturm)	May 6	1,450	Sameness in program, but "Summertime" was a big hit.	Bill Long at Co-Op Bookstore—sold all "Porgy & Bess" LP's and took orders for more.
SHIRELLES Scepter (Shaw Artists)	Oberlin Oberlin, Ohio (Paul Sturm)	May 8	1,000	Good, fast-moving program at dance. "This Is Dedicated to the One I Love," their big song.	Bill Long at Co-Op Bookstore—generally poor sales reaction.
RAMSEY LEWIS TRIO Cadet	Nebraska Lincoln Neb. (Lynne Morian)	May 3	608	Fantastic show. "In Crowd" was a big hit.	LaVern Sanborn at J. C. Penny's—no sales. Record Discount Center—no extra sales, but the group sell well all the time. Ron Petrus at International Super Store—Lewis' LP's don't sell here . . . he's about 10 years ahead of Lincoln.
FFERRANTE & TEICHER United Artists (Wm. Morris)	Iowa State Iowa City, Ia. (Charles Feldman)	April 30	1,700 SRO	One of the finest concerts presented on campus. Especially enjoyed their versions of Broad way hits.	Bob Mellicker at Harmony Hall—slight rise, but not enough to matter.
BARBARIANS Laurie	Harvard Cambridge, Mass. (Bob Foukles)	May 13	375	"Moulty" was their best number. They played for a dance.	Wayne Southends at Harvard Co-Operative Society—no sales.
SIMON & GARFUNKEL Columbia (Wm. Morris)	West Virginia Morgantown, W. Va. (Robert Welling)	May 7	3,000	"A Most Peculiar Man" and "Sounds of Silence" went over well; humorous songs and sketches helped keep show moving.	John Marshall at John Marshall store—ordered extra LP's for show, sales good. Mrs. Frank DeVincent at DeVincent's Music Center—sales fair on LP's, "Sounds of Silence" single sold good.
BO DIDDLEY (Shaw Artists)	West Virginia Morgantown, W. Va. (Robert Welling)	April 30	500	Diddley and band kept students dancing.	John Marshal at John Marxhall Records—no sales. Harvey Brooks at C. B. Fawley Music—no calls.
TONY BENNETT Columbia (Tony Bennett)	Seton Hall South Orange, N. J. (John Gallagher)	May 7	3,500	Bennett, backed by Bobby Hackett and Urbie Green Orchestra, was fantastic. Truly great performance.	Fred Baker at Discorama Record Shop—sold seven LP's as result of concert. Allen Heyman at Village Record Shop—no action.
MAGNIFICENT SEVEN Lemco (Magnificent Seven	Murray State Murray, Ky. (Ellis Mueller)	May 7	400	Fraternity dance. The group from Lexington, Ky., had tremendous sound.	Chuck Simons at Chuck's Music Shop—no sales as group does not have a new release out.
ISLEY BROTHERS CRYSTALS Philles (A. Damato)	Trinity Hartford, Conn. (Randolph Lee)	April 23	750	Block party by Interfraternity Council. Isley Brothers didn't do well, but Crystals gave excellent performance.	Belmont Record Shop — Isley Brothers have single that's selling, but concert didn't stimulate increase. Gene Ehrlich at LaSalle Music Shop—singles selling both before and after; LP's dropped in sales. No reaction, however, from concert.
TURTLES White Whale (Landerman Agency)	Trinity Hartford, Conn. (Randolph Lee)	May 13	800	Had to repeat their bit plus hit, "You Baby" twice.	Belmont Record Shop—sold several LP's. Gene Ehrlich at LaSalle Record Shop—sold several LP's but didn't attribute this to Trinity show.

MUSIC ON CAMPUS

campus scene are a sure way of making a successful weekend. . . . For Campus Day weekend, the Kent State Major Events Commit-

Billboard Magazine Concert Review. Murray State 1966

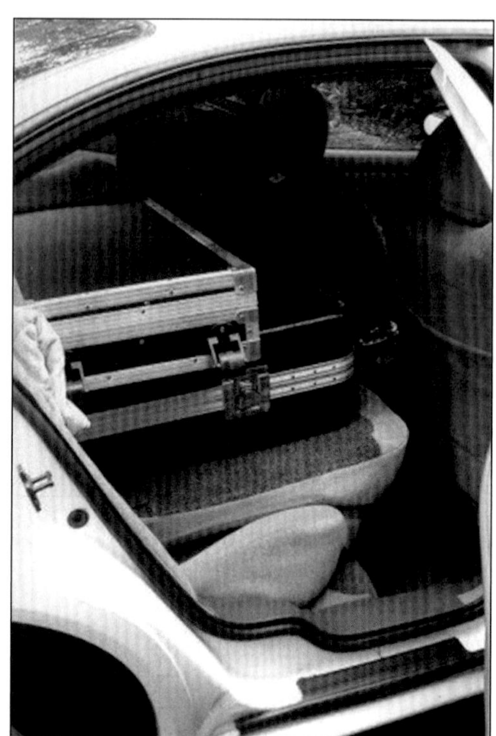

True Romance . . . Blue Highway, July 2010

Off the Charts . . . Mag 7 Horn Section at the Fireplace in Chevy Chase, 1970s. L-R: Paul Osborne, David Hall, Tom Brawner, and David Henderson. – Photo courtesy of David Hall

T.S. Then . . . 1968

T.S. Now . . . 2012

Candy Kisses in the park where I once played. Woodland – Courtesy of the author

The iconic Club 68 sign in Lebanon.

and the Lafayette High senior party the following evening for the Class of 1963. The summer about to begin. Near its end, I would leave a full-time job in a manufacturing plant I'd held since 1959 and go to college.

—∾—

I believed my Corvair had enough in it to pull a trailer. Renting U-Hauls seemed unnecessary anymore. I asked our neighbor next door to build me one. We measured the size of another I had rented. I gave him a sketch with details and a planned arrangement of our gear in the trailer. Mitchell Taylor could build anything. He crafted wood and steel, built a simple trailer, and painted it deep blue. I took it to a local sign painter, Joe Greer, who hand painted "The Temptashuns . . . Dance Band . . . Lexington, Ky" in white letters outlined in red on each of its sides. The trailer and contents were balanced well; the Corvair was just the right car to take it somewhere. Soon folks would begin to learn about a name and a place. They might begin to wonder what somebody did with the things they could not see in the blue box.

Engagements for July were light, an opportunity to exchange ideas and redefine ourselves for the upcoming fall semester at UK. The set list mirrored what each of us had begun to discover about ourselves.

August began poolside for Delta Tau Delta at the Congress Inn on North Broadway and a private party at the Red Mile racetrack. A year had passed since being inside Studio B. Would I ever go to Nashville again?

Would college take all my time?

My mind was a blur of uncertainties.

Picnic. A Labor Day weekend in Kansas. She takes a Continental Trailways bus bound for Tulsa to begin a new life. A patchwork of separate fields of Kansas farmland, make a quilt to spread on fertile the ground and have a picnic. Choices in a wind, in the middle of her own uncertainty. My own were not so different from William Holden and others at a picnic, on a bus, or riding the roof of a train car away from it all.

We played outdoors at Mr. Wiggs, just up the road from the Palms. After, I had a "poor boy" in a box at the Parkette Drive-In before going home. One more appearance: August 31 at the Imperial House for sweethearts and their dates, the brothers of Sigma Chi, ended the summer.

—∾—

I stopped by Graves Cox on Main for some nice things to wear for college before classes began at UK. I had $75 saved. Victor Bogaert Jewelers, on Main, sold fine things. Music and this band enabled me to have more than I ever thought possible: a fine watch, a college education, and, more importantly, the people I met.

I participated in the activities of freshman orientation on campus.

The watch, a Bulova Accutron, seemed all the assurance I would need to be on time. Sometimes on a blue highway coming home from an engagement out of town, I could hear the Accutron's tuning fork playing the only song the watch knew: a one-note piece at a frequency of concert F-sharp.

It was time to make a record.

—∾—

The Lexington Music Company, Lemco, was founded in the fifties by Cecil Jones. Lemco's office was located in a house on Southview Drive where he lived with his family. His recording studio was in a detached garage on the property.

The Temptashuns had been managed for some time by Cecil Jones Entertainment. Cecil managed other bands in Lexington and was our exclusive booking agent. He led the Jones Boys, his own combo, who played for social functions. Cecil produced commercial jingles, recording his band for a variety of local businesses.

When the Temptashuns did our first recording session at Lemco, the studio's space was not at all what one was led to believe it to be outside, an ordinary garage. Cecil was enthusiastic about the possibilities for a modest yet well-equipped recording studio. A lot of work remained to be done. Cecil needed volunteers. John Page and I helped Cecil insulate the walls and ceiling and covered it over with burlap. The work gave Lemco more desirable acoustics for recording and it worked.

Cecil later enlarged his studio, adding a separate control room at the back. We made some movable panels for drums, and he had an isolation booth for vocalists constructed. We added insulation and burlap to it all. He installed higher-quality four and more-track recording and playback equipment. Cecil would do a studio mix for playback in the recording sessions. Final engineering and mastering of tracks we recorded at Lemco's studio, was done at Owen Bradley/Columbia Records studios in Nashville. A fully equipped sound lab with state-of-the-art mastering equipment in the early years was not practical for a small independent label like Lemco.

Lemco was the label of Bluegrass artist J.D. Crowe, stand-in for Earl Scruggs for a time in the Flatt and Scruggs Band. J.D. Crow's first recordings were done in the Lemco studio, *The Model Church* album being one. We played on the same bill with J.D. Crowe and his bluegrass group on one occasion. *The New South* was fine ensemble of artists, including over time Ricky Skaggs, Doyle Alexander, Tony Rice, Jerry Douglas, and the late Keith Whitley. Their individual and collective achievements are remarkable.

The place appeared to be an ordinary garage from the street. A collection of interesting cars in the driveway and on the street from time to time may have given up its secret. Something not so ordinary was being produced behind closed doors. I believe the neighbors knew all along what we did there. Cecil expected nothing less than sensible and courteous behavior at all times.

We were guests in the neighborhood where he lived.

A neighborhood is like a family. Its trees are the big brother to the child, its paths the connections to each of its members. We all look to the same sky; we see the same sun, moon, and stars. We wait for the new clouds to come and the ones with us now to simply drift away on their way to another show, another neighborhood in another town.

Today, I live near this place where John Page and I spent time helping someone with a recording studio create and build memories with their friends. Little has changed since 1962. The trees have grown taller and older. Some are gone.

Such are things trees and people have in common: human nature and nature itself.

The kind of records we wanted to make were not to be set and broken. They were mixed blessings intended to be made and played. We approached making a record seriously, knowing the self-portrait nature of it all. Though recording lacks the spontaneity of a live performance, it does give recording artists an opportunity to present themselves in an unblemished form.

Before the summer of 1963 ended, we recorded the tracks of our first record, both instrumentals. I co-wrote the A-side, "Autumn Love," with Doug and Shelby. The B-side, "The Big B," was composed by John Edmondson. John was band director at Clark County High in Winchester and played trumpet in Cecil's combo. He charted all songs, for Lemco Publishing's songwriter agreements and publishing copyrights.

"The Big B," borrowed its name from a popular dance around town at the time. The "B" enjoyed enough favor around here for a name of its own, despite the enormous national popularity of "The Twist," Peppermint or otherwise.

I did the arrangement and organ figures for "Autumn Love." Doug contributed a nice and easy melody line on sax that suited the song well. The audio quality we achieved on both songs was remarkable considering the studio environment where the session was recorded. The tracks were captured surprisingly well on this, our first studio session.

"The Big B" is a horn piece. We used three in the original session: mellophonium, tenor saxophone, and fluegelhorn. This particular combination of three horns was unique, innovative, for a small ensemble in 1963. On a Sunday one September, someone other than Stan Kenton had a mellophonium section in their band. We did.

A difference. Making one was nothing new for the Temptashuns.

I believe John may have composed "The Big B" with Johnny Burrows in mind. We used Johnny on fluegelhorn to complete a brass flavor preferred for the song. The influence of Ray Charles rules the tone of the organ solo in "The Big B." I set the drawbars as near the way he may have done that I knew. All I heard from his Paramount recordings was enough to make it happen. The sound is high-octane Hammond organ.

—∾—

"Autumn Love" is a simple song rich in colors, a mirror to the season it honors. Had the studio had its own, "Autumn Love" would have begun with a piano. The organ accompanies Doug's slow-paced stroll in a late October wood. Walking with a lead melody, played well on a Selmer tenor sax, was a fine experience to savor. Doug selected his notes carefully. Reverb, born deep in the heart of a Hammond organ, is not an easily forgotten part of the piece. There's a warm dialogue between sustained notes and the space between. John Page, Larry Kelley, and Shelby came along beautifully on bass, drums, and guitar, the deeper into woods we played. A romantic interpretation if you will.

Today, I like to think of it that way.

"Autumn Love" and "The Big B" were recorded in a studio, which at that time had no control room isolated from the studio space. Songs were recorded in a live session, meaning we were there, musicians, vocalists, and engineer recording at the same time on the same take in the same space. If a note or chord wasn't the right one, the entire piece was done again from the beginning.

We put down the first tracks of our first record using an Ampex reel-to-reel tape machine placed on a folding metal chair and a pair of fine-quality microphones in the right places. I don't recall how many tracks Cecil's equipment had that September afternoon. Two tracks are most likely. The sound was fresh, a song, about love in a season on its way, recorded in another about to end.

The stress of recording was hidden in the newness of it all. This was it for us for all we knew. We may have figured we might not get the chance again. A recording session was never commonplace for us. Hearing the band in a way we never knew we sounded in the playback after a take was like opening an unexpected gift. How good would the quality of the final mix be? How would we sound on the radio or a record player? We believed in each other enough to know the band would do its music well in any room.

This was a tight bunch of friends playing with a lot of confidence.

Soon after mastering was done in Nashville, Columbia Records in Terre Haute made 1,000 copies, two boxes packed 500 to the box. The first shipment came in, and Larry Kelley and I took 500 to Barney Miller's. "Hi, we are Tony Stallard and Larry Kelley from Lexington. We are members of the Temptashuns Band. This is our latest record."

We were no stranger to the personalities of radio in Lexington, among them Nick Clooney, Denny Mitchell, Billy Love, Bill Carroll, and Tommy "Little B" Wallace at WLAP Tiger Radio and Artie Kay and Robert McDonald at WVLK.

Playing our record and commenting about us on their programs meant a lot to the band. The friendly confines of my hometown were but a momentary comfort. The time had come for Larry and me to hit the road for a little promotion work. Our first stop one afternoon was in Morehead at the college radio station located on its campus.

"Hi. We are The Temptashuns and this is our latest record."

Standing tall, Kentucky's next homegrown teller of stories in song replied, "Nice to meet you. My name's Tom T. Hall." Larry and I were asking the next down-home lyricist of common and ordinary to play a simple song. Tom T. Hall would someday write about some problems in a small town, the PTA, and hypocrisy. He painted stories of watermelon wine, old dogs, and little children, other things he loved, the days when ordinary folks like Clayton Delaney died. The genuine truth of that day and his stories is an undeniable tether I hold onto.

We had met before then.

Tom T. Hall had filled my MG with gas in the late afternoon at a small gas station in Olive Hill, Kentucky, on previous occasions. I knew Olive Hill would be asleep when I came back through in a few hours. The same was true for other towns and their gas stations whenever we played in Ashland. Tom T. Hall was the first radio personality outside Lexington to play our first record on the radio. He became a writer of simple truths.

Larry and I visited other towns nearby—Harrodsburg, Danville, and Winchester—to meet their radio personalities. The story was the same—We don't usually get visits from recording artists. Thanks for taking the time to visit us here at WSTR, small-town radio.

Tom T. Hall took his songs and a Cadillac to Nashville on January 1, 1964, not long after our visit that fall to Nashville. He met a lady named Dixie, got married, and became famous. Tom T. Hall, the Poet Laureate of Mercury Records, gave us laid-back, serious, and sensitive lyrics and line produced by Jerry Kennedy.

—∾—

Shelby Singleton was recording director and head of recording at Mercury in Nashville. Mercury, the first label to locate in Nashville, had no offices there. Their artists used the Quonset hut at Columbia Recording Studio. Cecil Jones knew about Singleton through Buddy Killen at Tree Publishing Company and a friend, James William (Bill) Denny, at Columbia. Bill was the son of Jim Denny who, with Webb Pierce, had founded Cedarwood Publishing in 1953. He later became president of Cedarwood Music. Cedarwood's offices were located on Sixteenth Avenue across the street from Owen Bradley's Quonset hut.

Cecil sent "Autumn Love" to Buddy Killen and Bill Denny, Mercury, and other major labels. A&R folks might take a chance and sign the

Temptashuns to a seasoned label. Fred Foster's Monument Records was an independent label. Monument already had Roy Orbison, Bob Moore, and Boots Randolph. We had little chance.

The response we received from people hearing us play our first record live made waiting bearable. "The Big B" played well, and couples danced. Johnny Burrows had been along with us on all engagements by then.

Johnny joined the Temptashuns on September 21, 1963, the equinox.

"Autumn Love" did well, immediately. Before the leaves in my hometown began to turn a brilliant color, eyes beyond Lexington, beyond Kentucky, turned to a fresh new sound in the Bluegrass.

—ᴥ—

HAVE YOU HEARD 'The Temptashuns' recording of 'Autumn Love?' If not, do so. I think you will like it muchly. It carries the 'Lemco Label.' The Temptashuns are a swinging group of Lexington musicians.[25]

—ᴥ—

I UNDERSTAND that the fine recording by the hometown boys known as The Temptations and labeled 'Autumn Love' is going great. It should—I personally think it is BIG TIME—and I hope the kids make it. There is an unreleased story back of this record. I feel it would make a wonderful publicity copy—but that is only my opinion—(I used to be in show business and I can sense good publicity a mile off!)—Why waste it?[26]

I came across this from saved artifacts of the band. What she is referring to remains a mystery. I believe she may have learned of lyrics being written for "Autumn Love."

—ᴥ—

The doors to the Student Center will open at 12:30 p.m. and the fun will start at 1 p.m. sharp. The Temptashuns will make the 'B' music until 2:30 p.m. we will be introduced to the beautiful shapely pledges until 3 p.m. in order to be rested for the game. After all that dancing there will be a concert by The Traveler's Three until 5 p.m.[27]

—m—

The Traveler's Three were a nationally known folk group at the time. Kentucky was one stop on their tour of college campuses and other venues.

I was getting my first taste of college. Now being a full-time student at the university enabled me an abundance of fresh experiences. Having seen many of the same faces at parties and places we played in the early sixties, helped make the walks of a shy freshman across campus to classes bearable. Being recognized by strangers was to me a sense of belonging.

Still, it all was sometimes frightening.

The times at UK were often mirrored in a coed's face on a polished sphere about to meet a varnished plane of wood between two alleys at Wildcat Lanes. They might be found in the smile on a coed's face waving from a car. An Austin-Healy sports car now and then. Bass Weejun loafers, or a parade in the afternoon down a street named *Rose*.

Cars slipped past Columbia Ave., the AD Pi house and a Lutheran chapel, past Tri Delt, and Chi O' houses, and Maxwell Place, Fine Arts building and the Guignol in it, across the street.

The parade soon said goodbye to Stoll Field and its games, before crossing Euclid.

The Avenue of Champions.

Coach Paul "Bear" Bryant and Saturday's heroes came to mind when I was just a kid.

The intersection of Rose and Euclid with 1963 and my once upon a time.

The times continued on their way by the Paddock Club bar down Rose to Kalmia, a parade's last stop that day. The only silence at a house on a corner was a two-wheel cannon's bore in its yard. Old South weekend and its parade were one of college life's diversions then.

You could have a sandwich with a date on the steps of all that was left of a dream on Elmendorf Farm or visit the graves of Whirlaway and Citation at Calumet Farm. Freedom, seemed more a gift than a right back then. The air on country roads around Lexington was rich and clear, the heirs to such wealth quite blessed.

—m—

Architecture was a new dimension in my life, one shaped by people named Louis I. Kahn, Eero Saarinen, Alvar Aalto, Frank Lloyd Wright, John Lautner, Richard Neutra, and Lawrence Halprin. I was introduced to the work of Morris Lapidus. His wonderful Art Deco, its lines of gentle curves and colors, lay peacefully warm in the bright Miami sun and on my mind.

Frank Lloyd Wright had died in 1959, my senior year in high school, the year of the Guggenheim.

I was particularly drawn to the work of Bruce Goff through one of the professors, Herb Greene, an architect who had come to Kentucky from Norman, Oklahoma, the same year I enrolled. I learned about Goff's creative use of utility-type structures. His use of Quonset huts and corrugated metal to go with a use of common materials in uncommon ways was a creative exercise in adaptive use. My studies were all about space, learning ways to define it.

And, learning how, ultimately, space and time and music would define, at age twenty-two, the rest of my life.

—𝔪—

October came; a record deal appeared imminent. Mercury's Shelby Singleton in Nashville had expressed an interest in "Autumn Love." The preparation of contracts and songwriter/publisher agreements seemed an undercurrent below the surface of calm I felt more comfortable with, the music itself.

We were in a predawn. The Age of Aquarius had not yet arrived. A new and different sun would rise, less than five weeks from the moment. Nothing after would be the same once our lives had been betrayed. Leafless trees one late autumn afternoon in Arlington mirrored how naked and vulnerable we, as a people, had become. Much that remained of America's innocence after that November day would seem to withdraw within itself.

Acts of civil rights and wrongs would shape and misshape the music to follow. Something was beginning to happen, a cloud-like presence in a prelude of things to come. How unclear, what it was, no one really knew.

I was attending a weekly Friday lecture with classmates on South Broadway. Kentucky's College of Architecture was located in the Reynolds Building, an old R.J. Reynolds tobacco warehouse. My car and band trailer were packed, parked, and waiting. I planned leaving Broadway after the lecture ended at 2.00 p.m. to begin a three-engagement weekend.

The guest, from Washington, D.C., was speaking when our dean, the late Charles P. Graves, came to the front of the room to say something had happened in Dallas, and the class needed to end immediately.

"Something is wrong here, something terribly wrong." A prelude to a time of discontent, a pretty lady in a pink suit, a parade ending, a sudden nightmare on Elm Street. So began a stain that spread from Dallas to tomorrow, leaving a nation wounded, wandering and wondering.

"From Dallas, Texas, the word, apparently official, President Kennedy died at one o'clock central standard time, two o'clock Eastern Standard Time, some thirty-eight minutes ago," Walter Cronkite told a stunned nation on CBS.

After November 22, 1963, we were left to learn to face tragedies of this dimension many times over. It is from here in my generation, milestones have since shaped and reshaped us as a people and individually.

Sadly, we would never be the same again.

A recording contract Cecil had signed between Mercury and Lemco was in Nashville that day. It would remain unsigned by the label. Popular music would not be played for four consecutive days. Radio lent its time to more appropriate and solemn classical-colored tones of music. Billboard's Top 40 rearranged itself the following two weeks.

Things were black and white until the color of an 8mm ribbon of Zapruder film. We were left with the cold stillness of a dark November's sky. Until then, the definitive turning points in the experience of a generation were the color of James Dean's custom black 1949 Mercury, red jacket, white tee, and blue jeans and Elvis.

We were scheduled to play an afternoon jam session 3 till 5 at Delta Zeta sorority. I left the Reynolds Building immediately for the DZ house, hoping events in Dallas were not as serious as they seemed. No one really knew. The story was still breaking. I learned of the president's death in the sorority. All plans for that afternoon were cancelled.

I left immediately for the Kappa Alpha fraternity, where we were scheduled to play that night. We sat in the basement stunned by the news, all of us. The KA party that evening was cancelled as were our two appearances for the next day, at Centre College in Danville and Hamilton House in Lexington. All classes at the university closed until a nation could lay a slain president to rest on an Arlington hillside.

For "Autumn Love," a destiny in late November became the first hard frost for an innocent song. Today came suddenly. The Temptashuns continued to be shaped in 1963. We let the seasons pass. By the time

October's leaves began to fall, a year away from yesterday, "Autumn Love" was high on the local charts and the band playing more engagements than ever in its history.

What was the likelihood we would ever have been signed by anyone larger than Lemco anyway? I'd like to believe, had Dallas not happened, Mercury would have signed us. The season was right for the song. Mercury Records had indicated their confidence in our potential beyond "Autumn Love." The horn-driven "Big B" was more than simply the other side of "Autumn Love." When Cecil told me about Mercury in Nashville, the unsigned contract, and the likely reason we didn't get a record deal, the thought of "what if" lingered for a time. He explained, "Many times, that's the way this business is." Cecil Jones encouraged us to look to the next chance, and the band played on.

The Temptashuns' next engagement after Dallas was November 26 at Morehead College. December was a good month for the band. My final project in my first semester design class in architecture was judged better than I expected.

We learned the signature design project for our class for spring semester beginning in January would be to design a memorial gravesite for John F. Kennedy in Arlington Cemetery. Dean Charles P. Graves was never one to waste time getting to the point. What more challenging design problem could he find to shape an ensemble of innocents in our first year? In a sense, he was the consummate mentor. He was all a dean should be. The creative energy of our freshman class in the Reynolds Building that spring was memorable. We grew up quickly.

The assassination of President Kennedy and Vietnam changed everything in a very profound way. "We went from clarity to confusion."[28]

Shelby, a member of the Army National Guard's 100th Division, had recently left the band to report for active duty at Ft. Chaffee in Arkansas. The Temptashuns traveled to the Country Club in Glasgow the day after Christmas 1963. A player from the area was found for the engagement; the evening was played unrehearsed. Carter Hackney was a zoology major at UK from Bowling Green, and a member of Phi Delta Theta fraternity.

Carter played a Gibson guitar, using my Fender amp and reverb gear thereafter. He introduced me to the fine work of Johnny Smith, a jazz guitarist. Smith's "I Cover the Waterfront" began a fresh look at jazz and the guitar in it for me.

The first song I remember the band doing with Carter that evening was "Honky Tonk (Part I)." Bill Doggett's 1950s classic begins with a nice long rhythm and blues-styled guitar lead. The sax slips in and takes the song home. It is the rhythmic shuffle beat and Doggett's Hammond organ that is the heart and soul of the tune. "Honky Tonk" is classic Bill Doggett, King Records, one of the best dance tunes ever recorded. Carter's versions of Freddie King's "Hide Away" and Lonnie Mack's "Memphis" were played well. Carter replaced Shelby on lead guitar.

As with jazz, when you play rhythm & blues, abundant opportunities arrive for one to play off other players and vocalists and what they are saying. Interpreting this language of note, chord, time, and phrase is a sweet, sweet spirit, gentle on a soul. We listened carefully to each other, now more than ever, one of the most wonderful collaborative experiences to be found in music.

More visits with Doug and Larry Orr to Barney Miller's made it necessary for me to chart new set lists, reflecting an ever-changing turn to the choices of music the Temptashuns were learning. The year ended with a New Year's event at the Phoenix Hotel for Lexington's Junior Chamber of Commerce. The first of others for the Jay-Cees in the years to come.

Looking back over the year that had just ended in the early hours of 1964, I sensed we were now seven individuals composed in a way I hoped wouldn't change for a while. The old *Chicago* upright piano in the room sat silent, a testament to giving something the time necessary to find itself. 1963 had been a very good year. Our collective experiences seemed to fit together well. The night was dark and still. Winter had arrived. Nice and easy fell like snowflakes.

The road to Uncommon had been taken.

9
Compelling Messages, 1964

1964. I was twenty-two. A year of fresh opportunities lay ahead for the Temptashuns. The bounty of their wake began in Louisville for Kappa Sigma fraternity, January 11. The second four days hence in Lexington for the same Kappa Sigs at their house on fraternity row. We played rhythm and blues on the Avenue of Champions. Larry Orr put on a show for his Sigma Nu brothers at their venerable house on Euclid. The rest of January was taken with fraternity and sorority appearances exclusively.

February began at the Tri-Delt sorority on Rose, playing all their favorites. If the first month and a half were any indication, the Temptashuns were going to be a busy band.

—ɷ—

Social Sidelights by Nancy Loughridge:

Well tomorrow is going to be a very social day, in fact this weekend should leave the party goer weak from dancing.

The afternoon will be filled with jam sessions, that ever-popular UK recreation. The Delts will be tripping off to the Palms with the Theta's for an afternoon of fun. The Temptashuns will be on hand to make it all possible.[29]

—ɷ—

Eleven weeks after President Kennedy's assassination, what America faced ahead would be changed by four faces from Liverpool. A silver plane arrived at Idlewild, recently renamed for the fallen president. The Beatles changed the face of popular music forever with lyrics and melody line. "I Want to Hold Your Hand" . . . from Abbey Road, to US, with Love.

Common sense and imagination seemed all one needed to fall in love. Freshness and the way they looked, beyond compare, way beyond anything we'd seen before. The Beatles were a farmer's market of new harvest. We all fell in love with it.

America was still in the shadow of November when the Beatles made their first appearance on *The Ed Sullivan Show*. The events of a sunny day in Dallas last autumn seemed like yesterday yet a lifetime of seasons since. The Beatles brought a fresh new enthusiasm to music. They were the rise of sunshine long before George would sing about its coming someday. England would redefine and wear the crown worn in the House of Rock & Roll. A little more than ten years had passed since the Hilltoppers' first appearance on *The Perry Como Show*.

The Hilltoppers and the Beatles share similarities. Both numbered four, were young, energetic and, relatively unknown. Each had a producer with seasoned experience. The Hilltoppers, Randy Wood. The Beatles, George Marin.

America was new country to the Beatles, New York City new country for Bobbie Ann Mason's Fab Four from Western Kentucky State College. Liverpool and Bowling Green were worlds apart. The Hilltoppers once had moments in popular music's sunshine.

The Beatles following one of their own.

The Temptashuns first performed our Beatles set at Kappa Delta sorority, an afternoon jam session on February 28. We had learned five tracks off their first album, a Capitol LP titled *Meet The Beatles*. "I Want to Hold Your Hand," "I Saw Her Standing There," "She Loves You," "All My Loving," and "That Boy" had found their place in the bluegrass.

Larry and I did McCartney and Lennon harmonies with the same confidence Wendell and I had done Don and Phil Everly. Doug and Carter chimed in when a song needed three or more-part harmonies, such as the richly textured "That Boy."

Songs from their movies, *A Hard Day's Night* and *Help!* opened a door for the Temptashuns to present ourselves as vocalists and instrumentalists. Those around campus had grown accustomed to our kind of rhythm and blues. The Beatles being so popular, their songs fresh changed our course, though momentarily. We learned and played many more, staying close to their early style for a while.

The subtle sophistication of their music gave us opportunities to show versatility beyond anything we had done before. Chord structure, melody line, and the changes in their songs were fresh. We presented their work in our own special way, enabled by horns and organ.

Carter did George Harrison's guitar solos with confidence. John Page and Larry Kelley were solid on bass and drums, a mirror of Paul and Ringo. I provided fills and added depth on the organ to compliment the otherwise guitar-influenced sound of their early recordings and George Martin's brilliant arrangements. We did their songs pretty well. Their early work was particularly happy. Caught in the gravity of Liverpool and Muscle Shoals, Memphis and Nashville, New Orleans and Detroit, and the two coasts, we could only get better.

And we did.

The music of the Beatles and other British groups was unique in the ways it mirrored yesterday, an America not so long before their time. They drew upon early rockabilly and blues influences—the Everly Brothers, Chuck Berry, Little Richard, Gene Vincent, Buddy Holly, and the artists of Sun. The Mississippi Delta, Clarksdale, and its crossroads weighed heavy on England's blues scene. Through the coming years, our own sense of blues and its importance would reawaken, for some the first time, for others again.

Producer George Martin took the Beatles beyond themselves. Innovative producers and engineers are the pen and recording studios the paper on which fine sound is written. One often overlooked aspect of the Beatles' uniqueness is in their sound and the equipment. George Martin's guidance was instrumental. Martin was the soul of their creativity, the center of their gravity.

Their equipment was the heart of their sound. Paul played a Hofner "Cavern" bass left-handed. I liked that. George and John played Gretsch and Rickenbacker guitars run through Vox amplification. Later, Epiphone's Casino became John's guitar of choice.

Up to that time, James Burton was the only guitarist I remember playing a Rickenbacker, in Ricky Nelson's band on *The Adventures of Ozzie and Harriet*. Rickenbacker's West Coast high-style design mirrored life, timeless in the sun in a live-and-let-live California kind of way.

I'd heard about Rickenbacker. At the time, no one around here I knew had one. Distinct sound and simplicity define how a unique and lasting moment in music can begin. A Fender doesn't sound like a Gibson or a Martin. A Wurlitzer Electric piano and Hammond organ are their own, sounding unique to the instrument they are. A Rickenbacker and twelve strings helped put the Byrds on an eight-mile high.

It was all about the choices you made.

We continued building a collection of songs during the British Invasion, beginning in the mid-sixties, till our set list numbered about twenty-five. The Temptashuns covered songs of the Rolling Stones, Animals, Kinks, Zombies, Dave Clark Five, and others. Rod Argent's terrific piano solo on "She's Not There," played on a Hammond organ, was nice using Jimmy Smith's drawbar setting.

I designed some portable staging. We had them built. Tops featured red carpet, edges finished with polished, fluted stainless-metal trim reminiscent of a 1950s diner. The skyline of the band's backline was a city of sound in silhouette. We used this setup for limited special appearances only. We had no road crew then.

The music was new; however, we never let go of the rhythm & blues that had gotten us where we were that spring. Unlike many other bands in the area, the Temptashuns stayed with the one we brought to the dance, and she never forgot us. Her name was Soul, about as pretty a tune as we could get around here.

We weren't a Motown band, though we did do what came to be called big chill music. What we presented was, however, more influenced by what was being done in a Memphis theater and Muscle Shoals, Alabama, than 2648 West Grand Boulevard in Detroit.

Willie Mitchell was recording R & B at Hi Records in Memphis. Mitchell's "20-75" was an instrumental we did featuring our horn section.

Elvis had gone from Tupelo to Music Row and back to Memphis to record before his sun's last set. Sessions recorded by Elvis at American Sound Studios in the seventies in Memphis were produced by Chips Moman.

Once upon a time, darkness came to Graceland before a summer and its echoes ended.

I took my family to Memphis in the eighties. We had come to Memphis that morning on a blue highway headed south out of Murray, Kentucky. We passed through Hazel, Jackie DeShannon's birthplace, near the Tennessee state line and Paris, Tennessee. There was stillness down the road at Camden. We were near the site where Patsy Cline and others had died in 1963. The last picture show, a sad one that one never hopes to see.

We reached the Mississippi River, Mud Island, child's play, and a picnic lunch. Leaving Beale Street for Graceland, we caught a glimpse of a lonely house from a boulevard. Passing the gates of Graceland, we left Elvis for another Memphis neighborhood.

The old theater on McLemore Street was abandoned that day. Its marquee-neon, sadly dimmed, its patrons long gone. I sensed the rhythm of life, and the blues without it—an empty shell of yesterday at a moment broken by the innocent question of a child.

"Daddy, what did they do here?"

Stax Records, founded by Jim Stewart and Estelle Axton, was located in the old Capitol Theatre, 926 East McLemore. Stewart and Axton converted a Memphis theater into a recording studio, the perfect room for Steve Cropper, Booker T. Jones, Donald "Duck" Dunn, Al Jackson, Chips Moman, and a brass section, the Mar-Keys. Stax was the landscape that enabled these players to compose and play behind a solid collection of rhythm and blues artists, including Sam and Dave. Rufus Thomas, a local radio personality, and his daughter Carla. Otis Redding, and Isaac Hayes.

Carla Thomas's "Gee Whiz," was the first national hit on Stax in fall 1960. Records were sold in the theater's original lobby. Satellite and Stax were the new candy of the Capitol since 1960.

The message told by large red letters on the theater marquee simply read "SOULSVILLE U.S.A." The Capitol was a mirror in a neighborhood setting. King on Cincinnati's Brewster Street, Decca, Columbia, and RCA Victor on avenues south in Nashville, and Lemco on Southview in Lexington shared a similar kind of down-home setting.

The rhythm, blues, and blended soul of Memphis and Muscle Shoals fit together well with the Temptashuns. We played a lot of southern-made soul music over the years. Larry Orr put his own into anything we did by Otis Redding and Wilson Pickett. You stand by it, and the music of soul will never turn you loose.

What we refer to today as the Muscle Shoals area didn't even exist until the 1920's when the city incorporated and Wilson's Dam obliterated the dangerous shoals after which the region was named.

The area in fact is made up of four towns whose metropolitan population comes close to 125,000; Florence, Sheffield, Tuscumbia and Muscle Shoals itself, the smallest of the four. They sit on either side of the Tennessee River in separate counties (Colbert and Lauderdale).[30]

A recording studio was located above the Quin Ivy's drugstore. FAME derived its name from Florence Alabama Music Enterprises. The place to record soul music in the sixties was there, the recording home of Solomon Burke, the King of Rock and Soul.

Rick Hall, considered the father of Muscle Shoals music, owned FAME Studio and Publishing Company. Hall produced Arthur Alexander's hit "You'd Better Move On" and helped a lot of young musicians to establish themselves as session players, including Duane Allman. Muscle Shoals was a sweet spot, soul-filled music, a blend of the region itself.

The Temptashuns couldn't get enough of what we found to be tasty as sweet, sweet corn.

Percy Sledge recorded "When a Man Loves a Woman," and the first hit record came out of Muscle Shoals. The place soon became a nationally recognized recording center. Jerry Wexler came down from New York to record Aretha Franklin, Wilson Pickett, and Otis Redding. Buddy Killen brought Joe Tex to Muscle Shoals in November 1964. Killen and Sam Phillips both shared the distinction of coming from Florence, Alabama, as had W. C. Handy; Helen Keller, from Tuscumbia.

Buddy Killen would turn his attention further down the road in time to seven players a little north of Muscle Shoals. Our set list was ever-changing, ever-reflecting the influences of soul's triangle on the Temptashuns.

Stax in Memphis, Muscle Shoals, and Atlantic represented the dawn of a new sun about to rise again on the South in a few years. Two brothers and some friends would ride to midnight from a big house to Atlanta's Piedmont Park and Fillmore East out of a Macon mist.

The Allmans bathed in Phil Walden's pond of music at Capricorn.

"In the Midnight Hour" was made for the Temptashuns. To many who followed the band, it was our anthem. We did it well, best the times Doug played a baritone sax. The bari put the bottom in our sound.

The 1964 Kentucky High School Basketball Tournament was being held in Memorial Coliseum on Kentucky's campus. Dreams had come true in the Coliseum since 1951. The last game of the night had ended; the joy and sorrow in the moment had passed. We, the Temptashuns, had reserved seats, courtside, at midcourt. We were there to entertain them.

Tonight, all would be winners.

Memorial Coliseum seated 11,500; the hall was filled for the two remaining quarter-final games on a Friday night. We set up in view of folks remaining, with no chance for a sound check. They stayed around to spend ninety minutes to dance in socks, inside the lines on a 50-foot wide by 90-foot long polished wood floor to our music. Memorial Coliseum—where legends danced a ballet, delicately choreographed by Adolph Fredrick Rupp, in Chuck Taylor Converse All Stars.

Near all the state of Kentucky was represented by those in attendance and we knew it. This was our opportunity to make an impression on a lot of people, even increase sales of our latest record "Sexy Ways"/"Strawberry Man." Any proms we might be asked to play would have to wait till next year. We had no open engagements.

Larry Orr introduced us to no fewer than 5,000 that night. We ended the anticipation, beginning the show with "Green Onions." Larry and I did a righteous rendering of "You've Lost that Lovin' Feeling." Doug played "Soul Serenade" as if King Curtis had never left the building. Carter led us through "Memphis." I relied on Memorial Coliseum's friendly echo to help me make it through "Runaway." The song's solo on organ and the band in the room's reverberation never sounded richer.

"She Loves You" and "I Want to Hold Your Hand" were done by popular request. We painted the Rolling Stones and Animals "Satisfaction" and "We Gotta to Get out of This Place," with our own colors. Johnny Burrows slowed things down with Erroll Garner's classic, "Misty." Our first set ended with Horace Silver's nice jazz instrumental "Song for My Father." We presented this fine song many times over the years. What a mellow piece of music to play.

We held the attention of everyone in attendance during intermission. We saved some of our best for half the second set, ending the evening with a thirty-minute nonstop collection of songs, borrowed from James Brown's *Live at the Apollo* 1963 album. Our 'Apollo' set mirrored the band at its best at the time. The James Brown set was always a popular request from those who ever heard us play it.

We closed out the evening, taking all attending home on the "Night Train."

The night ended; the train eventually disappeared down the line. Reluctantly, my mind said farewell to the evening, but not without a question. Would we entertain as many people or play Memorial Coliseum or any place like it ever again? We sounded big, and the band had a professional look. The Temptashuns showed a lot of poise. We were winners that evening, and you don't forget those nights.

Being destiny's choice is special. You've been asked by someone you know, even a stranger, if a dance with you can be their own. You are the one at a place on their prom card with a favorite song or moment on it that is mutual.

It can be beautiful, frozen in time in a place called forever.

The air about her was fresh. The girl was tanned and lovely, looking straight ahead, not at anyone on her walk by the sea. Bossa nova was a breeze popularized by Brazil's brilliant composer Antonio Carlos Jobim, in concert with Stan Getz, and Astrud Gilberto. "The Girl from Ipanema" was but an introduction. Then, Stan Getz and Charlie Byrd gave us a moment named "Desafinado." Bossa nova music was light, romantic. Such is love.

We decided to cover a version of "Sexy Ways" for our second recording session. This record was the band's first to feature our new singer Larry Orr. "Sexy Ways" had been written and recorded by Hank Ballard and the Midnighters in the fifties on King, a label long considered a giant voice in rhythm and blues, located in Cincinnati. Though Hank Ballard was best known for having written "The Twist," it was another's version in the early sixties that made Chubby Checker and the song and dance legendary.

I composed an instrumental and arrangement for the record's B-side and named it "Strawberry Man." Organ was the lead instrument. The song's arrangement was timely, appropriate since bossa nova was enjoying its moment. The sigh of a hummingbird on the air before it's gone.

Larry Kelly played the entire piece with brushes on the recording. His use of brushes and a Hammond organ made it light. Bossa nova's nice and easy style takes one's self to inner peace. Jobim, Gilberto, and Getz read each other like a butterfly does a breeze. This and the "Mais Que Nada" of Sergio Mendez was more than nothing. It was everything to me. I loved it.

We did the session on a Sunday afternoon in the newly improved Lemco recording studio. Although the record's release would feature "Sexy Ways" as the A-side, I hoped "Strawberry Man" would find a share of its own radio play.

I phoned Columbia Records in Nashville for advice regarding the best use of microphones to record a Leslie speaker in their sessions. Columbia's audio engineer indicated a preference to take the organ direct to the control room's console if a Leslie speaker's "rotary effect" wasn't planned for the session. The speaker's signature rotary effect was best recorded with a microphone on the Leslie. He preferred two to best capture the highs and lows.

Cecil had recently installed a new Ampex master console. He wired the instrument direct to the console's board as recommended. We were happy with the tone and sound. The organ's lead melody track of "Strawberry Man" was about as clean as you could get in 1964. We were pleased with the quality of the Lemco session on both its tracks. Cecil asked me to take the recorded tapes of the session to Nashville.

—∞—

The reason for my fifth visit to Nashville was unlike before. It had been a while since my last. I asked John Page to go with me. It happened to be a weekday, late February. The weather outside was bleak. We took a break, away from Pence Hall and architecture. The rain never stopped on the way down to Nashville. Aspirations of seven people were on a ribbon of hope, safe away from the storm.

All that remained to be done was a well-engineered mix, possibly added effects, and mastering. Cecil had used Nashville's Columbia Records' facility, formerly Owen Bradley's, in the past. Columbia had the latest state-of-the art audio equipment, experienced audio engineers, and a fine mastering capability.

John had not been to Music Row.

The Parthenon, located in Nashville's Centennial Park, was a study in classical architecture. We decided to stop by on arrival. The rain had become a downpour by early afternoon. We left the park for lunch on West End and our appointment with William Denny at Columbia Recording Studios. I felt the familiar pulse of the Quonset hut, the closer we came to the heartbeat of Music Row. John and I walked through a door I had only ever looked into, beginning in 1961. Bill Denny, of Cedarwood Publishing Company, was a friend of Cecil's and an important connection with Columbia at that time in Nashville. Cedarwood alone would've been enough. Cedarwood, one of the most influential and lucrative agencies representing many of the most well-known artists in country music, was now located across the street from Columbia.

Denny had arranged for us to meet with Columbia's recording engineer assigned for the work that Cecil needed done before sending the masters to Columbia. Cecil had placed an order to Columbia's production plant in Terre Haute for a first production run, 1000 records for distribution and sales.

Bill Denny met with us in his office. We talked a few minutes. While there, I placed a call from his office to BMI at the Life & Casualty Tower in downtown Nashville. I needed to obtain songwriter and publisher information necessary to assign label credits for "Sexy Ways." BMI confirmed Lois of King Records in Cincinnati had published the song and Hank Ballard had written it.

Bill Denny, John, and I went to a room on the second floor, where he introduced us to one of Columbia's audio engineers. All that had been done on this property to that day had begun in March 1954. Ten years later, someone was saying to John and me, "Nice to meet you."

He said his name, then, "Welcome to Columbia, Nashville.

What would you boys like your record to sound like?"

We sat with him at the largest mixing board we'd ever seen. He put our ribbon of hope on the spindle of their reel-to-reel deck. He tried reverberation and echo on both songs. We listened intently to variations. Collectively we felt only "Sexy Ways" was enhanced with a touch of echo. "Strawberry Man" was solid, the organ recorded well at Lemco. I thanked him for his advice on how best to record a Leslie speaker and Hammond organ. He recalled my earlier phone conversation before our session in Lexington.

The last time I remembered things had seemed this quiet was in the middle of the night in the middle of Shakertown in the middle of time between the last sound and the next. He broke the silence to say, "Unless you want to sound like somebody else, what you have here is quite good." He did his work on the board with confidence and ease.

We spent an hour or so with an audio engineer going about the final mix. He indicated he would complete mastering work the next day. He most likely used the same lathe as on the masters for an album I had at home titled *Tom & Jerry / Guitars Play the Sound of Ray Charles*, on Mercury Records. The album, produced by Shelby Singleton, had been recorded in Owen Bradley Studios in 1962. One of the two, Jerry Kennedy, later became head of Mercury in Nashville, signing Tom T. Hall to the label.

"Autumn Love" remained a bruise long to heal. Its destiny may have been written on a dark November day. On a rainy day in Nashville, being so near an echo of the ghost on an unsigned contract was more than a passing thought.

What "Love" might have become the autumn of 1963, I'll never know.

We returned with him to the first floor to collect our things, leave for dinner, and find our way home. It was now dark. Columbia's office staff had left for the day. Our raincoats were behind locked doors—two strangers to Columbia's reception area.

He called Bill Denny at home, telling us Denny was having dinner with his family. Denny suggested he show us to the studio, where we could wait. It would be an hour or so. A session was in progress. The "Session in Progress" sign was on.

He waited for a playback to end, then led us through the door. Leaving was the last thing on my mind, inside Owen Bradley's Quonset hut. I was beyond the threshold to a dream with a yesterday to remember.

A shade tree, an MG, a sandwich, salted Planter's, Nabs, bottles green, and a silence.

Just me, and all that.

Once upon a time was in it all. Then was now, the moment he led us through a door into Owen Bradley's Quonset hut. I'm in the country in the middle of a summer in a back porch swing in the south. Looking out where my world goes only as far as the darkness will let me see.

My thoughts in verse in the key of kindness. Unending.

John and I sat quiet and out of the way, witness to music made the way they did it in Nashville. A Mercury artist was recording a new album that evening. The session musicians behind the voice were stellar: Grady Martin—whom I had met before in Studio B—other A-Team players, and the Anita Kerr Singers.

I had seen their faces before, in photographs on albums of their own and in trade publications. My research around recording in Nashville 1955–1964, suggests Harold Bradley, Owen's brother, was most likely playing his "tic tac" styling on a six-string electric bass on the session. The collection of players and chorus featured with the artist on the session had played on some of music's best-known hit records. Bill Denny arrived somewhere in the middle of a typical Nashville three-hour session. We left quietly, returned to find our coats, thanking him for everything.

Music Row was now dark. We left for home; the rain had ended, the rainbow in the darkness that night was the one inside my mind. A sound engineer at Columbia had sprinkled a little stardust on "Sexy Ways" and "Strawberry Man," then christened our music by saying, "Hope your record does well." All that remained was mastering and for Columbia to do their magic in Terre Haute.

Tree International Publishing seemed little more than just another house in an old and changing neighborhood when we passed 905 Sixteenth Avenue up the street from the Quonset hut on our way around the block.

Tree International and someone named Buddy Killen were familiar voices in the music business. Other than that, I didn't think more about it, turning right on Grand on the way to Seventeenth, back to RCA Studio B again. Goodbye was long to escape my mind making it back to Broadway and out of town. Leaving that evening put the echoes of five visits away for a long, long time. This was my last chance to be in Nashville. My experiences till then were my velveteen rabbit it might seem.

I am convinced I never really ever wanted the boy I was to ever go away.

After Owen Bradley and his brother Harold sold the Quonset hut studios to Columbia Records in 1962, Columbia's new Studio B was built around the original Quonset hut, leaving a narrow avenue of space along its length, a court if you will. Locked inside all that's new is a living fossil of the past: one of Gene Vincent, Buddy Holly, Wanda Jackson, Brenda Lee, Patsy Cline, Loretta Lynn, Bill Monroe, the Everly Brothers, Marty Robbins, Patti Page, Johnny Cash, Tammy Wynette, Ray Charles, and Bob Dylan. The beginning of Music Row and me.

The facility has grown even more to all it is today. Sony Music bought the studios from Columbia and never missed a beat. The Quonset hut was converted to an art department for the labels of Sony Music—Sony, Columbia, Epic, and Monument Records. All lived for a time at 34 Music Square East, formerly 840 Sixteenth Ave. South, before being absorbed into the giant Universal South.

The property was subsequently purchased and restored by Mike Curb. The facility actively functions today in a teaching/research role for The Mike Curb School of Music Business at Belmont University. Curb had done the same to save RCA's Studio B years before.

Bob Dylan went to Nashville and put a new silhouette on the skyline on Sixteenth Avenue South in the Quonset hut, using a new homegrown generation of Nashville A-Team session musicians: Charles McCoy, Kenny Buttrey, Pete Drake, Charlie Daniels, Norman Blake, and Bob Wilson.

Buddy Killen's Tree Publishing, Acuff-Rose Publishing, Cedarwood Publishing, Pamper, and Fred Foster's Combine Publishing were houses for some of the most influential music being recorded, and it was all there. I could park my car and wander around in the wonder of it all. It was tangible then. Sessions produced during that time by these people represent a body of music reflecting a sensitive experiment carefully crafted. Somehow, I feel close to that time and place, beginning on a day in August 1961. I happened to be in the neighborhood around the time an abundance of things was taking their place at the table of time. The tastes of the bounty have been good.

—∞—

45-rpm records were sold in a paper envelope with a circle cutout to display the label. Occasionally, 45s would have two songs on each side and be sold in sleeves similar to the ones used on 33-1/3-long playing albums. We had considerable interest in our first record "Autumn Love" b/w "The Big B."

We decided the second time around to release our record in the album version sleeve with the band pictured on each side. Our photo shoot was on a Sunday afternoon at Bedford Studio on Harrodsburg Road at Rosemont Garden (now a Shell convenience station). While there, we decided to include a friend in the picture. Meade Brown, a graduate of Louisville's Atherton High, knew Larry Orr. Larry and three backup singers, once members of the Temptashuns, were graduates of Waggener High in Louisville.

Pictured in the photograph is a polished-looking bunch gathered around a rather Bohemian type seated on the floor. Fresh strawberries in a plate are held in one hand, a handful of juicy ones on their way to be tasted in the other. Blue jeans and bare feet, a sleeveless sweatshirt, stained with juice, an earlier sampling of fruit eaten before the photo was taken. The look defines the imagined sort of character a strawberry man might be.

I did the layout and artwork for Cecil, including my liner notes written about the band, the session players, the instrumentation, and the credits. He decided not to include the narrative.

New and higher-quality recording equipment Cecil ordered was coming soon. We were confident knowing our second record had an added polish to go with our look and sound. Sessions down the road would be even better. "Sexy Ways" was a good song for Larry. The studio recording captured the full sound of the Temptashuns. Our expectations were high. The song and record did well on local radio charts, popular with our audience. The record received its share of radio play in Cincinnati and Louisville after its release.

Parents were listening too. Some thought "Sexy" an inappropriate term for their teens. A few local radio personalities were being asked to stop playing the song on-air till the lyric and title was changed. Cecil Jones was more aware of the discontent than we. Despite rerecording a renamed track, we never played the "Pretty Ways" version anywhere.

No one complained.

Hank Ballard's other hits in the fifties included "Work with Me, Annie;" "Let's Go, Let's Go, Let's Go;" and "The Twist," recording for Cincinnati's own King Records. King was home studio for a stable of R & B artists known for the portraits they painted on the canvas of the day: Bill Doggett, Little Willie John, Earl Bostic, Freddie King, the Platters and Mr. "Please, Please, Please" himself—James Brown.

Hank Ballard and the Midnighters were advertised as appearing for one night at Brock's, a nightspot on Richmond Road near Mt. Tabor. I decided to go out for the show. I told Ballard during one of their breaks we had recently recorded one of his songs. "Sexy Ways," was selling well, sitting in the Top 10 on the local charts, and climbing. He could've just said, "That's nice, Tony," but instead he asked if I had a copy with me. "Yes, Hank, I do." We walked to my car, and I took the top off a box of ten or so remaining; rare vinyl—a white band doing fifties R & B.

Here's one to keep.

Hank Ballard put our new record on his old, well-traveled 45 rpm record player in his tour bus that night then smiled. He gave "Strawberry Man" a listen. We returned to the club, and Hank took the stage and completed his show.

He told me something I never forgot: "Good songs can get lost on the other side of an A. 'Strawberry Man,' you got a real nice tune there. Tell the band Hank Ballard said so." In a while, the bus, our record, Hank Ballard, and the Midnighters were away into the night. Northbound.

Cecil Jones received a call two days later, from Cincinnati. King Record's owner Sydney Nathan wanted to talk. Hank Ballard was there urging him to do a session with us in King's Studios. Nathan had listened to our record and thought with the equipment, engineers, and personnel he had at King, we could get a higher-quality sounding record.

He wanted to sign the Temptashuns to a record deal.

When James Brown wasn't appearing at the Club 68 in Lebanon, the ballroom at the Holiday Lanes on Georgetown Road, and Lyric Theater's stage on Third Street in town, he was live at the Apollo Theater in Harlem. King Records was James Brown's label.

JB was King.

King Records was once the nationally known den of R&B, blues, country and bluegrass. Its office was at 1540 Brewster Ave. in Evanston. King was owned/operated by Syd Nathan. Nathan started King (with Federal Records as a subsidiary) after someone came into his pawnshop with a stack of 78's to pay off a debt. Syd accepted the records, sold them in a few days and soon realized he could make money in 'music.'

King went on to rival the Stax, Chess, Sun and Specialty labels with its influence on the R&B, rock & roll and blues communities. Freddie King, John Lee Hooker, Charles Brown, Hank Ballard, Joe Tex, Jackie Wilson, James Brown, Little Willie John, The Platters and Billy Ward & his Dominoes, Earl Bostic and Bill Doggett were just some of the artists on the King roster. Some of bluegrass' earliest pioneers including the Stanley Brothers recorded here. King's country artists included Hawkshaw Hawkins, Cowboy Copas (both died with Patsy Cline in March 1963), the Delmore Brothers and Grandpa Jones.

According to legendary producer Jerry Wexler (in Peter Guralnick's book *Sweet Soul Music*,) Nathan 'got the job done.' 'When Wynonie (Harris) did "Good Rockin' Tonight," it was recorded on a Tuesday and out on a Friday. Usually records take months. But they made the records and did the art here. King had everything right there.'

Nathan had an all-under-one-roof-system: a record pressing plant, mastering lab, recording studio, art department, 26 sales promotion people and 48 national distributorships.[31]

Cecil set a date, a Thursday. We left Lexington early. King Records was unusually busy when we arrived on Brewster Street in Cincinnati's Evanston neighborhood. The place "I Got You" enjoyed on Billboard's record charts in the US was the reason. King's record plant had been working around the clock for the past two weeks to meet the song's sales demand. The Temptashuns were already doing his current hit along with others he had recorded.

Larry Orr's voice was well suited for a James Brown tune.

When James Brown returned to King in the spring of 1965, it was on his own terms, with almost every concession he had been seeking: his own publishing, a vastly improved royalty rate, a minimum of 25,000 singles and a comparable number of LP's in 'Free goods' to be distributed as he saw fit; and continued—and expanded—artistic control. In May of 1965 he delivered the completed tape of his new single for mastering to King. It had been a year and a half since he last entered the King Studio in Cincinnati. The record was entitled 'Papa's Got a Brand New Bag.' 'Papa's Got a Brand New Bag' was the first Top 10 hit of James Brown's career.[32]

By 1964, James Brown was supervising his recordings for King. . . One result was a move away from conventional song structures and dance. The breakthrough recording was 'Papa's Got A Brand New Bag' (1965), a number that is more than four minutes long that devotes less than half its length to a sung delivery of its lyrics, which celebrate dancing. Papa begins with the briefest of intros: a sustained full-volume blast from the band—three trumpets and a trombone, four saxes, and a rhythm section of organ, guitar, bass and drums—that plays with a fierce precision from start to finish.[33]

Syd Nathan wore black-rimmed glasses. Their lenses were heavy. He was dressed in a suit, tie, and shined shoes and held a cigar held in one hand. I guessed the cigar to be an expensive ensemble of leaf. He was the "King" of King, a wealthy man. I can't say the first blush was a warm one.

My car, the band trailer, and I were parked on the street. I rolled the window down to ask where he wanted us to load in. His gruff voice made it clear: "Everything you will need is already in there. Most drummers do prefer using their own kits." He led us to the studio, emphasizing the place was valued at about $1 million. The first thing I saw was a Hammond C3 organ alongside a Leslie. The C3 was the church model of the mighty B3. That instrument was no doubt the one Bill Doggett once played, having recorded "Honky Tonk" and other hits in this place in the fifties.

King had a big room. Neumann and Shure microphones in abundance, a vibraphone and celeste and tympani, music stands—the works. The studio's control room and its recording console was impressive, more importantly the man behind its sloping window's glass. Gene Redd, King's chief engineer, would be producing our session.

This place was built to make hits in the fifties, and James Brown was keeping the doors open. Maybe the Temptashuns would benefit from the experience in the home of a nationally known record label. The songs

King produced over the years are considered important contributions in American music history.

Before Sam Phillips ever produced a record, an asthmatic, cigar-chewing bespectacled Cincinnatian named Syd Nathan was doing what Phillips later got credit for: mixing black and white songs and styles among black and white artists.[34]

Hank Ballard was present at the session. He played tambourine on one of four sides the band recorded that day. We decided to use two drummers on "Strawberry Man." Larry Kelley played his own. Meade Brown, a friend of the band, also a drummer, had come along to Cincinnati. He used King's in-house drum kit that Mr. Nathan had mentioned to me earlier.

We recorded two songs I had recently written at King that day, one an up-tempo R & B Ray Charles-inspired song I named "You're Gonna Cry." The other, "Love Gone, Love Return." I arranged both to feature our horn section more effectively. Horn figures, accent, and phrasing were more uptown than we had done in earlier sessions. John Edmondson charted them all. We recognized the energy big horn sections brought to bands behind Joe Tex and James Brown. Later Billy Stewart's big sound.

Little Milton's band had a touch of swing others were without. Big and Mellow.

We were on our way to where we wanted to be. It would take time. Bigger-sounding performance was the band's heading. Another track or two we never had before would be available on newer studio recording equipment than we were using at Lemco. Our horns and backup voices would find their place on the train.

I was writing more musically complex material at the time. "Heartbreak Overdue" was one. Two others, "That Certain Something" and "Once in a Lifetime," were never recorded or published, finding their way to the yard of oblivion, dying for want of rehearsal.

Their time wasn't right. Most gigs we played were not yet ready for more complex music, its chord structure, horn figures, and its changes.

This was probably true at the time, but when Columbia released Blood, Sweat and Tears' debut album, *Child is Father to the Man*, in 1968, it affirmed for me my idea I'd had in 1964. The *Transit Authority* roared out of *Chicago*. Later, the five-piece horn section, Hammond B3, guitar, bass, and drums that defined Ten Wheel Drive with singer Genya Ravan was sounding great at the Atlanta Festival. Right about then, horns became the voice of rock's big sound. I believe we could've been a homegrown ensemble of similar description by 1968.

All this jazz-influenced rock and rhythm was stark in contrast to a white rabbit or a trip on the Jefferson Airplane. Doors were more than objects to walk through in a purple haze in search of a watchtower or an all-white album. Parents were told to teach their children well. . . . Was there enough time?

"You're Gonna' Cry" opened with a tympani drum and an instrumental spiritual-inspired "Amen," that became an up-tempo something else in the middle. The song ended with a repeat of the way the song began. "Amen." The track was a beginning, middle, and an end. A story.

"Love Gone, Love Return" relied on our horn section and Larry Orr's vocal interpretation of its lyrics. Carter added a nice augmented chord, where it was written to be, on a Gibson. I got to play a Hammond C3 on each track. I appreciated the effort of the band on these two songs. I was beginning to feel the only way to play the kind of music going through my head was to learn more about music itself. I enrolled in a music theory class in the Fine Arts Building, using the only elective I had available in an 18-hour schedule that fall semester.

My two new songs and "Strawberry Man," originally published through Lemco Publishing, were transferred before leaving Cincinnati that day. I signed a songwriter's agreement with King Record's Lois Publishing.

King may have been the only recording company at that time that had all the pieces necessary in the recording business under roof. We recorded our songs, staying around to see them engineered and mixed. Mastering was done there by King another time. Gene Redd, King's A&R and chief engineer, cut a disk with a stylus on acetate for me of "You're Gonna Cry" and "Love Gone, Love Return" as a courtesy. It remains the only record of this session for these two songs.

We were shown to King's photographic studio. Promotional photographs were taken of the day's session. We visited their art department. The original artwork for King's 1963 James Brown's *Live at the Apollo* album was on the wall in its frame. The piece, on exhibit, was a nice watercolor by King's graphic artist Don Quest. Dried colored water and the spell of it is a near LeRoy Neiman expression before its time.

We were given a brief tour of King's record production plant. Workers pressed raw acetate like music waffles. Hits, with edges trimmed, were labeled, boxed, and sealed then taken to the shipping department to be loaded in a truck at the loading dock. A truck, train, or plane would put "I Got You (I Feel Good)" in record stores and homes all over the world. All could be done from right there on Brewster Street, as simple as that.

All or nothing at all.

The Temptashuns returned to our beloved Danceland that evening to be a part of Henry Clay's senior party for the Class of 1964. We played for four hours on the banks of Town Branch. This time Doug and I weren't on the outside listening in. The Temps were playing rhythm and blues inside Danceland. That night, or any night, Charlie Bishop, Little Orbit, Johnny Ballard and the Houserockers, and Bill Pace and the Pacesetters could've been playing along with us or at home dancing.

We were that good.

We had recorded four sides in the home of a history-rich, nationally recognized record label. I learned the importance of being in tune with the times in the music business and finding the truth in the artist you are working with.

Unlike Ahmet Ertegun, Herb Abramson, and Jerry Wexler at Atlantic Records, Mr. Nathan thought the future of a band like the Temptashuns lay in the fifties. His fingers were not on the true pulse of change. With it all at his fingertips, Syd Nathan and King Records were not the same in the years following James Brown's leaving the label for Smash, a subsidiary label of Mercury.

Mr. Nathan died in 1968 in Miami. Hank Ballard, March 2, 2003 at his home in Los Angeles. King had been acquired by Starday, and things were never the same ever again in Evanston. I drove my wife there just before Christmas 2016. Brewster Street had become a blended echo of a theater on McLemore. King and the Capitol were two flowers a long time passing.

Papa acquired a brand new bag. The seventies could have been kinder to King Records. King had flourished as a label for nearly twenty-five years, beginning with Merle Travis and country in the late forties. The label of rhythm and blues that influenced a whole generation in the fifties had a real opportunity to merge with the new winds of the sixties. Things were different now. Memphis, Motown, most everything in Muscle Shoals, Alabama, and Atlantic put a spell on the Temptashuns. Theirs was music with arrangements and a quality more suited to our own.

"Pretty Ways" and "Strawberry Man" were released on Federal, a subsidiary label of King. Some of James Brown's million sellers bear the Federal label. We were on a promotional tour in July that summer. I saw our record on King's Federal Records for sale on a record tree in a drugstore in Canton, Ohio. You see your name on something and with it the notion of being for sale. The bigger things got, the more it seemed I was coming to sense the less of myself that I owned.

Knowing that feeling again, though fair to me, didn't seem to be so for the band.

Midsummer came calling. Other voices in other rooms had heard. Thus began our first promotional tour. First stop, new faces: Owosso, a small town northwest of Detroit, due west of Flint, Michigan. Arthur Miller's *Death of a Salesman* was packed away with notes along with *The Crucible.* I was taking a literature class that summer. Both were the body of my final exam early Monday morning. It was Thursday afternoon. The band trailer was loaded, the Corvair ready for the road. A long Fourth of July weekend began. I believe Doug and Johnny Burrows rode with me. John Page brought the others to Owosso.

I don't recall how long the drive was. We were still south of Detroit, midnight somewhere up ahead. We passed a place to stay in Bowling Green, Ohio. A family relative had long owned and operated a motel there. Signs soon began to read Toledo, Ann Arbor, Detroit, and East Lansing. Somewhere in Friday's early hours, a dimly lit signpost came into view.

Welcome to Owosso, Michigan.

A band from the Southeastern Conference had arrived to give the Big Ten a taste of rhythm and blues, the way it's played south of Motown and north of Muscle Shoals. Who was going to come to listen to us tonight? To North Water Street at West Exchange Street, on the banks of the Shiawassee River in downtown Owasso.

Who would come to a vintage 1915 armory there?

We checked into the Central Motel, 2247 East Main, "Telephone, TV, Tubs and Showers, Air-Conditioned and Standard Rates." All the amenities necessary for tired travelers were kind. The owners also managed the place. "Welcome to Owosso," the desk clerk's first words.

The hour was late.

One of the passengers, a lady, had just collected her ticket for a flight on TOPAC Airlines while telling the desk clerk she was from Owosso, Michigan. John Wayne was her pilot; no one knew what secrets the sky held for them in *The High and Mighty*. What secrets did Owosso hold for the Temptashuns? Enough time remained to get the rest we needed before becoming familiar with an armory.

Sleep came quickly.

I began to sense this might be a bigger event than we thought while loading-in and during our late-afternoon sound check the next day. We had been engaged to appear on this stage to play twenty minutes an hour, for four hours. The night's host was nearby Flint's most-listened-to radio personality. More than 800 teens and college-aged students came to see a band named the Temptashuns. They had been hearing two songs being played a bunch in that part of Michigan: "Sexy Ways" and "Strawberry Man."

Larry Orr was at Air Force ROTC summer camp, I brought back some of our old material from the days before Larry joined our band. "What'd I Say" and "Tossing and Turning" and our new record "Sexy Ways" were presented the best I could. We played more than our usual set of instrumentals, "Strawberry Man," repeated by request.

We had asked Meade Brown to join the Temptashuns a few days earlier. Larry Kelley had left the band to pursue other interests at the university. Larry Orr's absence on the trip and Meade being the newbie was the "jam band" opportunity we'd been given to show to a new audience.

"Hello, Michigan. We are the Temptashuns."

Meade may have been new, but we knew something was special. Destiny had made its choice again. Meade gave us a lot of drive. I remember handing out a bunch of the band's business cards to folks that night. Before fall semester had begun, Cecil Jones and I had received letters from different fraternities and sororities from nearly every school in the Big Ten. They wanted the Temptashuns to appear on campus or for one of their fraternity or sororities.

Indiana, Ohio State, and Northwestern were close enough. We could travel there. But we were college students with time demands. Regretfully the band had to let the chance go by. I wish they could've heard the Temptashuns with Larry Orr. We were already booked solid in Kentucky and southern Indiana for the upcoming semesters.

We could've spent the rest of the year in the Big Ten.

The master of ceremonies announced, after our last song, that Jimmy Gilmer would be appearing live in Owosso on the same stage the following week. Jimmy Gilmer's "Sugar Shack" was a *Billboard* hit and voted Song of the Year in 1963, one summer before that night.

Our record continued to do unexpectedly well in this part of Michigan. We made enough money to satisfy the band's part of the production costs with a little left for each of us. What remained we left in our account to make our third record.

I met a local girl from Owasso at the dance. We talked a while before I left the venue. She thought we were special, different from most bands that had appeared at the Armory. I gave her a copy of our record and the band's business card. We exchanged addresses and said goodbye.

I thought I would never hear from her again.

She sent a postcard to me while on vacation with her family later that summer. It came from their second home, by a lake somewhere else in Michigan. I remember Helen, a recent graduate of Owosso High, was much like my own daughter would be many years from then. I wonder what became of her. I hope her life's been good.

The band had taken three rooms at the motel. I was alone in one. The others were in their own winding down. I was the one with the final early on Monday morning at UK when we got back to Lexington. It was late. I studied till falling asleep at the part where Willie Loman was trying to come to terms with life and himself. Arthur Miller's remarkable gift, touching the bare essence of an American's experience, lay open in my arms.

We woke the next day, a Saturday morning, and had breakfast. The band checked out, leaving for a long day's drive to play a couple of hard day's nights in Canton, Ohio. The town Hank Williams never made it to during the early hours of a New Year's Day in 1953 drew us south again.

Arriving in Canton, we found a motel, checked in, and left for the Parkway Manor. After loading in and a sound check, the band left for an early dinner. Steaks prepared just right, a meal appreciated, and a healthy tip for the waiter were enough for six players leaving the restaurant for an evening of song.

We missed Larry Orr's absence again on the first night in Canton. A second chance to jam with Meade. We played some older songs, from a long-ago set list, for no more than ten friends out on the town.

"You know this one." "Let's play." "That's a keeper."

I recall a guitarist in another room of the Lounge, a local player originally from England. He played a wide-body Gibson fine and sang "The Days of Wine and Roses." His accent was undeniable.

The Parkway Manor was a nice motel with a dining room, a lounge, and a dance hall. The hall, a large room, had been closed near a year for renovation. The Temptashuns were the first band booked for its impressive new and improved stage. Promotion for the reopening was nonexistent. Few in Canton knew about our show. Someone noticed, impressed enough to get the word out. Hurriedly but effective.

The second night we sold some more records, and patron attendance was enough to make the evening worthwhile. The owner announced popular singer Johnny Tillotson would be appearing at the Parkway Manor the following weekend. "Poetry in Motion" in 1960, was one of Tillotson's nine top hits early in the decade. We ended the night tired, not knowing then how much the experience would mean. People didn't forget the sound or the name of a band. The Temptashuns were working on a hit of our own.

We left Canton immediately after the last dance, returning to Lexington during the night. I let another drive a few miles. The three or so hours of back seat sleep helped me make a ten o'clock appointment with *Death of a Salesman* and my final.

Literature class went well for me that summer.

Larry Orr was back. We next played at Freedom Hall on the tenth for a collection of fraternities and sororities from the Lexington, Louisville, and southern Indiana area. The band was set up to play on the concourse level. Freedom Hall is a big room to fill with a band's sound.

Attendance was more than expected, making the night memorable. Guests were pleased, leaving satisfied with the evening. We sounded fine and gave them a ton of show, about to get our first taste of playing in a big-time nightclub.

Monmouth Street in Newport, Kentucky, leads to the water's edge. Bright lights of the Cincinnati skyline shimmer reflected in the motion of the ever-changing current that is the Ohio River. The Ohio was a broad mirror of lights: night-lights like diamonds in the crown of the Queen City. Newport, in its heyday, was known to be a place where gambling was open, among other things associated with it.

Once upon a time, an Art Deco-style nightclub lived there. The walk along its length at the street was custom-designed, deco-patterned concrete. To me, it was a fossil of an earlier time. I witnessed remnants of a visit from Detroit's Purple Gang, frozen in time. Theirs was a message of stated purpose, just to let folks know the mob was keeping watch. Left in its wake on the face of the custom-designed walk in front of the club, a random moonscape, the voices of a purple rain of machine gun bullets. Empty ghosts. In contrast stood the modern, bright, and colorful splash of Glenn Schmidt's Club, among others less so scattered here and there.

Monmouth and York were streets of desire and fun in their day. A Cincinnati native and sports hero running for sheriff was framed, a woman part of the setup. He was going to clean up the town, once known as "Sin City of the South." When the Temptashuns got there, Newport was somewhere between the good and bad, the ugly and the beautiful. Newport was a still life of nightlife and lights in the sixties. Neon and others, the gas preferred for the highways on a road map of its night. Strip steaks and strip joints and a game could be found somewhere, somewhere over the rainbow of glitter. Newport, Kentucky, in 1964 was a place with a storied and colorful past where its clubs remained open well past the midnight hour.

The Flamingo Club was located at 633 York Street. The Temptashuns were appearing live, from 10 p.m. till 5 a.m. for two consecutive weeks. We loaded in, set up, did our sound check. The club's owner showed us to the basement. We stored our equipment cases, organ dollies, blankets, and spare gear there, among the dusty inheritance of the Flamingo. Silent, still. Asleep.

Roulette wheels, gambling tables, and a horse racing game, once located on the bar, among other relics, were a closed exhibit in a museum of what the mighty Flamingo had once been. You could wager a few on the horses that ran in slots down much of the bar's length, an avenue for friendly games of chance.

The owner told us the Flamingo Club could be the "casino" it once was in twenty-four hours. I sensed some truth in what he said. It was the look in his eyes in a damp and dimly lit quiet peace, below what would soon be a noisy room above.

The Flamingo Club welcomed its patrons through custom-designed, well-crafted front doors leading to a long entrance hall. Here was an avenue lined with promotional posters and framed photographs of previous entertainers to have appeared on its stage. History was a random collage of objects on gloss-finished walls of painted color.

A gallery of yesterday.

Soon, the Temptashuns would earn a place in the "Now Appearing" playbill, beyond the face of glass on the club's front wall outside. Joey Dee and the Starliters were headed here in the coming weeks before their return to Manhattan's Peppermint Lounge in New York City.

The Flamingo shared a colorful past with its neighbors on the streets of Newport. The history of entertainers to perform on its stage was impressive, including the Champs, Ventures, Lonnie Mack, and other big-name artists. Patrons came to be entertained, ushered through its doors to walk a red carpet avenue to other doors at its end. They opened to the world of the room, a diamond in its night.

Welcome to the Flamingo.

The club's owner told us to expect between 800 and 1,000 or more before the night was over. I recall extended breaks, often taking forty-five minutes, at midnight each evening. The club's patrons might leave to make room for others across the river, not wanting their evening to end. Cincinnati's nightspots closed at 1.00 a.m., and many would come over to Newport and its fun.

Not long into our first set our first night in Newport, we sensed our set list and its British-influenced song and sound wasn't true to the music tastes of Cincinnati and Northern Kentucky. More than any other area we played, the folks in and around Cincinnati loved rhythm and blues. R&B was in the soul of Cincinnati, her history of blues-based music a long one. They wanted to hear what we were known to play: rhythm and blues, the heart and soul found on the Top 40's best hits. The Temptashuns were now promoted as King recording artists.

They could get all they cared to hear out of England on the radio.

Everything changed for us in Newport when we delivered the songs of James Brown, Marvin Gaye, Little Milton, Wilson Pickett, Otis Redding, Gene Chandler, and others our first night on the Flamingo's stage. A mutual love affair began with Newport, the Queen City, and the Temptashuns. They would remember beyond our years a band who gave eighty hours of our best rhythm & blues on this stage for a month and more.

That night began a two-week long stay, hard days and nights, a.m. to p.m., ten till five. I drove back to Lexington each morning, with just enough time to shower, eat breakfast, and go to class. Life was home, sleep, study, eat, and drive. I gave Johnny Burrows a ride to 633 York every one of those days. We were two of seven Temptashuns on our way to seven hours of being a better band. And, more.

The engagement at the Flamingo ended, leaving a long-to-be-remembered impression.

—∾—

The times were a montage of many moods near summer's end. Our expectations continued to soar. We needed space to renew our music and ourselves. Some members of the band lived in a house on the corner of High and Mill. There, our customary two weeks of tight rehearsal produced enough current hits to present for fall semester at UK. Our harvest was the Bramble Bush Sessions, a soul-filled set list of songs to show a campus and the Bluegrass.

—∾—

September 1964 began what would be a long relationship with the Club 68. Lebanon was a small community where spirits were legal and weekends made to order for thirsty counties nearby, courtesy of its owner, Mr. Hyleme George. He owned the Club 68 and others. It seemed he owned the town. People, many young, would come to Lebanon by the hundreds on a weekend to nightspots named, Golden Horseshoe, and the Club 68, down the road on US Highway 68. The Club Cherry was another, on Cherry Street.

Hyleme George was no stranger to the nightclub business. In the mid 50's he had built the Club Cherry on Water Street, which catered to African-American audiences. Some of the biggest names in the history of 20th century music appeared there.

Club Cherry played host to Ike and Tina Turner, Little Richard, Fats Domino, Bo Diddley, Chuck Berry, Count Basie, Otis Redding, Ray Charles, Hank Ballard and the Midnighters, the Shirelles, James Brown, the Platters, Al Green, Percy Sledge and Lloyd Price—to name only a few of the black artists who played in Lebanon.

By the mid-1960's, however, the Club Cherry was no more. The building had burned and was not rebuilt after the fire. George felt Lebanon was ready for a mainstream nightclub featuring big-name entertainers, with a first-class supper club, drawing patrons from outside the immediate area. . . . It was billed as the largest nightclub in the south (at more than 1,500 people, the 68 was big in 1964).

Opening night, December 20, 1964, was an extravaganza. The featured star was Lloyd Price, who had recorded the hit 'Stagger Lee' a few years before. It was an elegant affair, the band in tuxedos, the crowd dressed up as well.

Many artists who had played the Club Cherry came back to Lebanon to play at the Club 68 for a mainly white audience. Ike and Tina Turner showed their loyalty by playing at the Club 68 when they returned from a European tour. Nat King Cole played at the Club 68 for a booking fee of $500.

It was a classy night when the Tommy Dorsey Orchestra played at the Club 68. Then Hyleme George made a fateful decision that changed the Club 68 and marked a whole generation of central Kentuckians. He started booking rock-and-roll bands from Louisville. The Epics were the first Louisville rock group to play at the Club 68. . . . Soon other groups were booked: the Sultans, the Trendels, the Monarchs—all from Louisville and The Magnificent Seven from Lexington.

When the fans saw the fine facility at the Club 68, they spread the word and the crowds kept coming and the Club's fame kept spreading. As students from Lebanon enrolled in colleges around Kentucky, they found that their new classmates almost invariably knew Lebanon as the home of the Club 68. Not all the talent booked at Club 68 was local. Nationally known artists also played the Lebanon stage as well. Other nationally known groups that played Club 68 included Jerry Lee Lewis, Creedence Clearwater Revival ('Bad Moon Rising), Steppenwolf, the Coasters, the Platters, Black Oak Arkansas and the Kingsmen.[35]

We were aware of the impressive list of artists who had performed on its three-level stage. Seeing your name in lights on the same sign becomes timeless in its echoes. Returning to the past seems more often the only way to hear them. Not having taken photographs of the sign with the name of the band in lights is my regret. I hold dear those nights we shared billing with others appearing at the 68 on the same weekend. Some I remember vividly, in particular the nights the sign read "Ray Charles, Friday night; The Temptashuns, Saturday night." Or "The Ike and Tina Turner Revue" or "James Brown and the Famous Flames; The Temptashuns," another night. Most times, it might be near dark when we arrived. Time was precious, a mind on other things.

Still, I wish I had taken photographs.

Maybe Ray had left his glasses or James his coveted J&B cufflinks, the ones in diamonds. Would there be something Tina or an Ikette may have left in the dressing room on a rushed exit to the next town, a gown in its closet?

The dressing room "For Performers Only" at the Club 68 was just off the top tier of its three-tiered stage. Few places we played had an accommodation this nice for the band. Mr. George spared no expense at the 68.

Stars were making a stop somewhere on their way through the big time. We were having a big time on our way to somewhere. Mr. George knew people wanted a good band and a good place to dance. He was confident in our special blend of rhythm and blues. Hyleme George knew the Temptashuns could fill the Club 68 with as many guests as other famous entertainers could.

We loved this place, and we did just that.

—~—

From the pages of the student newspaper, a half-page ad. Publicity Photo, the Temptashuns, King Records. — *The Kentucky Kernel*, Friday, Sept. 4, 1964, page 4.

—~—

When the horses run at Keeneland, I'm reminded of an appearance we had made at Keeneland in September. Some of yesterday's faces have faded. Places we played have lost little clarity over the years in my life. October and November were filled with places to play, seldom less than two, sometimes three on a given weekend. No two engagements were the same. Place was defined by a distinct personality it called its own.

Place itself could define your own.

Seasons are all things passing on the way to equinox, then solstice. There is the notion autumn is for many things the end of its days. Second chances may be found in autumn's message. Winter, spring, and summer help us wait a while to know them.

Love returned in autumn to Kentucky. Nearly a year had passed since the wind of last November had come and gone away. Our first record "Autumn Love" found itself a home on radio and its charts. The WLAP Tiger 30 Survey, October 10, 1964, had "Autumn Love" at No. 31, an "Exclusive," a single week after being named a "Tiger Target." James

Brown's hit "Out of Sight" was No. 8 and the survey told of his appearance at the Holiday Lanes on Newtown Road on Monday.

"Autumn Love" had come around. She stayed on the local charts in 1964 for six weeks.

A fine piece of time in the sunshine for a nice song that would not go away.

The night was going to be good; things felt right. The Temptashuns arrived at Lexington Country Club to play one of our favorite rooms. We loaded in like a circus come to town, setting up, tuning true, and performing a sound check.

The server for an older gentleman eating alone in an adjacent room came over to say, "Mr. Brennan is having his dinner." She politely asked if we could go about things quietly. I turned to see whom she was speaking for, replying, "Ask Mr. Brennan if he would like to hear something like 'Misty'?"

Walter Brennan dined; Johnny Burrows and I proceeded to treat Walter Brennan to a quiet acoustic version of Erroll Garner's classic piece. The piano, a baby grand, always there in this room on the road to Paris, was the perfect accompaniment for a trumpet's song. Walter Brennan may have been in town to attend Keeneland's fall sale.

Homecoming '64 All-Campus Jam Session at the Grill 2-4.[36]

The 1964 Kentuckian yearbook headline proclaims, "Sigma Nu's to move to new house next fall." This would mean the familiar 'Freshmen Women Register Here' sign would be a thing of the past. "Although the Sigma Nu's will sorely miss their women's registration booth, they will have plenty to entertain them socially as they have had this year with rush functions, jam sessions, Christmas parties, and the traditional White Rose Formal."

Larry Orr was a member of Sigma Nu. When their new home at 422 Rose Lane opened November 7, 1964, the Temptashuns were engaged for its dedication and first house party.

Another band was playing on the same night a few houses down Rose Lane at the new Sigma Alpha Epsilon house. The SAEs had moved from 230 South Limestone to Rose Lane. We went to listen to the band on our first break. I recognized the sound.

I had first heard the Escorts as the Candy Men, Roy Orbison's touring band at Orbison's concert in Freedom Hall. Charlie McCoy's signature harmonica was a reminder of another time. I had last seen them in Printers Alley, July 1962. They were a great band.

I hoped they would come up the street to hear us. Larry was a member of Sigma Nu; it would no doubt mean a lot to him. The Escorts took a break and came to hear us that night. I spoke briefly with Charlie McCoy before our next set began. He was particularly impressed with the range of the band's material and attention we gave to our arrangements. I appreciated the favor from a first-call session player for many artists in Nashville.

—∾—

I found the quiet of a room and time alone after my family reflected on our blessings and a Thanksgiving meal. J. M. W. Turner's painting titled *Rain, Steam and Speed* provided the perfect setting to go with a thought and a song I wrote that day, "In Mist and Rain." A changing mood in a season presents itself when least expected at times, so it is with late November. I guess that's what the last of its days will forever be. A November afternoon in 1964 was little different from ones before. It was windy. Clouds were dark, swiftly on their way across an even darker sky. I may have sensed a metaphor in its signal. Something was on its way from where it was to another place. They could be two lovers on their way from one another to another.

Cold had arrived too soon.

Turner is one of my favorite painters. His Impressionistic style mirrors his passion. One look into the painting and you can sense its moving parts. The rain, the steam, and the speed in it all is more than a feeling. Feel the power of a steam engine emerging from the storm in the rain of nineteenth-century London. I wrote the song in my room at a piano, a Chicago. My original thought was the song's tempo would be a slow one—two lovers breaking up, then giving love a second chance. "Can it be you want me back again? Eyes full of tears try to explain. You whisper words in mist and rain."

"In Mist and Rain" would find a place with another not long after in our next session at Lemco.

—∾—

We had decided to record a cover of a Marvin Gaye hit the band had been doing for some time. The song had originally been released on Tamla Motown, Detroit's hit-making label, charting at No. 46 on *Billboard* in 1962. Our own version was being well received.

Lemco 882 became "Stubborn Kind of Fellow" b/w "In Mist and Rain," the A and B sides of our new record.

The recording session was on a Sunday afternoon in Lemco's new and improved studio. Cecil Jones had installed a new recording console, mixing equipment, and new playback speakers. Air was fresh, and we were well prepared before we went in the studio that day. Relaxed and easy defined the moment.

Our confidence was high about the session from the beginning. We had the right players and a strong arrangement for "Stubborn Kind of Fellow." We sprinkled some spice on the session with a chorus of three singers. Martha and the Vandellas sang backup on Marvin Gaye's original 1961 recording. Ours were another version: Gary Edwards and Bobby McCaw—lead singers in their own bands—and Robin Reed, a backup singer in another.

It was November 29, 1964, a Sunday afternoon.

This was our fourth session, the third at Lemco. I believe it was Doug who asked Alonzo "Snooks" Robinson, tenor sax player in the Houserockers, to join us. Doug could play his baritone sax on the session, thanks to the Houserockers, Lexington's early sixties powerhouse R & B combo. The lyrics were handwritten. Our horns used no charts. It was simply, "Let me try this," and "How is that?" Then, we laid down the tracks. We didn't have a bunch in those days. The train took us somewhere on the ones we had. We recorded our parts in the same room, all together at the same time until we got to where we wanted the songs to be, the smoothest track of tracks to get the Temptashuns there.

That day was particularly special. The blend of talent assembled was fine. It seemed we had always played together. There is little doubt in my mind the eleven of us could've done anything with soul in it, then or any day after.

The Temptashuns were in a creative sandbox, a little naive how good it all was at the time or how good we were becoming collectively. Exceptional, we were truly in the moment on this session.

We recorded "In Mist and Rain" after the others were gone.

Larry Orr and I met with Cecil at the studio the following day. His new four-track taping capability was an extra track to create something. He suggested we try something that until that morning had not been done at Lemco. Larry did a voice-over narrative track introducing folks to "Stubborn Kind of Fellow." He added a second vocal track on "In Mist and

Rain." The up-tempo British-inspired twin voices left me pleased with the way the "Mist" recording turned out.

Larry did them well.

"Here's the one you've been waiting for all night—Stubborn Kind of Fellow," would associate an audience, with a song and the band from then on. Our signature—The moment I had been waiting for since 1959, had arrived.

Seven players believed in this record. It was who we were, in the best of our years to then.

One thing remained to be done.

Cecil asked me deliver the tape to King in Cincinnati. I was off to Evanston, again the following afternoon. Gene Redd, King's chief sound engineer, added a "live audience" track to our original recording of "Stubborn Kind of Fellow." This wasn't just any long-forgotten track retrieved from King's vault of yesterday. Redd had originally engineered the recording of James Brown's *Live at the Apollo* album at the theater in Harlem for King in 1963.

He held the original audience track in his hands.

He engineered a piece of the Apollo into our own studio recording. Gene Redd gave us a small piece of the past to shape a bunch of our future. The Temptashuns met Harlem.

"Stubborn Kind of Fellow" had its wings.

Cecil decided to release our record on Lemco, not King, this time around. All hoped for more promising results, a positive choice by a confident band and Cecil Jones. The tapes of both recordings were delivered to Columbia in Nashville, mastered, and sent to Columbia Records in Terre Haute. A sizable production run was ordered.

We had final exams in early December. The Temptashuns appeared at the Lexington Country Club. We played at Transylvania College two consecutive nights at Spindletop Hall and Phoenix Hotel on the twenty-second. We entertained an audience of color on December 23 at the Second Street "Y" on the corner at Jefferson. The band was well received. Our music and the band's ever-growing reputation for bringing the spirit of Motown, Muscle Shoals, and Memphis to a stage was why we were there. Those four hours were too brief.

The audience made the night better.

Christmas Day, December 25. We traveled to Mt. Sterling Country Club for a private affair in the afternoon. We left our gear in place, returning on the twenty-eighth for Delta Tau Delta and their dates, a holiday dance. Following private affairs in Winchester and Lexington in Southland on the twenty-ninth and thirtieth, one more show remained for the band to play.

Goodbye to 1964 began with promotional photos taken in and around the Phoenix Hotel downtown in the afternoon. We sounded fine with a show for acquaintances young and old alike, the Jaycee's annual New Year's Dance in the Hotel's Convention Hall.

I spent the last of my silence letting go of a year that was no more.

10
Our Kind of Stuff, 1965

1965. I was twenty-three. The World's Fair came to Flushing Meadow, Queens, New York. *Help! and* Stanley Kramer's *Ship of Fools* were hit movies. *Days of Our Lives* premiered. A year had passed since a tide was high and Paul "Bear" Bryant's '64 National Championship at Alabama. Joe Namath was Rookie of the Year in a football league they called the AFL. President Lyndon B. Johnson visited Kentucky. His Great Society program became his domestic signature.

Then, he ordered the bombing of North Vietnam far away. Deep, beyond far, the first walk was made in space.

Small steps, on the way to giant leaps.

Everywhere, *The Sound of* was seen, its *Music* heard. Rogers and Hammerstein contrasted sharply with the silence of Simon and Garfunkel. Lennon and McCartney, even more. Bob Dylan, far beyond. NBC launched a thirty-minute evening newscast, the first network to do this. World news was thought for food brought straight to the family dinner table. *The Fugitive* paused to receive an Emmy, and the chase went on. Cassius Clay changed his name, but not before an unexpected change arriving at another doorstep.

We had become a mighty good band. The next eighteen months would put a nice wrapping on a gift each of us would open years down the road to their twilight.

—∞—

Our first engagement brought us to Christ the King School on January 2. Doug and John Page headed for Florida's warm beaches and a few days in Fort Lauderdale. Doug indicated they would see us again at 7:30 in Lebanon on the ninth.

We began loading in Lebanon's Club Cherry around 7:45 p.m. It was well into dark by then, except for the lights of a nightspot on Cherry

Street. The Club Cherry catered to people of color only. They came to hear seven people that night. The weather wasn't favorable. A cold rain and snow mix had followed us on the drive down US Highway 68. Where were the others? I wondered how the return home would in a few hours. Things were going smoothly for the Temptashuns. I put the possibility of anything else behind.

We came to Lebanon to play from nine till one, and at nine o' clock sharp, with Meade Brown's downbeat and Carter's blues-flavored 9th chord, my hands kissed the keys, my feet the pedals of a Hammond organ. The Cherry Street Five began to speak the language of Smith, Montgomery, McGriff, and Brubeck. All were in fine company. Playing a Hammond organ's bass pedals is like rhythm in motion. I like dancing with the instrument.

We were in a jam, and jam is what we did, sounding relaxed as I recall. "Take Five," passages from Jimmy Smith's "Blues for J," and "The Cat." I touched the early voicings of "Slaughter on Tenth Avenue" with care. We featured Johnny Burrows on a couple of sweet Chet Baker numbers. "Round Midnight" and "My Funny Valentine" painted a seldom-seen chance to exhibit our capabilities and the depth of our musical tastes.

Meade was in a Joe Morello state of time on drums; Carter blended Kenny Burrell and Jim Hall into the personality of his guitar. We were playing licks we had heard or learned on our own here and there. Larry Orr added spice to "Stormy Monday" with a touch of Bobby "Blue" Bland.

Larry sang a couple of others, saving his best for three sets and long night remaining.

Collectively, the Cherry Street Five was a memorable ensemble. The patrons were at home with us. The music was softened by the cool that is jazz and the folks in the club. The gods were smiling down. Our set of jazz tunes by the likes of Smith, Montgomery, and McGriff was limited. We played the set, announced the others were on their way, and took a break. "Slaughter on Tenth Avenue" would not become the same on Cherry Street.

The night's walk on the wild side had better odds going to heaven than 6 to 1.

Two well-tanned apologetic band members were there for the second set. Rhythm, blues, and the soul in it was the "Special" on the menu. They helped us make it through the night.

The easy-going mood of the Club Cherry and its patrons changed the moment we took them for a ride on our night train, beginning with a near thirty-minute nonstop set from *Live at the Apollo*. We gave them "I'll Go Crazy," "Try Me," "Think," "I Don't Mind," "Lost Someone," and "Please, Please, Please." We closed the set with JB's classic "Night Train."

The night was October 24, 1962, revisited again by a band and its audience.

We began our last set with Horace Silver's "Song for my Father." Little Milton's "Who's Cheating Who?" sounded fine. This was our kind of stuff. Gene Chandler's "Nothing Can Stop Me," Booker T. & the MG's "Green Onions," Otis Redding's "Respect," and "Satisfaction" left most in the club well pleased. We lightened it all with "Try a Little Tenderness" before putting our blessing on the evening with "In the Midnight Hour" and "Hold on, I'm Coming."

Our last offering was the King Curtis classic "Soul Serenade."

We were redeemed.

—ɱ—

A blue highway had turned to white in the early hours, January 10. My mind was on a new semester and its spring. The snowy landscape along an empty Highway 68 silenced the conversation I had begun with a trumpet player. Johnny was asleep before we reached Harrodsburg. The road was a lady in a beautiful state of mood just before becoming frozen in the still of itself.

A winter morning snow told me that Robert's frost had fallen in the night, all there for anyone's embrace. Nothing would've brought more peace than to be that someone in a village, leaving an MG to do a shadow dance with snowflakes, silhouettes in white against the darkest sky. Moonlight fell on the palisades along the river on the road past Shakertown. A river shimmered. I heard its silence then left it all behind.

Johnny Burrows was not with us on the sixteenth when we played the Alpha Gamma Rho fraternity. He was making a guest appearance with his good friend Jonah Jones in Louisville.

—ɱ—

—From the pages of *The Kentucky Kernel*. The "Merry Go-Round" . . . by Gay Gish.

"Kappa Alpha will entertain with the big sound of the Temptashuns on Friday night as bands seem to be appearing all along the 'row.'"[37]

—~—

We entertained George Headley and his invited guests at a private party on the twenty-third at his farm on Old Frankfort Pike. Mr. Headley was married to C.V. "Sonny" Whitney's sister. The Whitney's represented, for many, an elegant class of all it meant in those days to be a horseman with a racing stable in Fayette and its surrounding counties. You lived on your farm in the bluegrass a few days in a year. Lexington was, for you, a rest stop on a map of the world's exotic destinations: Saratoga Springs, the French Riviera, on safari somewhere. You went by way of a silver plane or ocean liner. Some, the *Orient Express*, a train. Wealth and social standing enabled one to be of here, someone with a Thoroughbred stable in a time when racing was known as "The Sport of Kings."

George Headley was an internationally known designer of bibelots, precious-jeweled objects. The Headley Whitney Museum, itself another on his estate farm, was a jewel designed to exhibit his work. Headley, also a painter, had selected his guests as carefully as the jewels for his next object of fine art. The party for which we entertained his guests was in the artists' studio located behind the main house on the property. Here was a taste of the Bluegrass waiting to be had; all lay just up a gentle slope above a lake. Weeping willows lived on its banks. Swans moved lightly among their branches, a whisper on the plane of its face.

His guests were a mixed collection of some thirty some people, ages from early teens to older, seasoned friends. The room was intimate.

I remember this as the night the Temptashuns went acoustic.

Larry sang his vocals with care; microphones were less their normal gain. Guitar, bass, and organ were kept to a whisper. Meade used brushes most of the evening. The horns played naturally. Doug's tenor sax was nice on "Desafinado," his alto fresh on "Take Five." Headley and his guests were in exclusive company. These folks experienced us in a way few ever did. That evening was the most acoustic moment in the band's history. Our sound was clean as ever I remembered.

Unplugged . . . Uncommon . . . Unforgettable
Unplugged . . . Uncommon . . . Unforgettable
Unplugged . . . **Uncommon** . . . *Unforgettable*

—~—

We traveled to Ashland on the thirtieth to appear at the Moonlite Gardens on Carter Avenue. I made my customary stop in Olive Hill to fill my car's tank with gas. Tom T. hadn't been around for some time. He'd left the Morehead College campus radio station early in January 1964 and driven a Cadillac to Nashville. He was writing songs and had a record deal with Mercury and a lady named Dixie. Tom T. and Dixie Hall have been together ever since. Life has been good to them.

"Old Dogs, Children and Watermelon Wine" tells a story that says a lot to me about me.

This was not our first appearance in Ashland at the Gardens. The one they had been waiting for all night was the first song we played at Moonlite Gardens that evening. We could have sold a bunch of records. Johnny Burrows and I had heard "Stubborn Kind of Fellow" on Ashland's WCMI Radio, arriving in town. Some in attendance told us stations in nearby Huntington and Charleston, West Virginia, and WIRO Radio in Ironton, Ohio, were also playing our record.

Near that time, a young nurse had left her struggle in Ashland and was living in Lexington with a new daughter named Christina. Maybe Naomi Judd once visited Moonlite Gardens as a teenager or danced to the Temptashuns. I wonder if she ever heard "Stubborn Kind of Fellow" on the radio while that bridge, the one love built, was being put together.

Naomi Judd was a teenager then. She had moved to Lexington in the fall of 1964. I suppose the windswept memory of Chanticleer, Morrill, Big Hill, and Berea was still fresh on her heart. Commonplace is where you'll find it. For some it lasts a moment, others a lifetime.

A Chanticleer for anyone is rare.

—~—

Larry Kelly, former member of the Temptashuns, is pictured with other members of the Centennial Ball Committee on page one of *The Kentucky Kernel*, January 15, 1965. "Members of the Centennial Ball Committee are Gil Kingsbury, alumni member of the committee; Peggy Parsons, student member; Larry Kelley, cochairman; Mrs. John W. Oswald, ex officio member; Dr. Douglas W. Schwartz, faculty member; and Mrs. Richard Crutcher, alumni member. The Centennial Ball is expected to be the highlight of the One-Hundredth Anniversary of the University."

The Centennial Ball committee selected the Lester Lanin Orchestra to provide the music for the evening. The dance was held in the Student Center Grand Ballroom.

University President Dr. John W. Oswald and his wife hosted a reception in the Alumni House on Rose Street for students. We were engaged to provide the music at the event. The university's student newspaper, *The Kernel*, pictures Dr. Oswald, noting the president was there to meet the sophomores as part of the centennial celebration at the university in 1965. This was one of a number of centennial events the Temptashuns would play a part in during a milestone year in the university's history.

Dr. Oswald was always there on behalf of the students. The student body at Kentucky was a priority to its president. Such priority was rare in the sixties, particularly the deeper we all walked together into the decade. He later became president of Penn State University. President and Mrs. Oswald were kind to us, complimentary of the music we provided for the occasion.

We left immediately following the reception for Lebanon and the Club 68.

—m—

Snow began lightly falling, appearing like an innocent child on the night. We made it to Lebanon safely. Johnny Burrows rode with me. We probably talked about what was fresh on Verve Records or Lexington's own Les McCann and the Jazz Crusaders. James Bond books and girls.

Topics like that.

We sounded good that night at the Club 68. The place was packed. Ike and Tina Turner Revue had been on stage the night before. We shared a place together on the sign out front. Other nights before or after Ray Charles or James Brown and the Famous Flames rolled into the Club 68.

Thinking if I could make it down the hill to the bridge, then up the winding road on the other side of the Kentucky River, getting the rest of the way to Wilmore and home might be forgiving. The palisades along the river were cold this time around. Crevices weathered in the rock face held deep shadows. The only arms reaching out to capture the moon's light in this hour were Kentucky cedar trees. Others, their leaves long gone, were stark in silhouette, bare of a blanket to ward off the wind. Snowflakes danced. A cotillion on window glass.

All was well with my soul.

We left the scene behind; snow began falling ever more quickly, a naked land soon to be clothed in purest white. Too soon. I hoped not.

The Lexington Drive-in Theater was located at that time on a long gentle rise along US Highway 68, the Nicholasville Road. An easy climb was not to be this night. I settled in for a long, slow assent, easing a Corvair and band trailer to the hill's crest. We passed the Windmill Motel on the right; enough coffee left in the Thermos to still the chill of the moment in my hand.

Chef Sears Restaurant was darkness in silence up ahead on the left.

Words and a tune—"Someone to Watch Over Me"—shared a place in my mind with imagined tastes of the chef's southern-style menu. Southern-fried chicken, mashed potatoes and gravy, creamed peas, and homemade buttered rolls with sweet tea were a tasty diversion to a moment. It ended at the top of an uncertainty.

Burrows was asleep. No one else was on the road at this hour. It was approaching 3:30 a.m. I let Johnny be till arriving at his apartment on Walnut near Third. I left him with the thought maybe all of us could all go to Chef Sears sometime for Sunday dinner. Leaving for home, it was past 4:30 a.m. What began as the poetry, that is a night sky in a season defined by the innocence of snowflakes, had ended with its signature on the landscape, where winter had signed her name.

—ɱ—

An advertisement appeared in the student newspaper:

The
Main
Record Shop
224½ East Main Street
Phone 254-0155
'STUBBORN KIND OF FELLOW'
By The Temptashuns (Lemco Label)[38]

Larry Orr is pictured in the same issue as one of the newly appointed 290th AFROTC Cadet Wing Staff for Spring Semester.[39]

—ɱ—

If the Temptations didn't hit the big time until their seventh disk, it wasn't for Motown's lack of ingenuity. Back in 1962, the group went so far as to change its name to the Pirates for one release—a cover of Nolan Strong's 'Mind Over Matter'—issued on Motown's subsidiary label, Mel-O-Dy Records.[40]

The Detroit Temptations had their first hit "The Way You Do the Things You Do" in 1964. We had our first record, "Autumn Love," released in 1963.

We got there first. They got there bigger.

Our manager Cecil Jones received a phone call one morning from Detroit. An attorney for Barry Gordy's Motown Records had a message: "We can't have this."

—w—

Record companies typically establish more than one label for the music they produce, sometimes to create different identitics that will attract a variety of listeners, or to feature the work of a specific producer or artist. In the early 1960s another reason to market a variety of labels was to get the maximum airplay; at the time many radio stations avoided appearing to play favorites with one particular label.[41]

Motown Records was described in the book *The History of Motown* as a "Music Factory" with different departments. Barry Gordy had learned this from observing manufacturing of automobiles at Ford Motor Company. Syd Nathan had operated King Records in this manner since the mid-fifties in Cincinnati and even manufactured the product (the records themselves) under the same roof.

—w—

River Deep—Mountain High, The Supremes, and the Four Tops, Motown album MS 717, *The Magnificent 7*, 1970. Less than five years later, Motown just couldn't seem to get away from us.

—w—

The Temptashuns, a bunch of college guys in Lexington, Kentucky, had awakened the Motor City giant living at 2468 West Grand Boulevard from its long sleep of success. "Stubborn Kind of Fellow" had quickly become a

Billboard Regional Breakout in Northeast and Midwest markets. Motown was telling us, "You are not to record or perform as the Temptashuns anymore."

One band was in for a change—a name change. Our own.

Destiny's choice arrived again on a cold February morning. I went to Lemco Studios on my way to classes and typed a few simple lines on a blank piece of paper.

February 9, 1965
PLEASE DO US A FAVOR
Change the name of the group
On Lemco 882
'Stubborn Kind of Fellow'
from The Temptashuns
To
The Magnificent Seven
THEN PLAY IT.

We sent notice to radio stations and record stores in Kentucky, southern Indiana, Ohio, and larger cities south in Tennessee. Cecil wrote a letter explaining it all to *Billboard* magazine in Nashville, *Music World*, *Cashbox,* and *Record World* magazines. I put them in the mail after leaving Pence Hall on my way home after design studio.

I don't recall who suggested the Magnificent Seven for a name. Others didn't seem to define our aspirations. They were high, near the middle of an ever-changing decade. We made the positive choice. Agreement was unanimous.

Magnificent, seven or otherwise, was a name with something to live up to.

I spoke with Cecil. Columbia Records needed a name to put on fresh labels printed for a record production run scheduled for the next day. I told Cecil who we were. He phoned Terre Haute, an order placed for 1,000 records.

Copies remained bearing the band's original Temptashuns name on the label. Cecil needed help. I did camera-ready artwork for a small Magnificent 7 label. A local printing business printed copies. In a day or so, Doug and I had put a few hundred new labels on records in the bins of Lexington's record stores. Labels on others not yet to distributed, still fresh in their boxes, at the studio were done by Cecil.

Immediately, on receiving the new record shipment, we sent fresh copies to *Billboard*, *Music World*, and other trade publications. We hoped they would give our record a listen, maybe even a review. "Stubborn Kind of Fellow" was moving on charts published by radio stations in Lexington. Request-based Top 40 charts as distant as Kansas City, Chicago, Detroit, Cleveland, and Boston mirrored its local popularity, particularly on college campuses.

Oh, what a sweet, sweet feeling. Priceless on a midwinter night in February. In Kentucky.

Distribution of "Stubborn Kind of Fellow" was uninterrupted while the song was enjoying its popular demand, the ninth of February, 1965. It's nice to be No. 1 in your hometown. You can turn the "No Vacancy" sign on for a while.

—∞—

The Magnificent 7 broke the attendance record on March 20 at Moonlite Gardens in Ashland with 700. Cecil had arranged for the band to meet and talk to a couple of radio personalities from nearby Ironton, Ohio. The promoter had expressed interest in the Mag Seven appearing with Bo Diddley and Lonnie Mack.

Back on campus many things continued to be exciting: architecture and music, how could it not be? We sounded great at an afternoon jam session in Keeneland Hall, a girl's dorm on Euclid. We backed a Keeneland coed named Diana Brewer on four songs. "What a voice" can be found expressed in my notes. Diana soon became lead singer with another group, the Titans, managed by Cecil Jones. They also recorded for his Lemco label. Harrison Underhill, the band's lead guitarist, was an exceptional player. Cecil asked me to be another ear in the control room during two of their studio recordings. I helped with an arrangement and a backing vocal on one of their tracks, "How Long Must I Wait." This part of music's creative expression—studio recording, arranging in particular—appealed to me.

The Titans were a terrific group to work with. They had no idea how good they were. Ever open to suggestion, the Titans sought the opinions of others and listened. They were a reminder what we once were. The Temptashuns, in the early years, was mirrored in some of the young new bands now beginning to flourish at Lemco.

—∾—

News about us in the pages of the *Kentucky Kernel*:

The AFROTC Sponsor Corps will hold a jam session to introduce the 21 Sponsor finalists this week. To mark the occasion 'The Magnificent Seven' will entertain. The jam session will be held from 3 to 5 p.m. on Thursday at Buell Armory. Price of admission is 35 cents stag, 50 cents per couple and 'free' to cadets in uniform."[42]

On "The Merry Go-Round" . . . by Gay Gish: 'Chi Omega has reserved the Imperial House for its formal Friday, and The Magnificent 7 will provide the rhythm.'"[43]

Those on campus began referring to us as the Mag 7.

The Mag 7 band had a special evening sounding big for the Alpha Gams at the Imperial House on Waller. Jimmy Dorsey's orchestra played elsewhere on the same night at the Phoenix Hotel. The pleasure of such company as a Dorsey, though a few blocks apart, is rare. The nearness was enough for a memory.

Jimmy Dorsey's "So Rare" remains my favorite big band piece of instrumental music.

—∾—

We broke our own attendance record on April 10 in Ashland at the Moonlite Gardens with 750. The trip in the rain back to Lexington was long, near tragic. I was pulling the band trailer for what would be my last time. Johnny Burrows was with me. A stranger was walking in our lane of travel. I left a narrow two-lane highway near Salt Lick. The trailer disconnected from my car on its way back to the road. Hope lay beaten in the road. A concerned motorist, who stopped to offer help, gave Johnny a ride back to Morehead for assistance and a wrecker. I remained on scene keeping watch. My car illuminated the accident enough to alert the few on the road that evening. Rain fell like tears.

I couldn't determine the extent of damage. A frail object lay broken in a downpour, an ominous signal that would be a defining moment for the Magnificent 7 Band. How much courage could we draw upon in the coming weeks? What would we learn about the character of each other and our friends? The station owner stored the trailer and its contents safely indoors till we could come again.

Two hours after we left a rain-covered highway near Morehead, the cause of sadness, a stranger, continued on the way down a road safely, as if nothing had happened. We had a lot to be thankful for in the early hours of Sunday morning. Johnny and I had not been hurt. I drove us to the house where most of the band lived and told them the news.

The road trip on that weekend ended in my garage.

I returned to Morehead with friends a day or so after. We unloaded the material world of a band into a rented U-Haul at the station. The next few weeks were trying ones. I lost the trailer I owned. Its sale was cancelled. My instrument had been damaged beyond use. Other gear—instruments, amps and sound equipment—were fine. Things could have been much worse for the band and its members.

The song guardian angels play is sweet; it seemed always to be with us.

The owner put an abandoned trailer at a lonesome corner of a secure fenced lot at the service station. There, it slowly met tomorrow, long after that night. Each time we passed by in the coming months, a hurt was painted in words on its sides. All that was a memory was on its way to fade. The Temptashuns; dance band; Lexington, Kentucky.

Then, one day, it was gone.

—∞—

Ray Sousley sold Cadillacs on Richmond Road, across from Mt. Tabor, near Brock's. Sousley's was a unique car lot; he sold only used Cadillac hearses. We found one well suited to keep and carry our instruments and other gear in comfort with little modification. Warm in winter, cool in summer, a terrific radio, and a smooth ride. The Magnificent 7 band had a long black Cadillac with wide whitewall tires and lots of shine, all mirrored in polished black lacquer and bright chrome.

This was style.

The first road trips led to our only choice for dependability. We equipped her with a pricey new set of high-quality truck tires in Cincinnati.

—∞—

The next challenge I faced was getting my instrument repaired. Shackleton's, the authorized Hammond organ dealer, recommended the local certified Hammond services of Jack Hurd. The organ was insured. The cost to repair and replace damaged wood cabinetry, some broken keys, and vacuum tubes was going to be high. Otherwise, the heart and soul of the instrument appeared to be untouched. I considered another possibility, meeting with him again at his home workshop on Wichita Drive. He looked at the colorful LP album in my hands. Could he make me one of these? The album's cover pictured a smiling Bill Doggett and his Hammond B3 organ. He studied each detail carefully. Jack Hurd was a quiet man.

"I can, but it may cost a little more." I was confident by his reply. He knew his trade well.

I continued renting gear from players in other bands who had an open date on the same night we had a gig. Studies continued in architecture. Time often seemed at a still, the wait to see what he had crafted unending.

—∾—

John Edmondson had originally charted the music of our first record when it was published. He had found a songwriter living in New York City named Cynthia Medley who was interested in writing lyrics for "Autumn Love." She did, and music was charted. I received a letter from John in October 1965 with news he was sending "Autumn Love," with lyrics, to Anita Kerr.

Anita Kerr, her singers, or anyone recording "Autumn Love" was a rush. John had a notion Nina Simone might be interested. Delicious to me. I've not found anything since then in my discography research, however, suggesting Nina Simone ever recorded "Autumn Love."

An interest expressed or otherwise by Nina Simone about anything is an awakening.

"Autumn Love" and its lyrics on the canvas of Nina Simone's mysteriously beautiful style was perfume; what she could do for any song was near spiritual.

She was life itself when it came to a song.

Johnny Burrows appeared once again with Jonah Jones on May 1. We alternated with Cecil's band at the Phoenix Hotel's Convention Hall for Westinghouse Corporation the same night.

Margaret Hall was an exclusive Episcopal Prep School in Versailles for young girls of social standing. We played for the girls of Margaret Hall on the fifteenth. Young men from an academy elsewhere were invited to attend as their dates. The dance was formal. The gentlemen left with their chaperones after we played the last dance. We began to pack the Cadillac on a night in May to a song. The poetry in dreams on windows up above on Elm Street became self-evident. Motion was impeccably defined by girls, a dance in the age of its innocence appearing live.

Hushed noise was visible. Suggestive moves illuminated softly for our eyes only. Strangers to all else in their second-floor rooms, Juliets danced a song to Romeos in the band below. Girls in silhouette behind window shades pulled to cover panes of old glass. In college, in the middle of your own uncertainty, you don't forget the innocence of someone you will never meet again.

Often, life in a band isn't always what it seems.

—∞—

Doug, John Page, and Meade left for Florida's shores with the promise to meet the rest of the band at Irvine High, a prom on the twenty-first. And so it was.

We played for 700 in Ashland, confident and sounding big again at Moonlite Gardens. Larry Kelley substituted for Meade on drums. The US Navy borrowed Meade for a mandatory two-week summer cruise. Larry never missed a beat. I left 365 records. Folks in three states shared a common interest.

We met on May 26 at WKYT Television studios. A talented local teen had arranged to have the Magnificent 7 back her on an audition videotape she was making. The station was located near the Circle 25 Drive-In Theater then.

She was hoping to pursue a chance for a future in entertainment. The demo featured her vocal of "Put on a Happy Face" to recorded music. We backed her live on "Summertime" and "Misty." Her pantomime to our recording of "Stubborn Kind of Fellow" was taped after we left.

The band took a couple of weeks in June to rest. Summer and fall semester were well booked. "Stubborn Kind of Fellow" stayed busy on the charts.

The Magnificent 7 returned to the Club 68 on the nineteenth, playing to a full house. While loading out, we were told music had set off the burglar alarm at the Schenley Distillery in Lawrenceburg. I can't say for sure. Two guys in a Cadillac gave a pair of grateful ladies a ride back to Lexington. Their dates had abandoned Shelley and Kay. They needed a taxi, conversation, and a pair of gentlemen that night, and we were.

The Mag Seven played for the National Association of Student Councils on the twenty-second at Phoenix Hotel. Eight hundred teens representing fifty states attended. Some bought our record to take back home. "Stubborn Kind of Fellow" and "In Mist and Rain" might get the chance to be played in Alaska and Hawaii. Such are the whispers of coming so near the plane of unlimited possibilities in life's geometry.

—∞—

My new instrument was kind, at first glance the baby sister to the mighty Hammond B3 organ. She was dressed in ebony, polished and lacquered, a lady in her prime about to dance. Up close and personal, a well-crafted replica of a Hammond B3 cabinet held the original chassis and components of my L-100. The top folded on solid brass piano hinges to cover two manuals, forty-four keys, each hungry to be played, similar to a B3.

The cabinetry's open front was Hammond B3's most signature design feature. Expression and thirteen-note bass pedals were located below the body. Wiring for the power and pedal functions, contained in wood cabinetry at the floor, was carried in two solid brass tubes to the upper cabinet. He painted the organ, bench, and Leslie speaker ebony, rubbed to a satin finish. He recognized the unique opportunity he was given. I was pleased with his work and had a small sterling silver plate engraved. It lived inside at a special place in the cabinet's neighborhood.

At times it seemed I was driving some kind of sound machine.

—∞—

I was confident the Magnificent 7 was going to be better than ever. We looked like a together bunch on July 2, taking our music to polished wood and the smiles of couples on it. Shy pairs of dancers moved about, a hint of doubt in their eyes. What could it be, the something in their need that wasn't to be satisfied in these last days of summer?

Life and uncertainty. Were they simply two dancers on a "No Break" card?

The colors of our music painted on walls and trim, we left to dry on the finest of wood. Echoes of once upon a time slept there. One's soon-to-be fleeting summer lingered before slowing to an end. The Lexington Country Club was a near-perfect room to play.

Chambers of privilege, with its ghosts of long ago. Cotillions.

The dance floor was wood, portable, and nicely enclosed the next night for a debutante party outdoors on a horse farm. The setting was intimate. We played R & B in a paddock-like showcase, surrounded by nothing more than more of the same. Creative expressions written on a midsummer night are words on the lines in the kind of poetry one can only find in the Bluegrass.

The Mag Seven presented a summer jam on July 9. Soul arrived in the Grand Ballroom on UK's campus for the Student Center Board.

—From my notes: "It's good to play at the University again."

We finished out what remained of July with two well-attended appearances at Moonlite Gardens in Ashland and a pair of nights at Lexington's venerable nightspot, the Palms.

Johnny Burrows bought the complete set of Ian Fleming's James Bond paperbacks. A chronological order, as originally written, was included. *Casino Royale* was the first. Johnny was reading then lending each to me.

August 7. I was home off the road and a night in Ashland at the Moonlite Gardens. I began *Diamonds are Forever*, Chapter One. It was 4:00 a.m. A concert F-sharp played by an Accutron's tuning fork had me near sleep. She was with me through band appearances, college classes, exams, and most of the rest of my life. I had bought a Bulova watch downtown in another August two years past. Time was living in its case telling me a story of its life. I could hear the song of a timepiece in a quiet setting song in the night on a road. I sensed the essence of time passing all too fast, and I too swiftly through it. Sometimes I wondered would I ever see a roadside and all that mattered on it quite the same again.

I was bound for the fall semester at UK, about to fall into *The Age of Aquarius*.

John Page couldn't seem to keep a bass amp together. If the speaker wasn't failing, the cabinetry was coming apart. John had enough and sought a friend for help. Paul Shaw, the local acoustics and sound systems designer who had put the components of our first sound system together in 1961, designed a bass amp for John. The cabinet's proportions were designed to deliver an unbroken depth to color our sound. John's bass amp had a sweet, sweet piece of deep that stayed with you. Twin 12" speakers and some tasty wattage were not unlike a Harley standing at idle in a conversation with itself. This amp and the language of itself stood behind each note John played as if to say, "You want 'low' my friend? You got it."

I admire John's journey in the years since our college experience. I remember long nights in the Reynolds Building and Pence Hall design studios. There, we left ideas in pencil, with pen and ink on yellow paper trace or boards and models in our years for others to judge. That, to any lover of creative expression, is what life is.

The Magnificent 7 put a band on a stage to be seen and heard, to entertain, and to let a world around us be our judge. Guilty for being good was fine with us any day.

We celebrated John Page's twenty-first birthday with his family at their house on Westgate with steaks and a movie. I remember a nice evening, a simple outdoor cookout with six friends and John's family. This one, like so many other memories in the Magnificent 7, is priceless.

The end of summer's days was near. More than a week of consecutive long uninterrupted days of rehearsals began. We made ready an ever-evolving show and its songs to take to Kentucky's colleges and high schools and the people of the Commonwealth another year.

The Magnificent 7 was a confident band, more polished than ever.

It would've been nice to have recorded "You're Gonna Cry" and "Love Gone, Love Return" at Columbia's Nashville studios using a bigger horn section. Ray Charles could've sold a million copies of "You're Gonna Cry." We could've sold a few copies too. I believe the song would've been hard to beat in 1965, the way this band was performing.

—∾—

Rain, Steam and Speed, J. M. W. Turner's masterpiece, is one of the great moments in art. The imagery had been with me in the November of "In Mist and Rain." The power of the train becomes magnified by the rain, the motion of its speed, by the steam. The three are inseparable. He paints a landscape all in motion, all about escape, everything struggling to free itself from everything else. Turner is mystical. I find the train to be a metaphor of struggle in the sixties. Struggle wears a crown of souls and innocents gathered in their worship. The Brown Chapel A.M.E. Church . . .divine intervention. March 3, 1965, was huge, and Selma was waiting.

Echoes strained to be free to escape through opened stained glass windows in the Dexter Avenue Baptist Church. Echoes were born in this place to fly in warm, Deep South air. Ideals are born in dreams. The unchained dreamer walked across Bainbridge Avenue with little fear, ascended steps leading right to the front porch of power in Montgomery.

Canaan's fair and happy land was of the ages, for all ages.

We would be witness to a litany of walks across the Edmund Pettus bridges of our times, across the troubled waters of our own conscience. The stormy banks of uncertainty on the other side held echoes of the little children, the girls of the 16th Street Baptist Church. Birmingham was near two years past. How many others would there be and the years, how many? What of atonement in them?

Where was the center of one's identity to be found? Who am I? What's going on out there—over here? Dylan, Baez, Simon, the writers. It wasn't the Brill Building anymore. The times were heavy, brother—the harvest a heavy, heavy one to bear.

—∾—

The Mag 7 was in its prime doing "Monkey Time." Guys and coeds danced to our horn-driven blend of brass and reeds, a Hammond organ that looked like the mighty B itself, a drummer with a kick, and a singer who could deliver. Bob Dylan's message was beyond our times. For a moment, it seemed strange an audience was listening to what was being said. The Magnificent 7 first played Dylan's "Like a Rolling Stone" in October 1965 outdoors at Holmes Hall. The afternoon was sunshine filled, a day to be remembered by many as Limestone Revisited.

"How does it feel . . . to be on your own . . . like a complete unknown, like a rolling stone."[44]

The Mag Seven doing a Dylan tune? Bob had gone electric, and a lot of purists were really upset. Somewhere along Highway 61, he'd left his acoustic child. His now was a screaming Hammond organ, guitars gone electric—a renewed Dylan.

He gave some space to a Hammond organ, and it roared.

Like a Rolling Stone lasts six minutes, unusually long for a single in the pop music marketplace. The subject is also unusual: an overprotected person being pushed out into a cruel world. The song taunts middle-class American youth with images showing that it takes a tough, resilient spirit to give up the props of middle-class life.[45]

We played "Like a Rolling Stone." The dancing ended, replaced by an uninterrupted expression of serious frozen on young faces. Dylan's was a message piece, not rhythm and blues. People were in their prime on South Limestone. There was little doubt.

We gave them a taste of Motown, its song, and the Mag 7's sound. College guys and dolls left Kennedy's Book Store, the World Famous Two Keys and Jerry's Drive-in restaurant to dance in the street all the way from Euclid to Maxwell.

We connected with them. It was more than a feeling. The sixties were about a lot of things: Echoes from the generation of Jack Kerouac, flavored words from a collection of individuals perched on ladders reading poetry in coffee houses near campus. Lexington's own "Left Bank," was trendy. Acoustic celebrations of Joan Baez and others were being heard for one cause or another. We were going through the changes in our times.

Popular music was going to get the message out.

—ฑ—

—From the pages of trade magazines:
MUSIC BUSINESS SINGLE PICKS
R & B Spices New Releases
Chart Picks
MUSIC BUSINESS DISCOVERIES
THE MAGNIFICENT SEVEN
Lemco 882
STUBBORN KIND OF FELLOW
(Jobete, BMI) (2:16)-Gay, Stevenson, Gordy
Flip is 'In Mist and Rain'

(Lemco, BMI) 1:55)-Stallard
A new group on a label out of
Lexington, Ky.
Side was published by Tamla-Motown's firm,
Jobete Music, and it bears
a Detroit quality.

—ᴍ—

Someone in the business had taken notice. We were in the box with *Music Business* magazine's "Discoveries" in the February 27, 1965 issue. They had releases of their own on that date. So sweet it was to be in the company of others. Well-known artists needed no box: Motown's Brenda Holloway, "Come See" by Major Lance. Artists, Bobbi Martin, The Coasters, Bobby Comstock. *Reprise* 0350—Frank Sinatra's "Anytime At All," received the comment, "Frank swings out on this big tune that builds and builds. One of his best and it should do well on the charts." "Got to Get You off My Mind," by Solomon Burke was joined by Dee Clark, Dick and Dee Dee, Bern Elliot, Nelson Riddle, Toni Harper, and Jimmy McGriff, a fine Hammond B3 jazz artist.

If you played rhythm and blues, to be mentioned on the same page as Solomon Burke in the sixties, was special. If it all ended right there, being on the same page with Frank Sinatra just once, would have been enough. We were hoping for that elusive No. 1. Reprise had a good chance. Frank Sinatra and Nelson Riddle were an impeccable blend that made competition a meaningful experience anytime. Who knew? In the presence of great company, you have no idea what company may come calling.

—ᴍ—

Record World
Three Star Pick
Stubborn Kind of Fellow (Jobete, BMI)
In Mist and Rain (Lemco, BMI)
Magnificent Seven—Lemco 882
'Rousing slice done by a brassy group of artists.
Plenty of dance action here.'

—∞—

Our record received another favorable review from a national trade magazine. In the Record World issue from March 27, 1965, page 8: Three Star review recognition. Again, we were with other artists who had received Four Star reviews: The Four Seasons and the terrific "Woman's Got Soul" by The Impressions, shared places with The Shangri-Las, Brenda Lee, Chuck Jackson, Perry Como, Andy Williams, Olympics, the Four Lads, and Patti Page recording "Hush, Hush Sweet Charlotte."

Four Stars was not beyond reach; we knew that. Someday it would happen for us. Three Stars was a beginning; a lot of sky remained to be filled.

—∞—

Cecil Jones and Magnificent 7 signed a record deal at Lemco on a Sunday afternoon. Buddy Killen's Dial Records, a subsidiary of Tree International Publishing in Nashville, had become interested in the band and its song. Killen found evidence of seven undiscovered objects sprinkled about in the vast reaches of space on trade paper.

Buddy Killen put record deals together with independent labels like Lemco and his own Dial label. Exclusive to our agreement was the long-reaching distribution capability of Atlantic Records. A small independent label like Lemco simply didn't have the means to move a product nationally or worldwide. Stax, Volt, and Satellite labels in Memphis had recognized the benefit of Atlantic's sphere of influence with its distribution strength. We were in familiar company.

Buddy Killen was enjoying considerable success producing Joe Tex, who also recorded for Dial. The Magnificent 7 had the same kind of deal he had put together for Joe Tex. Atlantic Records in New York City would distribute our records nationally.

Atlantic is recognized as one of the most influential labels ever in the history of music. Dial Record's albums were issued in the Atlantic 8000 series with standard Atlantic labels. Dial singles issued had the distinctive Dial label. Atlantic had their fingers on the pulse of a generation of people in change.

Dial and Atlantic heard the pulse of seven hearts.

We signed the necessary papers, and the Atlantic Records distribution deal Cecil Jones and Buddy Killen had put together was done. The Buddy Killen of Muscle Shoals and the Buddy Killen of Nashville and Atlantic represented a long road that Sunday afternoon. We were somewhere on it. The connection had been made, one mutually beneficial for us all. A Dial/Atlantic representative headed back home with the agreement. Signed.

"Stubborn Kind of Fellow" enjoyed a second release, nationally distributed by Atlantic on the Dial label. We were part of something special, a world-class record company. "Stubborn Kind of Fellow" began to move. The one folks had been waiting for on its way to arriving in many towns.

—∾—

"In Mist and Rain" was destined to be in record stores all over the country. I had signed a songwriter's agreement with Atlantic Records on Sunday; my song now rested in Atlantic's Cotillion Music Publishing. Cotillion was one of three houses for that label. Walden Music and Progressive Music, two others Atlantic possessed. Progressive Music was most familiar to me, because I'd seen the name many times before, associated with Ray Charles's early times.

I received a modest royalty check from Atlantic Records a few months later, a writer's share of our record's sales for writing a song on the B-side of "Stubborn Kind of Fellow." The monetary reward meant less to me than the fresh air at the top of a small mountain we had climbed together.

Buddy Killen released the Magnificent 7's version of Smokey Robinson's original hit "Ooh Baby, Baby" on Dial Records in 1968. Atlantic distributed the record nationally. Killen later produced Exile in the eighties when they rose to achieve prominence as country artists.

Exile remains as fine a band today as it ever was.

—∾—

We were knocking on heaven's door in the mid-sixties. The prospect being pulled into a war seemed ever-present. Year upon year would come to be a momentary lack of vision of a war in which there were few parallels, a lapse of reason more than momentary. Latitude was only a line in this one. Few things would be crossed, either with or without the people of

America knowing about it. Truth is rare. When sensed to have been lost, truth has no place it would rather be than with the people it lives to serve.

We gave them songs. Others danced the night away. Such was a reason for being.

The Mag 7 played on.

We delivered music the way we felt. Folks liked the way we played. We expected a lot from each other, nothing was left to become routine. No performance was the same as the one before. Each was fresh, a significant reason for our popularity. We were a soul-based band.

Inherent truth can stand alone.

—ꟽ—

Our first Singles Review from *Billboard* magazine for "Stubborn Kind of Fellow" received a 4 Star Rating in the R&B Category in April.

BILLBOARD Singles Reviews

4 Star

R&B

Magnificent 7

Stubborn Kind of Fellow (Jobete, BMI)

Lemco 882

Billboard, Vol. 77, No.16, April 17, 1965, Page 41.

Others in the same R&B category were Sam and Dave and David Clayton Thomas, who later joined Blood, Sweat and Tears. Artists receiving 4 Stars in the pop category included Lenny Welch, Sarah Vaughan, Kitty Kallen, Sammy Kaye and his Orchestra, The O'Jays, and Stevie Wonder.

Another fine moment for the Magnificent 7—*Billboard's* coveted "Spotlight" rating was achievable someday. Out of reach, was out of the question in our minds.

—ꟽ—

SUKY

JAM SESSION

Thursday Sept. 9

2-5 p.m.

Student Center ballroom

Music By:

The

Magnificent
Seven
Meet The:
1965 Football Team
Coaches
Cheerleaders
—From a notice posted on UK campus in 1965.

—⁓—

On "The Merry Go-Round," by Gay Gish.

Capping off an active—and unusual—rush program, the Phi Tau's will hold a semi-formal dance at the Phoenix Hotel on Friday night. The 'Magnificent Seven' will provide the sound . . . and music by the Magnificent Seven will end the Pike's upper-class rush Saturday evening.[46]

LAMBDA CHI ALPHA
Pushcart Derby Weekend
Friday Night. . .
Dance with Trendells and Carnations
Saturday. . . Billy Love will M.C.
PARADE leaving Lambda Chi House at 12:30
DERBY RACE in Administration Circle at 1:30
JAM SESSION immediately after derby, about 3:30 p.m.,
with The Magnificent Seven.
COME OUT AND SUPPORT YOUR FAVORITE TEAM . . . Proceeds to Charity.[47]

We presented Stevie Wonder's Hit "Uptight," with an arrangement borrowed from Nancy Wilson's version. Bill Doggett's arrangement on Phillip Upchurch's "You Can't Sit Down" was another. The Mag 7 was who we were because the band looked for other colors to paint our music. We mixed them with a little of ones from our own imagination, leaving many to wonder where we got our arrangements.

—⁓—

The Pan Hellenic Council

I don't recall when the Pan Hellenic Council at UK sought to rethink their entertainment budgets as it were. Bands represented by Cecil Jones

Entertainment, including the Magnificent 7, were invited to perform live for members of the council and social chairs from each fraternity and sorority. Notice was sent to management agencies in Louisville and Cincinnati. Auditions were held in Memorial Hall on campus for five nights in September 1965.

The Pan Hellenic Council and social chairs reviewing the bands had heard us before. We were confident going band to band with anyone, especially in Memorial Hall.

Our price was fair.

The auditions showcased other bands represented by Cecil Jones Entertainment. The Magnificent 7 auditioned in the company of a collection of fine local players: the Classics, Formations, Titans, and Torques. Louisville bands of the Sambo and Joni agencies, which showed up, represented a clear sketch of the River City. The Driving Winds, with Carl Edmondson, and Casinos out of Cincinnati may have brought their bluesy R & B southbound as well. I don't recall.

The Mag 7 put a set of songs together to showcase the depth of our sound and the range of material in our catalog. Doug brought a borrowed a baritone sax along with his Selmer tenor, Carter his trombone for the evening. We featured three horns with a lot of bottom that night on a half dozen or so R & B songs. John Page moved to lead guitar. I played bass on the Hammond. A three-horn brass section was polished in Memorial Hall that September.

The Mag 7 sounded big in that room.

We gave them a one hour, near nonstop ride that evening with confidence. "In the Midnight Hour," "634-5789," "Monkey Time," "I've Been Loving You Too Long," "Respect," "I Can't Turn You Loose," "Night Train," and "Try Me" delivered a clear message to the council and others. For the money, you can't beat the Mag Seven for your next affair. We closed our set with "Stubborn Kind of Fellow."

Solid performances by other Lexington bands representing Cecil Jones Entertainment, Louisville, and Cincinnati made five nights memorable. The council learned their fraternities and sororities were engaging professional, high-quality entertainment at a fair rate. Our engagements became more frequent. I believe the five nights in Memorial Hall was instrumental.

Music flourished that week in between studies on campus.

The Mag 7 put more space between each of us on Memorial Hall's big stage. Memorial Hall made you feel good and sound big. This was our finest hour to this point in time. Many photographs were taken of the band over the years. Not being seen in the one someone took of the Mag 7 in Memorial Hall is the one I miss the most.

We were dressed in our concert attire and put a lot of space between each other on Memorial's big stage. My B and I were just beyond the edge of a camera's lens.

There, at the edge of a panorama, I knew the silence of anonymity once again.

The echo of a moment is the only thing between anyone and a long ago. I'm on thin ice. It's now, and time's breath is like a veil between where I am and, too often anymore, where I might rather be. The silent noise is played again on the very wind that lives to keep my porch swing in its motion.

The sweet, sweet arc that it is a song is beyond measure.

—~—

No one really understood what was blowing in the wind. The beginnings of change were sensed all around the watchtower. We entertained the SAEs, Thetas, PKAs and Chi Omegas at The Circle H on the banks of the Kentucky River on the ninth.

From my notes— "Stubborn Kind of Fellow sounded the best ever."

The Mag 7 enjoyed being a small part of the experience in venues like the Circle H, Danceland, Palms, Club 68, and Flamingo Club. There's a self-defining art form in each style of dance. I like the ones easy in their way. They give you time to think about your next move. Some songs, you never want to end. It is the innocent and forever "Love Without Mercy" Leroy Parnell kind of tempo that won't let you go. The Circle H and Danceland are reminders of so many nights we played while others danced the hours away. How could it get much better? They brought out our best. An afternoon at the Circle H in October was delicious.

We had dinner at the Circle H before leaving for Maysville to entertain 400 at the Tom Browning Boys Club. Fork, knife, and spoon on diner ceramicware were a soundtrack, the momentary intermission music for seven in a band. Catfish, hushpuppies and slaw, steaks and baked potato, with sour cream and butter, were on the menu that autumn. We washed them all down with iced water and sweet tea in clear glasses, chilled.

The Mag 7 was on the edge of heaven. So near we could taste it.

My first writer royalty statement from Atlantic's Cotillion Publishing House arrived in the post October 1. I learned our record sales had satisfied all Dial/Atlantic production, marketing, and distribution costs. Songwriters, like Oliver Twist, wait their time deep in the line of others to be fed. The times are often long for writers.

Sad of eye, we hold our empty bowl and hope.

"Stubborn Kind of Fellow" continued its bubble under the Top 100 on Billboard for a while. As time and the rivers of our own, the record eventually began to ebb away. Though we had not charted in *Billboard's* Top 100 Songs, seven sang in the sunshine.

Embrace all you can when you come that close. The wind blows and with it one's moment is adrift, only to fall to its rest somewhere, long to be forgotten. Warmed by the sun in the last of its days, a butterfly's tired wings lay still, and an echo is born.

Its own.

A concert notice, for the following weekend, appeared in *The Kentucky Kernel*, Wednesday, October 13, 1965. It read:

THE FOUR PREPS
Will NOT Be in
CARNEGIE HALL
October 16
They Will Be Here!
SATURDAY, OCTOBER 16
8:00 P.M. AT MEMORIAL COLISEUM
Tickets $2.00-$2.50 at the door
Available at Kennedy Book Store-Graves-Cox-
Dawahare's-Barney Miller's

I recalled their UK concert and two of the four with us at the SAE house, March 1963.

Not this time.

We were on another stage in Ashland at Paul Blazer High. I heard "Stubborn Kind of Fellow" on my way home on Boston's WBZ for the first time. I had heard our song on others. WLS in Chicago and Nashville's WLAC were two.

—⁓—

Listening to "Stubborn Kind of Fellow" on a 50,000-watt station in New Orleans is my keeper for always. The one I had waited for all night was being played in a bayou town. I just happened to end the wait by moving the dial on my radio. The place less traveled on the analog world of a radio's dial is life-changing. I was moving the dial on my own. Dial was moving the Magnificent 7. Buddy Killen had reason to be happy. October had been a good month for us all.

We played UK's Homecoming Dance on October 29 at the Student Center Grand Ballroom, breaking the attendance record for that room. The large room, adjacent to the ballroom, was opened. "Stubborn Kind of Fellow" was more popular on campus than we ever could have imagined.

—ʍ—

We played in Cardinal Valley Park on the thirtieth, and after, some of us went to hear a combo appearing at a nightspot in Gardenside. The Camelot booked good bands at the time, most passing through town, some of them jazz combos. The Chuck Peters Trio, from Philadelphia, featured a fine singer, Barbara Roman. She later joined the Glenn Miller Orchestra as its featured vocalist. The trio remains one of the most polished small combos I've ever heard. Instrumentals were tight, well-played by guitarist named Rudy Troccoli, a complete Hammond B3 player, and drummer Chuck Peters.

Barbara was a songbird.

I remember seeing Rudy on NBC's *Hullabaloo*, the popular weekly entertainment variety program. I believe he may have been a member of the studio band providing music for the show. Rudy's Gibson L-model guitar was wide as Moon River and mellow. Guitarist John Pizzarelli is a reminder of Troccoli's style.

The B3 player held a degree in electrical engineering from Syracuse. I don't recall his name. He asked how it came to be. His interest in seeing a smaller version of his Hammond B3 prompted my invitation to come see. He liked to tinker, confident an L-100 could be more than itself. I took the afternoon away from class the next day. He stopped by the house in the afternoon.

"I can improve the tone." He made some homegrown adjustments in the percussion section of my L-100 and changed out its vacuum tubes. I bought an extra boost section from a circuit he had designed for his own Hammond B3. He installed it that afternoon.

I listened. He played. The sound of my L-100 was bigger than before. Living in it was the delicious persuasive percussive tone characteristic with Hammond's M3 and B3 models. He left uncommon pieces of tomorrow in my keeping, an ebony Hammond B3-style cabinet with an L-100 parked inside sounding like something in between the two and its player.

—ꟿ—

Clay Gentry Arena on Angliana Avenue was a room inside a stockyard, unique as the event held there on November 6, the Beaux Arts Ball. Beaux Arts was an annual event presented by the College of Architecture. Two of the band's members were studying architecture. Who better to bring art, music, and architecture— all of it—to Beaux Arts than the Mag Seven?

Beaux Arts was a costume ball. John and I went to the Beaux Arts Ball as members of a rhythm and blues band that year. This was the first of two consecutive Beaux Arts Balls we were engaged to play at UK.

Clay Gentry Arena had an interesting history. A venue where country music artists frequently appeared since the mid-fifties. Local country artists Esco Hankins and Stan Corman performed there often. Esco sang, "Lies and Alibis" with Jackie, and Lexington had an Opry of its own. Bigger stars George Jones and Lefty Frizzell appeared in this galaxy on Angliana. A room in a stockyard was not the usual kind place for the Mag Seven to play, the Beaux Arts Ball not your usual party.

We played the Beaux Arts again the following year in a tobacco warehouse on Angliana nine till one. All were treated after hours to a uniqueness found in the bluest of bluegrass: J.D. Crowe and the Kentucky Mountain Boys. J.D.'s popular bluegrass group appeared regularly at Martin's Bar on North Lime, near Seventh Street. Bluegrass played in the Bluegrass didn't get much better. He passed the hat; you gave back, a plain and simple kind of cover charge. Everybody helping everyone else, that's how bluegrass works. Zydeco north, bluegrass is friendly music.

Bathed in plain truth with a language all its own.

They became J.D. Crowe and the New South in a later edition playing four sets, six nights a week, at Holiday Inn North on Newtown in the seventies. J.D.'s Lemco album took him all the way from Martin's on North Lime to Japan. A night in Clay Gentry Arena at a stockyard was in between. The clock had turned one hour past midnight, ours had ended. It was J.D.'s turn to put his kind of polish on Blue.

The Mag 7 Band and J. D. Crow & Co. on the same bill, near opposite sides of midnight, was music uniquely presented. In a mirror that is the Beaux Arts Ball. True artists need little else. J.D. is the consummate mentor, a humble player. He's faced letting go of folks like Ricky Skaggs, Keith Whitley, Doyle Lawson, Tony Rice, and Jerry Douglas. He sidestepped the loss of enormous talent; others accepted the space he gave to grow. Recognition of genuine truth, too often, is elusive.

—w—

Mickey Levy, a member of Alpha Gamma Delta sorority, is pictured as one of fourteen great-looking candidates for the 1965 "Miss Christmas Seal" in the *Kentucky Kernel* student newspaper, Wednesday, November 10, 1965, page 8. It was nice to see a former member of the Temptashuns doing well in the life of a university and its community.

—w—

December began on the road, invited to show again by Tom Browning in Maysville. I began to study for finals at the university, completing my design studio project for its juried presentation and other class studies. I hoped my 19th Century Art History class would never end. Art, its history in a dynamic century, and my professor fit together well. He shared his passion for teaching. I sensed a presence reminiscent of Miss Ruth Mathews.

He filled a wooden box of slides with styles and colors, subtly and splash, and the chances taken by others in their lifetime. The delicate sound of images on slides sheathed in glass made, one against the other, signaled he was on his way from his office down the hall.

Art is never-ending in showing itself to us. What were his choices today: Monet, Degas, Turner, Manet, Van Gogh . . . who? The fog of his insecurity went its way once an image met a white screen of tiny dust-like pristine beads of glass. Uncertainty left the room. Shadows overtaken by reflected light on a face mirrored a mentor more confident with each slide.

He wanted us to love . . . True Romance.

Craft, without one's senses to love, is nothing.

She is in the life of creative expression. Impressionism is my favorite period. An Impressionist's eyes, the composer's ear, the silent notions in a mind are shaped by the space where nothing appears to be. Ballet and sculpture breathe because of negative space.

A breeze is the gentle engine of an Alexander Calder piece. The shape of space is never the same in the midair waltz of form. What was nothing becomes the poetic motion of space, ever-changing, a work of art. The bounty of the in between knows no measure. Space between what has been written and written next is at the soul of what a story is. In a ballet of words, space means everything. Calder is art that works, the measure of something meaningful.

Edward Hopper saw motion in still life.

Fall semester ended.

—∞—

I met her in a painting class we were taking in the UK's Fine Arts building. We had our first date December 2 after an afternoon jam session for Delta Zeta sorority in the Student Center Grand Ballroom.

I took her home.

Nancy and I began a relationship that would continue to this day.

The Mag Seven resumed play in December at the Lexington Country Club on the tenth. We shared the night, and its stars on a painted sky, in Spindletop Hall's Louisiana Room on the eleventh.

—∞—

Mrs. Preston Madden entertained guests on the seventeenth for a special Christmas party at the Iroquois Hunt Club on Grimes Mill Road. Mrs. Madden engaged the band to provide her music. Anita Madden, always a most gracious host, knew how to entertain in a special way.

The Magnificent 7 were fortunate to have been a part of her entertainment on two such occasions. A guest of Mrs. Madden on that evening was rumored to be the "Black Velvet" Scotch girl for that year, can't say that to be true. I do recall she could've been the girl for any year in velvet.

Mrs. Madden invited the band to visit a Waterford Crystal bowl, a cut glass boat on a sea of fresh, crisp white linen in the harbor of the Iroquois. An invitation by a lady to another, elegant, shimmering glass, filled to the brim with boiled shrimp, impeccably chilled on ice, and waiting to be taken in a shower of cocktail sauce. Anita's unforgettable style. Priceless.

"Enjoy, help yourself to all you want." Shrimp, peeled and delicious; country ham; and buttered biscuits carried to the heart of me on a stream of tasty punch. It was so nice to be in from the cold. Such is the style of an unforgettable host.

Anita Madden and the Hunt Club, in a bluegrass kind of setting out in the country, was style painted on the soon-to-be enchanting season of winter unlike any other. Her own.

Merry Christmas, everyone.

—ꝏ—

We traveled to Somerset on the eighteenth to entertain the Ambers dance at the Hotel Beecher, then again to Ashland's Paul Blazer High on the twenty-third.

—ꝏ—

We were on the road north to Ohio on Christmas Eve to entertain the debutantes of Cincinnati. The annual dance was held at the elegant Cincinnati Country Club in Hyde Park. The Magnificent 7 alternated with another band of fine players in the afternoon from four until eight. The Charlie Kehrer Orchestra was high society in Cincinnati in those days. They had followed Stan Kenton's Orchestra in Cincinnati's Coney Island Amusement Park in September 1959.

The debutantes were treated to two versions of Buddy Morrow's "Night Train," one from the orchestra, another from the Mag 7 band. Compatible contrasts played on the eve of Christmas, fine tastes for the appetites of the social set.

We presented the only version of Henry Mancini's "Peter Gunn" that evening. "Slaughter on Tenth Avenue;" a horn figure, was carefully placed in another tune. Another, from Jimmy Smith's "Who's Afraid of Virginia Woolf," spoke to strangers. There was more to the Mag Seven than rhythm and blues. We sounded so fine, looking formal in an elegant setting.

I returned to Lexington on a snowy evening, stopping by to give Nancy her Christmas gift, Chanel's No.5.

We had two days off followed by gigs at Winchester Country Club on the twenty-seventh, the Country Club in Paris the twenty-eighth, and Lexington's Idle Hour Country Club the twenty-ninth.

—᧙—

One of two places to go is all you're given in Harlan County when you have an off-road experience, beyond the edge into an unforgiving piece of empty space or the side of a mountain. We were staying the night in Harlan's Mount Aire Motel. The band was invited to attend an after-dance party. Three of seven, near half the band, had gone to attend the party. John Page's Oldsmobile Cutlass got into a spin. John went to the mountain. John, Doug, and Carter were okay. Larry Orr had returned to Lexington earlier with a friend who had driven him up. Three of us decided to remain at the motel, needing rest. The delicate balance of life moved perilously in the house of time. An object left a highway.

I called Cecil Jones. Our next engagement, a New Year's affair, waited in Kenova, West Virginia, near Charleston. We left John's badly damaged car behind to be repaired. The journey in a few hours was long one for six by Cadillac. The road ahead wasn't to be kind, leaving Harlan early the next morning after Johnny arranged to get his car fixed.

Six players, a band, and its gear packed in a long black Cadillac left Harlan County alive.

Overnight's sleep put the hours ago in their place. The old road from Harlan to Kenova was long, the air cold. The owners of the Ashland's Moonlite Gardens, hosting the dance in Kenova, learned about the accident from Cecil. We phoned ahead to say we were on our way and would be late. I don't recall where.

The dance was held in Kenova's National Guard Armory. We performed on a portable stage halfway up telescoping wooden bleachers, the old-school kind. We began a year-ending four-hour show with Doug's sax intro and Junior Walker's classic "Shotgun." The Mag Seven opened the door for all there into the New Year with "Auld Lang Syne." We took the circus down at 2:00 a.m. and loaded out for the long road home. Faces of six of my closest friends looked the same as my own.

We were a tired bunch of players.

The year had ended with a stark reminder how quickly all we were experiencing could vanish. The fragile nature, life's hidden secret, can elude anyone young, and we were young.

My friends and the things around us all made this time in the life of the band the rich experience that it was. We were close. One of the others drove the Cadillac home.

It was way past midnight in Montgomery.

I spent the first hours of the new year deep asleep in the back seat of a white sedan, a Jaguar, in a heavy snowstorm. A new leather scent found my senses, like echoes in a dream. I was in it, under its British Leyland spell. One of an MG in 1959.

Unlike Hank Williams, I was in a different kind of car in a different state in a much different state of mind. Such is time's everlasting imagery. Snowflakes were all about in cold dark skies changing places.

Windblown.

The scene was surreal, born in a Turner painting, a white Jaguar sedan in a blinding snowstorm struggling to free itself. On the wall of my mind, a dream painted an impressionistic portrait of an escape.

From what I didn't know.

The random whisper of snowflakes held in an ever-growing snowstorm welcomed me to the driveway where I lived. I sensed a fresh new piece of opportunity waiting there. In winter, on a New Year's Day, there's the essence of a bride. She wears the gown of a new beginning. She sings a sweet, sweet song. All is white around her, and the notes keep falling.

I wish, I may—I wish, I might, know what is in the note's tonight.

11
Claim Ticket, 1966

1966. I was twenty-four. Some were being called Flower Children. The miniskirt made its debut. A hemline seven inches above the knee and love was all you needed or so it seemed. Things were definitely looking up. Sandy Koufax won twenty-seven games and announced his retirement. *Sounds of Silence* was a best-selling album.

If it was rhythm and the bluest of soul in 1966, we were playing it.

Half all television sets sold were color, *Batman* a new show about a couple of guys in a nifty car. Route 66 was nowhere to be found on Gotham City's map. The Joker, Riddler, and Penguin were perfect for color television. "Holy dark side, Batman." Elizabeth Taylor was outspoken in *Who's Afraid of Virginia Woolf*. Best Actress would be hers the following year. Elizabeth Taylor was a portrait in white in *Cat on a Hot Tin Roof*. She was sophistication in silk, a night woman to a fragile Lawrence Harvey in *Butterfield 8*. Willie Mays earned $125,000. LBJ said we would stay. The war went on.

Lies kept pounding rhythm to the brain.

What tapestry would seven threads weave in a time of social conscience? It began at Bryan Station High, a dance in the gym. The Mag Seven sounded fine, appearing in concert with the Chiffons on the twenty-first for the Gold Digger's Ball in the Student Center Grand Ballroom. We backed the Chiffons on their hits "He's so Fine," "One Fine Day," and others. "Stubborn Kind of Fellow" was moving well in local Top 40 charts, entering the Top 10 on the WLAP Billy Love Survey on January 22.

We were in the SAE house on the twenty-second, the KAs the following night. We played for a dance at Lexington Catholic High, the twenty-eighth, an afternoon jam session in UK's Student Center Ballroom for the Army ROTC and Phi Gamma Delta fraternity at the Phi Delt house, the twenty-ninth. January ended on the road to Trinity High in St. Matthews. It was good to be in Louisville again.

Memorable appearances in February included an event at UK's Prestonsburg campus on the eleventh. The Mag Seven sounded our best at Xavier University in Cincinnati on the eighteenth. We brought our music to the high school in Stanford, Kentucky, the following night. The customary after-dance invitation for early breakfast at the home of a hospitable Stanford family was accepted. We were grateful. It wasn't the first time for the band to have a meal in Stanford.

Small towns are warm, their food delicious, their ways kind.

The girls of Alpha Gamma Rho favored "Stubborn Kind of Fellow" the following weekend, Friday the twenty-fifth, a jam session in the afternoon at their house. We played at Henry Clay hours later till midnight. Four hours in Cardinal Valley on the twenty-sixth ended February.

March began at Kappa Alpha fraternity on the fourth. The Mardi Gras Dance for UK's student body, featured the best of our sets in the Student Center Grand Ballroom on the fifth. Teens danced to the music of The Mag 7 at Tates Creek and Henry Clay Highs on the eleventh and seventeenth. They wanted to hear "Stubborn Kind of Fellow." Young voices sang along with the band, their mind made up about us, it seemed.

"In Mist and Rain" enjoyed a place in the sun. Our live performances and unexpected play "Mist" was getting on UK's Student Center Grill jukebox let it be so. These were the warmest of times, being in the sun. All I needed to keep writing.

March 19, 1966. The Magnificent 7 played an afternoon jam session at Centre College in Danville. We were scheduled to play again that evening, nine till one at Delta Kappa Epsilon fraternity on Centre's campus. The DEKE house was an unpredictable bunch of party time. The Mag Seven was set up in the basement of the fraternity. Before beginning our first set began, it was suggested all go watch the final game of the NCAA basketball tournament at the Sigma Chi house. A reprise was momentary. The hope we could watch the game, load out, and go home a momentary lapse of reason.

The Kentucky Wildcats took the floor of the Cole Field House on the campus of the University of Maryland in College Park that night in March.

The Mag Seven had taken the floor of another stage another time not so long before then, engaged one autumn afternoon last November to play an always special moment in the life of the university. It was an honor to share the same stage with Coach Rupp, this special team, UK's cheerleaders, and the moment with the student body.

Seven hundred had come to meet a fine, fine basketball team and dance to soul music.

The Magnificent 7 were the entertainment for the affair. Few have the distinction of sharing the hope for another national championship just once in their college years. This was our second consecutive year to be a part of the annual introduction of the basketball team to the student body. The student body had gathered to meet their team in UK's Student Center's Grand Ballroom on campus. Being on the outskirts in the halo of a spotlight shining on the tradition of that afternoon is light that never dims.

Coach Rupp introduced his boys, "Rupp's Runts," as they've come to be known.

Tonight, we were on another in another town on another campus. Seven months of separation.

We had been as close to this team in November as the referee, about to toss the ball at center circle. I knew Pat Riley would get the tip; Larry Conley would set one of Coach Rupp's classic patterns in motion, orchestrated well. Louie Dampier, Tommy Kron, or Thad Jaracz would get the pass, score, and make it all look easy. Like a Derby winner.

March 19, 1966. Kentucky versus a team from out in the West Texas town of El Paso. The game, considered by many a milestone in college basketball, was a forty-minute, two-act play, white and black keys, sharp, flat, and natural. Ten players could augment or diminish the chord and shape the tone of the song. The song played in Maryland was sad.

Kentucky 65, Texas Western 72.

Choreography was played in time, in between and through the lines of a game. It was not to be. We played all the songs everybody wanted to hear at the DEKE house late into the night.

"If we had won, the story would have been commonplace."[48]

I drove on a trail of tears from Danville that night, taking time to let the team get back home before I did. I didn't stop in Shakertown. The hour was late. My friend was sad of eye on the sky that night. I never knew the moon, like the summer wind, to be fickle.

The Magnificent 7 finished March with exceptional performances, beginning in UK's Student Center's Grand Ballroom for UK's Donovan and other men's residence halls on the twenty-fifth. We sounded big again in the Phoenix Hotel's Convention Hall for Parker Seal Company after a brass-filled jam session the following afternoon for the ZTA's at the sorority the twenty-sixth.

—ꟾ—

'Thanks for inviting me into your homes and into your cars—but what are we doin' way out here?' 'If you're a Billy Love fan, you undoubtedly recognize the sign off slogan and you probably know Lexington's biggest DJ will bounce out of town Saturday for a new job in a new city. . . Billy's moving far away—Orlando Fla.—and just as far up—from a 5000 watts station to a 50,000 watter. . .' His 7:30-till-midnight show on WLAP Monday through Saturday is a refreshing production that equals top-notch programs in big radio markets...He uses his three-year experience at UK on his show to better cater to the college student. . . 'After the young kids go to bed, I play rhythm and blues and folk. I don't dare play a Dylan song before 10.'

His last show Saturday night, he'll play some of the hit songs popular in the past one and a half years he's had the show. One of his favorites is the song he uses to close out the program, and which provides background for the quip about parking. It's Autumn Love by the former Temptashuns, now The Magnificent Seven.[49]

The Billy Love Show was enormously popular with the college audience. Billy Herald was a genuine friend to the band.

—ꟾ—

Seven Henry Clay seniors wanted to be the Magnificent Seven in the school's annual "Student Night" program. The girls did a pantomime of "Stubborn Kind of Fellow," as the Mag Seven.

We were unable to attend but understand they were entertaining.

—ꟾ—

The Mag Seven returned to Lemco studio for a private recording session. We were engaged to record Lerner and Loewe's "Gigi" by a client of Cecil's, the family of a Lexington debutante. Invited guests attending a debutante party in 1966 at Idle Hour Country Club were given a copy by the family. Lerner and Loewe represented some of the finest music in America. I worked with Doug on an arrangement blending Broadway and our way. A single order for several hundred records was made, "Gigi" b/w "Stubborn Kind of Fellow." Copies of this record are rare.

She was one of the debutantes, pictured in the *Lexington Herald* newspaper, to be presented at the Blue Grass Charity Ball on June 17.

Debutante and family were happy. We placed rhythm and blues carefully, like flowers in the vase of America's great songbook. The arrangement stayed true to Frederick Loewe's melody. We added the spice of Muscle Shoals in refreshing figures played by our own horn section. The taste was good. It was the best we had to offer young sophisticated ladies of high society.

April arrived and in it a whisper of great expectations. Having become uncommon, how and where we had arrived seemed to be a mirage on a long ago. The quality of our own look, moves, and sound was more polished. Our confidence in each other mirrored the style of a show band we were fast becoming. We seemed to be coming to a place of unexpected ever-growing demands on the band and its members more and more anymore.

We traveled to Bowling Green, had steaks at the Branding Iron, before driving by Pauline's on our way to the hill. Pauline was Bowling Green's hospitable madame. Her establishment, a house, was located at 627 Clay Street. We were on the hill again to entertain the student body at Western Kentucky State College, now Western Kentucky University.

Western became one of my favorite places to play over the years. Bowling Green was Carter's hometown. It was more to me than Duncan Hines and Western Hills and pretty coeds. Western had its mind made up about us. It seemed at Western we were more than seven players and soul music at a campus on the hill at College Street.

The town was personal, I guess.

Memories packed away, one more for the Forever Road east back to Lexington.

We played in the Paul Garrett ballroom on the second floor. It seemed, when time came around for a Sadie Hawkins dance, Western's student body wanted the Temptashuns or Magnificent 7 to be their band. We spent the night at the McBroom Motel, down the road beyond the Barren River, on the outside of town. The next day heading out of Bowling Green on 31W, the Dixie Highway, I recall wanting to turn back, to head for Nashville, sixty or so miles away. Would an echo go that far?

Though we were reaping a harvest of something planted in fertile ground, I missed a time when it all was new. Fresh. Long since yesterday, it seemed we were becoming kind of big.

Such is the music business.

The Mag 7 played the Southland Hop the following weekend at Southland Pool and Campbell House Inn for Lafayette's Rex Club the following evening. The band left for Louisville the next day, a Sunday, to do a show in Freedom Hall, nine till one for the Podiceps Club of Bellarmine-Ursuline Colleges, a well-attended private event. Compensation, to do what we loved doing, began to reflect the benefit in having a record out that was doing quite well regionally.

I heard "Stubborn Kind of Fellow" again on WBZ, Boston. The song still had life out there. Other nights, the search in the glow on the radio dial in my car brought it all near me from far away: WLS, Chicago, WLAC in Nashville, and other powerhouses in Detroit and St. Louis.

John R. played the one I had been waiting for all night one night. I had heard the echo.

We were in the Student Center Ballroom on the fifteenth for Alpha Gamma Delta sorority's jam session and a spring affair at Sayre, an exclusive private school in town. The buildings and grounds were old, drenched in history like something from a novel. I felt the touch of John Knowles and separate pieces everywhere.

Many questions were parked on my mind. I had no answers for some of them.

April 16, 1966. I arrived at a watershed. A pair of polished metal doors opened at Memorial Coliseum around 11:00 a.m. The Avenue of Champions was a lonely avenue this time of day. The street, paved with a past, laid in between bookends: Stoll Field, where Coach Paul "Bear" Bryant fielded bowl-winning football in the late forties and early fifties, and Memorial Coliseum, home of Adolph F. Rupp's winning basketball team.

Memorial Coliseum began as a facility dedicated to veterans of World Wars I and II, and the Korean War from Kentucky who had given their lives for our freedom. The names of all Veterans from Kentucky who died in The Vietnam War were later added. Once there was a life. The price paid by each soul lost on Memorial's walls is beyond measure. Collectively, they represented unimaginable sacrifice.

They would forever be the first and the most lasting stars in this heaven of a building.

Memorial Coliseum was the house that wins and Coach Adolph Frederick Rupp built in 1951 for 11,500 people and two teams to play a game. We had brought our music here before on another night in March 1964 for more than 5,000.

It was good to be back in the room again. The Coliseum was a place for winners.

Today would be a defining moment for the Magnificent 7.

House lights were down, floor seating in its place. The whole of me was embraced by a single letter, a block K, a white one in a deep blue circle. Bound in a white ring on an ocean of varnished wood. Center circle in Memorial Coliseum was to me the center of basketball's universe. Kentucky's team picture was taken around the K, year by year. The faces changed from time to time.

The K, always there, never a question of what it meant or who it represented.

I was there at the place where, just before a game began, eyes of those attending and countless minds beyond the glow of a radio's face were to be found. Tonight, eyes would be focused on the band.

The Mag Seven would know how good a chance can be.

The Coliseum was hallowed ground, Kentucky basketball's home court. He walked over to me. I expected to be told to take my Hammond organ and that black Cadillac sitting out front and leave. Adolph F. Rupp, in his office on Saturday morning, wanted to know who I was and what I was doing in his house. "We have a big game to play tonight, Coach. The biggest one we've ever played." If Coach Rupp said anything at all to me that morning, it surely must have been, "Make sure you win."

The campus end of the Coliseum was dressed in a long stage, from sideline to sideline. Daylight found its way softly through tall panels of glass block units in glazed masonry openings above the Coliseum's main entrance. Glass units have a near prism-like quality defining the essence of light itself. Memorial Coliseum was a space with personality. Light in it was natural and subdued then.

I had seen Ray Charles perform on this stage in 1961. I saw others, too, while at UK, including Stan Getz and Dionne Warwick; The Fifth Dimension; Peter, Paul and Mary; Nancy Wilson; Brothers Four; Andy Williams and Roger Miller; Henry Mancini; Isaac Stern; and Peter Nero. Anthropologist Margaret Mead and other speakers told their stories on this stage. They touched the face of the sixties.

We were the Temptashuns when we told our own once before during Kentucky's State High School Basketball Tournament. Once is an honor in this place. The second time around, beyond words.

The serenity of Memorial Coliseum was defined by a quality only light can give a big room. We began an efficient staging of instruments, amps, and other gear for the sound check.

The Coliseum's sound engineer arrived to lower house microphones from the ceiling. He mixed and amplified sound from our own, sending it to the Coliseum's distinctive sound system. The taping of the concert by the Rocket Boys would've turned out better had they had been permitted to set the levels of their personal taping machine. Levels of our sound check were compatible with the house sound only. Regretfully, the Rocket Boys' tape, its audio quality, and the years could not save it from harm's way.

The Student Center Board had graciously included the Mag Seven band in the Little Kentucky Derby Concert, also featuring Chuck Berry, the Shirelles, and the Coasters in Memorial Coliseum. LKD was billed as "America's Biggest College Weekend," and at the time, it probably was. Peter, Paul and Mary had performed the previous year, 1965. Henry Mancini was a year away, in 1967. We were in between. I wondered if, after we were on the same stage with the stars, would folks still love us tomorrow?

When tonight was over, would there be magic in their sighs?

The band planned to meet around noon, load in, and do a sound check. Artists headlining the concert were scheduled in the afternoon for our brief encounter with their concert material. The Magnificent Seven were the opening act on the program and the concert's backup band for the evening. Chuck Berry, The Shirelles, and Coasters, the stars appearing, didn't come out that afternoon. We would be performing in a few short hours with each of them, unrehearsed.

The opening set was ours.

Two weeks were spent in rehearsal between studies, at the house on Rose where some in the band lived near the Paddock Bar. We learned the hits of legends. Collectively, their material was extensive, the songs making music history. The Mag Seven rehearsed our concert set to its best. We took some time of our own winding down where Euclid and Rose collide in the Paddock.

The Mag Seven was heard by a lot of people on our own home floor. Memorial Coliseum was good to us that evening; *Billboard* magazine was there. Chuck Berry and others headlined this particular concert. Maybe something about the performance of the Magnificent 7 would deserve comment. *Billboard* remembered us along with the stars in a subsequent issue with a nice piece. We were there again in the most important trade publication in the record business.

It was not unusual for performers traveling the oldies circuit to play with house bands or hastily assembled pickup groups. Chuck Berry is notorious for arriving minutes before Showtime, collecting his nightly fee, then alternately sleepwalking or duck walking through his set. . . .[50]

UK's concert coordinator told me, offstage, that Chuck Berry had arrived from Blue Grass Field. I was ushered to meet with him in his dressing room. Concern about an afternoon rehearsal that never was, I kept inside, eased by a legend's smile.

By spring of 1966, Chuck Berry had already headlined some of the best rock and roll and pop music acts with "Mr. Rock and Roll," Alan Freed, at New York's Paramount Theater. He starred in B-movies in the fifties about teens and their music in a time of change. Chuck Berry had influenced the Beatles, even performed with them, and, only recently, returned from Europe.

Tonight was our turn.

You meet a lot of folks in music. Most are unknown, some undiscovered. Then along comes one who puts a memory on a moment. This was mine. Chuck Berry and me, a few minutes alone with a legend, rock & roll's first-ever poet, a world-class Chess player.

"Hello, Mr. Berry, I'm Tony Stallard. Welcome to the Bluegrass."

I was on thin ice, till he suggested I have a seat. A too well-traveled instrument case was open, a red Gibson ES-345 guitar in it. It seems like only yesterday. We went over a set of songs, an order to be determined another time. Little concern most likely to him—with near 4,000 guests with tickets, paid,—Waiting.

It was near "Show Time" and the splash that goes with it.

He assured me the band would do just fine, and he preferred to be spontaneous with his show. "We'll just see what happens out there. Just watch my left hand."

The Mag Seven learned Chuck Berry's set list in a fog of being frightened.

I was with Chuck Berry, away from the crowd for a few minutes. The band had learned the songs in the keys to all of Chuck Berry's greatest hits. All that was left me to do was look to the place of his hand embracing the neck of a lady in red. A legend and his Gibson had been down a long road since 1955. Two for the road.

This stop at the intersection of him and me that night was a moment I would never forget. Chuck Berry put on his cuff links, telling me he planned to come and see our opening set. We shook hands.

A handshake ended the experience of a lifetime.

I left for the stage and the band with a piece of paper in my hand, the secrets of a random harvest. Moments after our concert-opening set, the Mag Seven Band would back a legend-to-be on any of the hits he wanted to do. We knew them all. I started learning from Chuck Berry in 1959 on the highway to a Stratocaster, on my way to a Hammond organ. My inner sense signaled the nearness of thirty minutes of the best of this band. The house lights dimmed.

We were at time's door. We opened it, stepped through, and came of age.

Tommy "Little Bee" Wallace, WLAP radio personality, was the master of ceremonies for the evening. Little Bee, as his father Cal before him had done in the fifties, played some of the best R & B around here, on the FM side of WLAP radio.

We gathered with him momentarily offstage before quietly making our way in the darkness to our instruments. Tommy Wallace stood ready to introduce seven to about 4,000.

Act I

Little Bee began, "Ladies and Gentlemen, the Student Center Board of the University of Kentucky welcomes you to the 1966 Little Kentucky Derby Concert of Stars. It is my pleasure tonight to present a band who is no stranger to you: The Magnificent Seven."

A 120-foot column of pure white energy raced the darkness. We were bathed at the speed of it in its warmth. The Mag Seven filled the room with our sound. The audience, though hidden in darkness, was witness that something special had just begun. The Mag Seven delivered a thirty-minute set, a program of our best, at its best. We signed our name on the night.

Presenting who we were and our sound at its best.

We were a show band smartly dressed in our finest. Our look and sound mirrored the concert setting of the event. We looked like Manhattan. Seven pieces of Jackie Wilson: burgundy slacks and jackets, white-pleated formal shirts with French cuffs, cuff links, black continental ties, and polished black boots. The Magnificent 7 sounded big and welcomed the applause with a smile.

Applause sounds different in a room that big. You don't forget it.

John Page and Carter mirrored the choreography of Doug and Johnny Burrows. Larry Orr was motion personified. Meade put down a solid R & B beat. I sat at a Hammond organ, one looking and sounding like the baby brother of the mighty Hammond B3. I had the keys to a Formula One machine, frightened yet calm, immersed in the sounds of a Leslie speaker.

The stage was epic, a frontier, and we put lots of land between us. We looked big, not fenced in by convention. Other acts watched from the wings. Our day had come, and we put our signature on "Respect," "Don't Fight It," "I Can't Turn You Loose," "In the Midnight Hour," and "Satisfaction." We closed our set with a James Brown's "Night Train."

Before the last note left the room, "Little Bee" addressed the audience, "Ladies and gentlemen, let's have a big round of applause for the Magnificent 7, Lexington's own Magnificent 7."

Act II

Little Bee introduced Chuck Berry. His amp developed a problem before he could begin the end of the line for a museum piece. I welcomed him to use my own. Got a glance, a smile, and a thank you. Chuck Berry was a star who needed a little help from friends to get by. The lifeline that ran from Chuck Berry's Gibson guitar to my Fender Vibrasonic amp was my connection to Chuck Berry.

A lifeline for a lifetime.

We began with his classic "School Days," playing behind an artist considered the first guitarist of rock and roll. We were unaware of anyone else in the place at that moment.

The Mag Seven played rock & roll, Chuck Berry and Chess Records' music and lyric as if we had been with him from "Maybelline." A student body and more were on a night out to school learning the Golden Rule and rock and roll from Professor Chuck Berry. He put folks in Memorial Coliseum with no particular place to go on time's echo back to 1957. A legend delivered us all from the night we were in.

The Poet Laureate of Rock & Roll finished his show, took a bow. He turned and smiled, unplugged his Gibson from my Fender amp, thanked the band. "Nice job, fellows."

He went away. We never saw him again.

We really wanted to back the Shirelles that night. The Shirelles, named for the lead singer, were Shirley Owens, Beverly Lee, Doris Kenner, and Mickey Harris. The girls put Scepter Records on the map of popular music, recording some of the best songs penned by songwriters in the shadow of the Brill Building, including Don Kirchner's kids.

Sadly, the Shirelles brought their own tour band, the Soul Rockers. A chance was not to be tonight, down the road someday, perhaps.

I was handed a note that read, "I'm sorry, but we brought our own band. Hope you're not disappointed. Shirley." Shirley Owens had broken a heart. I put the note from the group's namesake in my pocket. We never knew she was bringing her own. The girls were terrific in their sequined gowns; their smiles and lipstick and high heel shoes, all things one could ever imagine. She turned. "Baby, it's you." I'm thinking, "Can't be, not me." Where the dream of sequined gowns on young ladies comes from is a lover's question.

The Magnificent 7 backed the Shirelles near the Jersey Shore, during a northeast-to-southeastern swing early in the seventies. Dreams do come true.

Act III

We stood in the light again. Little Bee introduced the Coasters. Lead singer Carl Gardener and his friends were a West Coast blend of vintage casual conversation and message. We backed the Coasters on all their hits: "Poison Ivy," "Young Blood," "Searchin,'" "Yakety Yak," "Along Came Jones," and "Charlie Brown." They came on like a rose bringing the fifties to Lexington one night that spring. The songs of Leiber and Stoller arrived, special delivery from Los Angeles to UK.

They clowned around in a style for which the Coasters were known. The Coasters' guitarist, their only musician, stood close enough to say, just in time. "'Searchin'' in G." I got the word to the band somehow.

We wanted to end the evening with “Stubborn Kind of Fellow.” The concert folks told us the concert had gone past long. It wasn’t to be. The night ran out of time. We closed the concert with our take on the horn riff from James Brown’s “Think” and drove the night train home. The Magnificent 7 were good enough in the spring of 1966 to back most any entertainer UK’s Student Center Board engaged, with their music or our own, this or any other night. The light shined down on the boys in the band on a night in April.

The Mag Seven was in the spring of what we could be.

How far is far?

Leaving, late in the dark silence of Memorial Coliseum, an answer was deep in a heart in Kentucky. The other artists were on their way home. Who was richer because of the night? This one was over. I believed the magic in their sighs. I wouldn’t trade what we brought away for all the stars were given. It was 2:00 a.m., time to get my date Nancy to her house and me to my own. Chuck Berry was probably in the air on his way back to Wentzville, the Coasters and Shirelles on their way down a road to . . . somewhere.

The Magnificent Seven band was near the top of a long climb in the spring of 1966. On which watershed between the coasts of tomorrow and beyond would the sketch of one’s days to come be drawn? I felt tired, so tired. My mind fell lightly on giving endings serious thought.

—𝔪—

A review of the Little Kentucky Derby Concert appeared in the campus newspaper on April 18, 1966:

As the show started, most of the 3,500 in Memorial Coliseum Saturday night probably expected little more than the Magnificent Seven in concert. But the big-name attractions scored heavily with most, but provided little more than refreshing, nearly nostalgic relief, from today’s Beatle-type music.

From Chuck Berry’s ‘School Day’ to the Coaster’s ‘Along Came Jones,’ collegians were no doubt reminded of their own school days when those tunes were popular.

The Magnificent Seven, certainly not unknown to the jam session set, opened the show with Wilson Pickett and Otis Redding rhythm and blues soul tunes in a style that lived up to the adjective in the group's name.

The expert showmanship of Larry Orr, a UK English major coupled with the Mag Seven instrumental sound made some of the listener's remark, 'the rest of the show will have to be good to top this.' The guys didn't close with 'Stubborn Kind of Fellow,' but if they had, 'Here's the one you've waiting' for all night long' would have been appropriate.

After Respect, Don't Fight It, In The Midnight Hour and Satisfaction, The Mag Seven yielded to Chuck Berry, who squeezed that unique sound out of his magical guitar throughout his old hits. . . . The Shirelles, shaking like lime Jell-O on Meade Brown's drum heads, entertained with old rock, sock and roll favorites including Dedicated to The One I Love, Mamma Said, Tonight's the Night, (Will You Still Love Me Tomorrow) and Baby It's You. . . . Enter The Coasters. . . . Yakety Yak, Searchin', Charlie Brown and Poison Ivy.

The concert could have headlined The Righteous Brothers . . . Bill and Bob, who now have the number one song in the country according to Billboard magazine, cancelled because of TV commitments.

The three groups took home $5,500. The Mag Seven got $400, and should have been paid more and allowed to do more. This group is too good, too professional to deserve the status and frustration of a back-up band.[51]

The review was accompanied by a nice large photo by Rick Bell captioned, "The Magnificent Seven's Larry Orr sways to the soul music of Wilson Pickett's In the Midnight Hour, in the Lexington's groups part in the LKD show, held in Memorial Coliseum." A photo of Chuck Berry playing Memphis was beside it — Chuck Berry and his music living in my Fender amp, frozen in black and white.

April ended with three appearances at fraternities the following weekend. We were on the road to Huntington, West Virginia, at the Prichard Hotel for the KAs of Marshall College. The band returned to Lexington to rest before playing again at the Southland Hop the following night.

I would remember April, always.

May began on the road to Danville for a formal at Centre College, and days of finals. The first Saturday in May, the seventh, came a run for roses, the Kentucky Derby. The Mag Seven had a post time of its own the same day in Murray, Kentucky. The long road west led us to Murray State College. *Billboard* magazine was on hand once again.

—∞—

The following comments in the "Concert Review" appeared in the June 4, 1966, issue of *Billboard* magazine.

College Circuit
The Magnificent Seven at Murray State
May 7
Attendance 400
Fraternity Dance
'The group from Lexington, Kentucky
had tremendous sound.'[52]

—∞—

An engagement on May 13 in Frankfort brought us to Franklin County High for the prom. The Mag Seven set the pace for a dance at Westport High in Louisville on the fifteenth. It was good to be in the River City again.

The Fieldhouse at Morehead State College was staged for a Magnificent 7 performance on May 17. We played the following two nights at the Fireplace in Chevy Chase to a full house. Patrons waited in line beyond the door to Euclid Avenue to hear the Mag Seven play rhythm and soul.

May began its end on the twentieth with the prom at Boyle County High in Danville, returning to the Phoenix Hotel for a Junior Chamber of Commerce affair on the twenty-first. Destiny brought the Magnificent 7 to US Highway 68, the bluest of them all. The landscape of yesterday was a lady clothed in patches, wonder-filled and tied in tender ribbons. She held my hand all the way through and beyond Shakertown more than many nights.

—∞—

Telling them I was leaving the band wasn't easy. What had begun in 1959, as something quite simple, had suddenly become a business too busy for me. A once nice and easy breeze had become windy. Too much was going around in circles, and I not one to stay too long at the fair. I could've stayed through the summer. We had some exciting gigs in the coming weeks. I simply needed some time off, and someone special had come into my life. My classes, design studio in architecture, and related studies required an ever-increasing time commitment.

In my life up to 1966, this was the most painful choice I had yet to make.

I began working with Randy Evans, who the band had sought for my replacement. Randy was playing organ at the time in the Marauders, a band based in Frankfort managed by Louisville's Joni agency. I never doubted Randy would be a good fit. The Marauders were playing much the same material as we. I was confident the band had made a positive choice, and as things turned out, it was.

Randy became the organist at Market Square Arena, in Indianapolis, for Indiana Pacers Basketball down the road of years. Market Square Arena, the last place Elvis Presley performed, has since been razed.

The last picture show began in June with another prom on the sixth and Henry Clay Senior Party at the Armory on the Old Frankfort Pike for the Class of 1966 on the seventh.

Her father was a doctor. The fresh voice of Nana Mouskouri played softly on the stereo. The first weekend of June began. The Mag Seven provided music for a sorority in Danville, a private affair, in the home of one of its members.

Terry Travato, a KA and longtime friend of the band, was with us that evening, substituting for Meade on drums. Terry, an accomplished musician, had written percussion cadences for both the Kentucky and Indiana University marching bands. Terry Travato, from Louisville, played with the confidence of having been with us, always.

He was that good a player.

Saturday, May 11, 1966. Barney Miller's had one copy of Nana Mouskouri's album. I bought *Nana* and the memory before traveling to Lebanon and my last time as a player in the Magnificent 7 band at Club 68. I have it still.

—∞—

The Mag Seven Show sounded big, deep, and brass-filled then. The light from the sign played on my face a little longer. I drove away from the Club

68, for what would be the a long time until I returned. I spent a bunch of time along US Highway 68 those seven years. I never lost the feeling, falling in love all over again with an indigo dream. She had become bluer each visit to her roadside and the relics on it.

The night found me stopping here again, an appointment where eyes meet a moment and a sky full of stars mirrored on it. One last dance had been saved for me on Main Street in Shakertown.

The midnight player would forever be the delicate sound of wonder, its song a silent noise.

The Mag Seven hit the road west again to Hopkinsville, Kentucky. Tuesday, June 14, to entertain the Sub Deb Social Club. We headed north by northeast to Russell, near Ashland, for an event at the exclusive Bellefonte Country Club on the seventeenth.

Saturday, June 18, 1966. The last picture show began.

I stood in the darkness with Nancy at the back of the room. I learned a truth till then I'd only heard or read about. I was listening to one fine bunch of players. The Mag Seven had soul, about as good as it gets. You knew it from the first note.

The "door marked *nevermore*, that wasn't there before," had opened. I felt "how strange the change from major to minor"[53] can be. Goodbye found its time. —From words inspired by lyrics from Johnny Mercer in Henry Mancini's "The Days of Wine and Roses" and Cole Porter's "Ev'ry Time We Say Goodbye."

The Holiday Inn East, Lexington.

8:30-11:30

End.

A garden in the rain, I was there before she came along; then the sun came out again.

I left the Magnificent Seven in the summer of 1966 with mixed emotions, a fresh relationship, and architecture. Summer was the space I needed to consider the possibilities that would shape the rest of my life.

Gardens in the rain—isn't what this has been about all along?

Time passed. Blue-colored ribbons changed to ones I found looking back to what was, and is for me, a simple place. My separate peace rests on the last echo I will ever hear.

12
Epilogue

1966. Summer's time. I could be found "down by the banks of I'd rather not say."[54] It would be remembered like a long-playing multi-track record titled *An Emerging Preview of Coming Apart*. It doesn't happen here, not on our soil. If you can't speak out against something and a life is lost, something isn't right, wrong, or anything. Something was happening here, in America, her prairie vanishing as the heading turned to a new compass point. Her time in an age of innocence began its exit. An rpm was being redefined on college campuses. Voices would be silent no more.

1967 began. Time I had taken away from music ended before spring's arrival. School tuition and other expenses needed to be satisfied. Thus began a memorable year of nine till one, six days a week, in a house band at the Fireplace in Chevy Chase. Spring semester passed quickly. I embraced summer days about to begin and their uncertainty.

Artist Edward Hopper died on May 15 in his New York City studio. His was a lifetime seeing place as simple form: light, shadow, and color in the landscape of the ordinary.

How would I see the rest of my own?

The flower-filled summer of 1967 was to some the Summer of Love, one defined by the International Pop Festival in Monterey. Life brought me a bouquet of fresh warm summer nights in Chevy Chase, go-go dancers, and sweet soul music. I never lost sight how lucky I was to be who I was, what I was, and where I happened to be.

The Fireplace was a bar, once the Buffalo Tavern, in between the venerable bookends of the Chevy Chase Inn and Farmer's Jewelry on Euclid. The Toddle House, a diner Doug and I had frequented after playing, unwinding on coffee, pecan waffles, and hash browns, lived across the street.

A portrait of seven years before hangs on the, veiled, transparent wall of then. Two players—*Nighthawks*—creatures of pulp fiction, two silhouettes framed in a diner's window glass in the wee small hours of a morning. The mirage of Edward Hopper was in its gait on a midnight passage out of now to somewhere. Life itself was reflected in polished mirror glass along the back wall. Common and ordinary was brewing nearby across the long near-empty counter where we sat. Edward Hopper leaned across the counter's top to fill my cup to the brim and overflowing.

We were not a mirage. Doug and I were real. The Mag Seven was not a dream after all. Once, I wondered why I left the Magnificent 7. Ecclesiastes tells of a new season, a time for leaving and a reason for it all. The unfinished painting on the back of another canvas in time is the one we all must bear.

The house band at the Fireplace was fronted by its co-owner. Charlie Wiley knew how to manage a club, what it took to attract patrons, and hold their dedication. Charlie offered me a job in the house band. He had a Hammond M3 with a Leslie on the stage. I noticed a dusty Baldwin baby grand piano in a dark corner off the dance floor. I had a notion.

If he put the piano on the stage with the organ, I'd take his offer.

Charlie had the instrument on stage and tuned. My post time was 9:00 p.m. Monday night. The starting gate opened; the race began with the first note played. I became one of the boys in a band with no name, one with five pieces and a singer. We were Earl Grigsby bass; Eddie Beckley, guitar; Gary Falk, sax; John Oliver, drums; and Tony Stallard, organ and piano. We were Charlie's backup voices. He featured band members on some favorites of our own.

Bassist Earl Grigsby, later with the Mag Seven, toured with the Charlie Daniels Band. Earl contributed bass and backing vocals on the first three studio albums recorded by Charlie Daniels, including "Uneasy Rider," a track on *Charlie Daniels*, his first album, released in 1970. Earl worked with J.D. Souther and others in shows in Branson, Missouri, until he passed away a few years ago.

The band was a tight group of players with reason, twenty-seven hours a week, unrehearsed. We stayed together one year without change in personnel. The Fireplace featured go-go dancers, black lights, and a mirrored ball to complete its atmosphere. An image lived in this house. *Let us be* was a multi-layered body of escape, a sandwich held fast between two slices of life. One abstract, near mystical—the other, a tastier plain and generous helping of truth in sound. "Knock on Wood," "In the Midnight Hour," "Mustang Sally," "Ninety-Nine and One-Half," and "Try A Little

Tenderness." We painted Bobby Hebb with wildflowers fresh enough to gather for the sunshine bouquet he meant "Sunny" to be.

Billy Stewart's "Summertime" was a long haul.

Charlie would bring guest vocalists and other bands in for one and two-week engagements from time to time. The house band provided music between sets during appearances by the Casuals, Brenda Lee's Tour band since 1959, and Single Swingers, formerly the Mystics out of Louisville. They remain one of the best bands I ever got to work with.

We shared one night's stage with Vanilla Fudge, Billy Joe Royal, and Major Lance.

The Box Tops delivered "The Letter" to the Fireplace, first class. Local groups to show at the Fireplace while I was there included the Mag Seven, Wellingtons, and Exiles. The Mystics and Super Band came down from Louisville.

The place was packed every night. Three-hour jam sessions on Saturday showcased rhythm and blues and jazz-fused numbers. One could expect a ten-musician power plant at times. Energy in music was performed in a stunning experiment once. I remember eleven players delivering a long version of Chicago's "25 or 6 to 4."

Its echoes were with us when we took the stage at nine, the night of the same day.

August 29, 1967. Charlie Wiley knew the nature of human behavior well enough to realize we could stop the music to watch the final episode of *The Fugitive*. We found a seat next door in the Chevy Chase Inn, locally known as the CCI. The place is there today. Little has changed. We consumed chili dogs, pickled eggs, and Coca-Cola during David Janssen's last attempt to elude Lieutenant Gerard.

The company of "Red Eye," the bartender, was more than just another episode on Euclid. Absolute truth was a not-so-ordinary blend of characters in the CCI. We were suspended animation in between the Fireplace and a gas station on Euclid, around the corner from the Saratoga Restaurant. I sensed Edward Hopper had stepped away from his own painting of the scene to join us.

Sadly, the corner I once knew lost its charm, as others in Chevy Chase. The Saratoga Restaurant was razed years ago. Yesterday became a lost episode in a lifetime.

We slipped away to show patrons in the Fireplace the midnight hour and an appointment with one a.m. and a soul-filled set of good stuff.

We could be like anyone we liked. Mine was the spirit and energy of the Rascals. Felix Cavaliere became an important influence on me. He painted the summer of us all with "Groovin.'" Cincinnati found its way to the room nightly. The Casinos' hit "Then You Can Tell Me Goodbye" was one of the most requested songs we did.

"When a Man Loves a Woman" was in my bones. The Fireplace band played the song as well as I've heard it. A tenor sax and screaming Hammond M3 were our horn section. Others in the sixties would be different. 1967's summer played nice and easy.

Pat Riley frequented the Fireplace that summer. It was the place to be in my hometown. Pat was passing time until the NBA draft. He was recovering from back surgery following his senior season as an All-American at Kentucky, time before a reason to leave.

Pat bought coffee for Charlie Wiley and me at the Toddle House after hours one night, his last before leaving town. I found myself in shared company with one of my all-time favorite Kentucky basketball players for the last time. He left town the next day in a Corvette for southern California, sunshine, and the rest of his life. A sigh was heard in Dallas when the Cowboys realized the player they had drafted was not to be.

Ermal Allen made a choice and Pat Riley his own.

The 1967 Volkswagen I bought in August began a thirty-three-year, quarter-million-mile affair. The car was my escape back to simple things on the expressways of the heart. I was twenty-and-six. Three-hundred nights of full-time academic work at the university, and its toll left me no choice but to make one. This band was keeping the place packed every night. Each night mirrored an ever-changing way of life in ever-changing times. Yet, the nature of a night's scene in the Fireplace harkened back to another time.

And my sense that things had not changed that much at all, it seemed.

This nightspot, couples and singles, drinks, and dancing to good music played by a fine band, wasn't dissimilar from a big band dance hall experience of the thirties and forties. The Fireplace had a sophisticated character blended with the roadhouse of the forties and fifties.

America's escape from a bitter war in Vietnam was defined by things real and others not. Go-go dancers, white-pleated miniskirts, deep yellow-colored cheerleader sweaters, high tan boots, NBC-TV, and the girls of *Hullabaloo* were real to most, while others found comfort in the haze of a trip.

My own were imagined journeys to faraway places on a Vespa scooter or glazed tastes of long ago: Spalding's doughnuts in Gratz Park. Simply watching Catherine Deneuve dance in the fountain's waters there or the inner peace I found in a picnic on the quiet steps of Green Hills on Elmendorf Farm often seemed enough. These vibrations of silence on my soul would be forever missed were it not for the echoes.

The war remained an indelible bruise on the spirit of America. The latter part of the sixties was a contradiction of coming to terms; some tie-dying, others died trying.

Compatibility and contradiction were vying billboards all along the landscape of the sixties. Lessons learned were hard. Illusions were everywhere. Untold truths, held fast in a thick fog, momentarily mirrored our hopes, only to vanish like a vapor in the mist. The decade was a kaleidoscope turning at light speed screaming to its end. In it were ever-changing arrangements of love and hate, peace and war, in and out, black and white.

The Age of Aquarius in its dawn.

What used to be didn't seem to matter anymore. Regional beers were going the way of the blue highway, local color all but disappearing. Our lonely eyes turned, first to this, then that. Joe DiMaggio was gone, and Mrs. Robinson, what are you doing?

A field trip with architecture class during spring break brought me to New York City in 1968. She was a portrait in rose-colored glasses, aviator style, and a smile. Red light, I'm standing on the corner of Fifth Avenue and "Unforgettable" with Nancy Wilson. A lady embraced by perfume, with style and a most gentle persuasion. I wanted the light never change, to be forever red.

Two strangers—me, unknown; she, known by many.

Green light . . . an intersection. We crossed it together, side by side, then parted ways. She turned and entered Bergdorf's, never knowing how much I wanted to say, "Hello," and take her photograph with my Nikon.

The walk down the avenue to the Seagram building on Park Avenue and ice cream in Paley Park on Fifty-Third was alone. I put aside any chance of ever finding a songbird there, in the noise of the city in an oasis in midtown Manhattan. What seemed best to me after the moment, was to be in Central Park with my camera and a poem to write.

I was nearly two years since the Magnificent 7.

"Taxi."

I spent the next day with my class in New Haven and the work of Louis I. Kahn and Eero Saarinen and collegiate Gothic architecture that is the stone of Yale.

—∞—

The Wellingtons, a local band, needed a replacement on organ for the summer. They asked. I accepted. "All Along the Watchtower" and "Purple Haze" were heavy pieces to learn. Playing behind an exceptional guitarist, the late Harrison Underhill, was a blessing. Harrison, a longtime friend, had once been with the Titans, another band managed by Cecil Jones. His manner of play was effortless. I understand Harrison was offered a chance to join Edgar Winter's group on its tour later in the seventies. Somewhat shy, Harrison may not have believed he was good enough and declined.

Harrison Underhill could've been anybody's guitarist.

The Wellingtons rehearsed at the Carnaby. I was reminded of 1959, school lunch with friends, seniors in Wing's Cantonese Restaurant, now a nightspot on East Main, the Carnaby.

The two were quite different. I learned how quickly things were beginning to change that summer. Music in their sets told me so. 1968 was for many the beginning of the end of the sixties. Times had changed. Jimi Hendrix excused himself to kiss the sky. The contrast was distinctly different from the boy singing "Candy Kisses" to himself in the fifties. Such are walks and autumn leaves down one's path in Woodland Park. Such are the colors of change and my own.

An overnight stay in Delaware, Ohio, became the highlight that summer. We had dinner in the home of the Zwick family, parents of Bob Zwick, the Wellingtons' trumpet player. A blessing was said before the meal. Homegrown food prepared by Bob's mom was delicious. The dance we played in Delaware mirrored a night of innocence in motion. I fell asleep on a farm in Ohio with the notion of family, its values, and life's blessings on my mind.

The Wellingtons, having patterned themselves after the Mag Seven, enabled me to blend yet be myself. We spent the summer mostly on the road, mixing rhythm and blues with Hendrix, Buffalo Springfield, Cream, Spencer Davis Group, Chicago, and Blood, Sweat and Tears.

I looked to Harrison and listened for the Wellingtons. Playing behind his lead was an easy ride. Somehow things felt strangely different near that summer's end. Personnel, the music, and arrangements made it clear. Little seemed the same anymore.

Knowing the likely truth in that reality, when the summer ended, I did as well.

—ᴍ—

A Jackson Pollock painting seems to me a metaphor of times often perceived to be a confused random scattering of ideas. Pollock knew how to pick his colors. Each found their place on a chaotic canvas. He let it be so. What Pollock had resolved in his art wasn't always clear. It was resolved nonetheless.

The sound heard on the walls around us was the splash of an uneasy wake. Buffalo Springfield was happening out there in Laurel Canyon. Jefferson Airplane was near ready for its flight to surrealism and a rendezvous with a white rabbit.

Alice told me this was true.

Cream was beginning its rise to the top on the way to a station in a white room filled with sunshine and love. Rose-colored glasses couldn't hide the surrealistic display of unreal by folks on an eight-mile high. Summer didn't last long in 1968.

I managed enough to pay my tuition, books, and supplies for the next school year.

Silence pays a call and all that's left for an instrument's strings are a dance to mystical vibrations, in midair, alone on a tightrope between nut and bridge. The tone it makes is sad. I miss a shy smile, a simple gift he may have shared after a solo just played like no one else would've done. He never knew how good he was. —T.S. memories of a friend, Harrison Underhill.

—ᴍ—

Other times I'd get a call to substitute for someone. I played summer nights and weekends with the Eddie Everitt Band at the Congress Inn's Pub on North Broadway in the summer of '69. A band member had occasional summer camp and weekend obligations in a reserve unit

The Eddie Everitt Band was horn-driven, like a southbound freight out of Chicago. The instrument was a Hammond B3, the sound a Leslie 122. The music was blues; Blood, Sweat and Tears; and Chicago. As big and finely tuned as the music was, it simply wasn't enough. Little seemed the same anymore. Sadly, I had an up close and personal look at what I had once loved had suddenly become.

Opportunity paid an occasional visit in the early seventies. I worked with Earl Watkins and his band at the Circle H down under the bridges to Madison County. His was country music immersed in Merle Haggard, Conway Twitty, or Ray Price. The style was late sixties and early seventies. Country cooking on the banks of the Kentucky River was tasty. Shadows of two bridges rippled lazily on the shimmering current of a river on the county line.

There, I found the truth. I started loving it all over again right then, right there "classic country" at the Circle H. Bassist Johnny Ballard asked if I knew "Last Date." Floyd Cramer's slip-note style found a place beyond sheet music. The only way I knew to play these songs was by ear and memories. The piano wasn't a Steinway.

Though in the same space, I was no longer a player in a sorority and fraternity scene at the Circle H. The scent of beer and bourbon and the dancing were my only tangible connection to yesterday. A Gant shirt and tie, leather belt with a name engraved on a solid brass plate from a turf shop, khaki and madras and a pair of Weejuns were absent from the scene.

Gone was conversation with a cute coed some autumn afternoon at Sleepy Hollow on the banks of North Elkhorn Creek. The game had changed, not to be followed by another that night with Vanderbilt on Stoll Field.

Not long ago, seemed more than distant from where I happened to be.

Affairs of hearts were nothing new on Saturday night. This was the Circle H, games of chance and circumstance in a roadhouse dance hall, true romance as it were. A dance with a stranger to some; to others, the one you brought and love. Johnny Ballard could take anyone every fret of the way on a four-string bass.

Note by note, with every emotion the conscience of a note can hold.

We were together again. Johnny tugged my sleeve. "Nice crowd tonight, Tony." I led a blind friend around objects and past patrons standing there. It was never with the same sureness of a friend leading me around and through a song since the echoes of Danceland were born.

A Saturday night anymore was a honky-tonk and the truth under the bridges to Madison County. My river was between the banks of Town Branch and the Kentucky, my emotions somewhere in between Danceland and the Circle H. Going out near the top of one's game on the county line is a silent noise. The Circle H experience with the Earl Watkins band was tangible. I was a player, just another face in the place, another verse in the way the song would eventually play out. Now and then someone might call. "Tony, can you play this weekend?"

The long run ended in the early seventies. Time passed, the calls were no more, and I got on with the rest of my life.

—~—

The decade turned to another. Daria Halprin had a date with a stranger at Zabriskie. An appointment was more than just another strange point of rendezvous for two people in complicated times. A fast-approaching storm appeared on the mirror of my last college spring. Now was delivered to our doorstep time after time. Then was never far behind: a relentless war, Kent State, an ROTC building in flames, and National Guard on our own campus.

What had we to do with the crosses we would bear?

In the middle of it all, we were putting the last lines and polish on our architecture thesis projects in Pence Hall. Graduation day came suddenly. The whole world was watching and ceremonies were cancelled for the University of Kentucky Class of 1970.

All we ever wanted in the sixties was the truth.

Midsummer. Sunshine filled an afternoon. Our wedding beside a birch tree in her yard. The rest of our lives waited, like a swing in a shade tree's cool. We heard the voice of a summer wind.

The swing moved in an easy way.

—~—

Chances are, on some special evening, the Magnificent 7 was your band. Being with another, anywhere else, was simply out of the question.

Separate pieces of a band.

The Magnificent 7
Doug Hammonds—Tenor/Baritone Saxophone

Doug was mellow as nights outside Danceland, the two of us listening to rhythm and blues at its best. Doug and me waited for Charlie Bishop's band or the Houserockers to arrive on a night's train. Doug was Toddle House, pecan waffles, hash browns, and coffee in a diner on Euclid in Chevy Chase around 2:00 a.m. "Green Dolphin Street" was a song we both liked.

"Time to take me home, Tone."

Author's note: Sadly, my friend Doug Hammonds passed away in 2011 near Lexington. Doug, a musician all his life, later after leaving the Mag 7, became a member of the Tren-Dells during the eighties, featuring a fine, fine horn section. It's hard for me to think of R & B being any better; I believe it to be the best lineup ever for that band.

Larry Kelly—Drums/Percussion

Larry was the only true flower child I ever knew. Without compromise, he experienced everything the late sixties had to give and never changed.

John Page—Bass

John was complex and quiet, often distant. I can't recall a note he ever missed. John and I remain friends, sharing thoughts and ideas of music and architecture and life. I deeply admire what he has done with his own in the years since our college experience. I remember long nights in architecture design studio, putting ideas with pen and ink on sketch paper, boards, and building models for juried presentations.

Johnny Burrows—Trumpet/Flugelhorn

Johnny was somewhere between a lost little boy and a question: "I wonder whatever became of my friend?" Johnny was our most accomplished musician. He later changed his instrument of choice to valve trombone after a move to California in the seventies, when I last saw him.

Author's Note: John passed away three days after Thanksgiving Day 2005 in Salinas, California. John had come 'round right as the Shakers might say. I sent him a copy of the manuscript for this book in the months before he was gone. Despite illness, he was able to complete his reading, saying how much it meant to him. My question found an answer.

Larry Orr—Lead Vocals

Larry was often like someone out of a novel. A fresh story was written by the Temptashuns around his character sometime in the summer of 1963. An enormous talent, Larry could park a song in any space reserved for the band and its audience.

Carter Hackney—Lead Guitar.

A fine guitarist and solid musician. We liked the best to be found in all kinds of music, though our paths diverged now and then, my painting outside the lines of music theory.

Author's note: Sadly, my friend Carter Hackney passed away in 2016 in Lexington.

Meade Brown—Drums/Percussion.

Meade was a terrific drummer, serious when the curtain went up. He could put us where we needed to be. From countdown to song's end, from R & B to "Take Five."

Me—Hammond Organ/Piano

I'm on a time train. I go to Shakertown with Nancy now and then. Once a day, a stop at yesterday is more than a rule I live by.

—ᨓ—

January 1, 2000 . . . reflections on the twentieth century and the best years in my life.

The sixties changed us all. We could've remained relics of their years. We refused to let it be so. I found kindness and truth on the road to my inner tree. Loving will get one by most anything. I love you, more than enough.

June 20, 1999, Father's Day.

I stopped in Lebanon near the end of a day trip with Nancy. The Club 68, where the band had frequently played, was gone. One object remained where I remembered it to be. The nightspot's sign on Highway 68 was a not-so-ordinary piece of yesterday. Our name was once in its lights, silhouettes on the stage of an illuminated sky.

Appearing Tonight . . . Seven players.

The ghost of a faded memory was thick on the air on the face of an empty sign. I was the only one in the band appearing at the Club 68 that day. I took some photographs before leaving.

The sun was on a kind fade-away, to a place beyond the Pacific Ocean's sky.

How near we came to something thought to be out of reach, we'll never know. The Magnificent 7 went away winners with no regrets. I can only imagine what the band may have become had we stayed together. I can think of nothing better than to have been a collection of players, deliciously playing "Who's Cheatin' Who." Soul with an unmistakable hue, creatively presented with a bunch of energy sounds about right.

As near Little Milton's band as I could hope for.

We could've had Paris.

This ten-year affair with life was no ordinary experience. An uncommon history shaped by visual gifts wrapped in ribbons that are yesterday's blue highway. Ours led to creative expressions on a ribbon of magnetic recording tape. It happened in my life, all the way from the Hilltoppers to the Beatles, from one "P.S. I Love You" to another, 1953–1963.

We went from Buddy Holly to Woodstock, 1959–1969.

Ten years shaped by what defined an in between and a coming-of-age.

People come to empty fields for different reasons to plant themselves. One's history can be found in the wake of harvest. I carried Emily's echo all the way from *Our Town* to your band.

"Oh earth, you're too wonderful for anybody to realize you. Do any human beings ever realize life while they live it? Every, every minute?"[55]

The End

Acknowledgments

An unconditional gift from others is priceless. I am grateful for the steady and determined support of Patricia Ranft. The encouragement of Mickey Settle and advice given me by the late Don Edwards. The guidance of author, Milt Toby, and my publisher for helping me take this book to the street. Those who followed the Temptashuns and Magnificent 7 when life was still young, who continue to remember the band beyond its years. The late Cecil Jones for believing in us, enough to give the band a chance. Radio personalities who played our records and tracked our charts. Mike Marsh and the *Rocket Boys* for their taped documentation of sound, in a band's beginning. Creative session players on the coasts and in-between during the late 1950s and early 1960s who did it right.

A memory, whose silent voice told me there was a deeper meaning to the pieces in it all.

—A.S.

Endnotes

Chapter 1

1 Simone, Nina, "Wild is the Wind," Dimitri Tiomkin and Ned Washington.
2 Lightfoot, Gordon, "The Wreck of the Edmund Fitzgerald," Mouse Music Ltd.-CAPAC, Reprise REP 14451, music from the album Summertime Dream.
3 From the Negro Spirituals.

Chapter 2

4 Lee, Harper (novel) and Foote, Horton (screenplay), from the film To Kill a Mockingbird, Universal International Pictures, 1962.
5 Guthrie, A.B. Jr, The Blue Hen's Chick: An Autobiography, University of Nebraska Press, 1993, originally published, 1965. p. 22.
6 Lexington Herald, July 16, 1953.
7 Granata, Charles L., Sessions with Sinatra; Frank Sinatra and the Art of Recording, A Capella Books, An imprint of Chicago Review Press, Inc., 1999. pp. 115-117.
8 Words spoken by Grace Kelly, To Catch a Thief, Directed by Alfred Hitchcock, Paramount Pictures, Hollywood, Calif. 1955.
9 Lee, Brenda, Little Miss Dynamite, The Life and Times of Brenda Lee, Hyperion Books, 2002. From Little Miss Dynamite, p. 30.
10 Guralnick, Peter and Jorgenson, Ernst, Elvis Day By Day: The Definitive Record of His Life and Music, Ballantine Books, 1999. p. 106.

Chapter 6

11 Granata, Charles L., Sessions with Sinatra; Frank Sinatra and the Art of Recording, A Capella Books, An imprint of Chicago Review Press, Inc., 1999. p.115.
12 Guralnick, Peter and Jorgenson, Ernst, Elvis Day By Day: The Definitive Record of His Life and Music, Ballantine Books, 1999. p. 66.
13 Murray, Robert K. & Brucker, Roger W., Trapped! The Story of Floyd Collins, Kentucky, 1979. p. 220.
14 Ridington, Amber, Ph.D., Rovers, Wrestlers & Stars, 'The Quonset Auditorium.' Folklore from the writer and Producer of this documentary presented on KET, Kentucky Education Television, 2010. Permission to use was granted by the Writer/Producer.
15 Eng, Steve, A Satisfied Mind, The Country Music Life of Porter Wagoner, Rutledge Hill Press, Nashville, Tennessee, 1992. p.108.
16 Jennings, Waylon with Kaye, Lenny, Waylon, Warner Books, Inc., New York, N.Y., 1996. p. 116.
17 Jones, Margaret, Patsy, The Life and Times of Patsy Cline, HarperCollins Publishers, Inc., New York, N.Y., 1994. p. 85.
18 Lee, Brenda, Little Miss Dynamite, The Life and Times of Brenda Lee, Hyperion Books, 2002. p. 78.

Chapter 7

19 Jones, Margaret, Patsy, The Life and Times of Patsy Cline, HarperCollins Publishers, Inc., New York, N.Y., 1994. p. 151.
20 Jones, Margaret, Patsy, The Life and Times of Patsy Cline, HarperCollins Publishers, Inc., New York, N.Y., 1994. pp. 194-195.
21 Jones, Margaret, Patsy, The Life and Times of Patsy Cline, HarperCollins Publishers, Inc., New York, N.Y., 1994. p. 195.
22 Words and inspiration from the Negro spiritual.
23 Lyrics from The Big Book of Country Music, Hal Leonard, Winona, Minn., 1997. p. 11.
24 Eng, Steve, A Satisfied Mind, The Country Music Life of Porter Wagoner, Rutledge Hill Press, Nashville, Tennessee, 1992. p. 132.

Chapter 8

25 Nancy Loughridge or Gay Gish, The Kernel, ca. autumn 1963.
26 A comment by Nancy Loughridge or Gay Gish in The Kernel, ca. autumn 1963.
27 Nancy Loughridge or Gay Gish, The Kernel, ca. autumn 1963.
28 KET, West Point, a documentary program presented on Kentucky Educational Television, Lexington, Ky., January 30, 2002.
29 The Kentucky Kernel, Friday, Feb. 14, 1964, page 3.
30 Guralnick, Peter, Sweet Soul Music, Rhythm and Blues and the Southern Dream of Freedom, Harper & Row, Publishers, New York, N.Y., 1986. p. 177.
31 Schuster, Joe, "Long Live The King", EveryBody's News, Cincinnati's Free News, Arts & Entertainment Weekly, Issue #289, March 25-31, 1994.
32 Guralnick, Peter, Sweet Soul Music, Rhythm and Blues and the Southern Dream of Freedom, Harper & Row, Publishers, New York, N.Y., 1986. pp. 240-242.
33 Crawford, Richard, America's Musical Life, W.W. Norton & Company, Inc., 2001. p. 797.
34 Editors of Country Music Magazine, The Comprehensive Country Music Encyclopedia, Country Music Magazine/Times Books, a Division of Random House, Inc., New York, 1994. p. 236.
35 Ward, Terry, "Teen Landmark Vanishes," Montage … A journal of life in Marion County, Vol. 8, No. 2, pages 14-19, The Lebanon Enterprise, summer 1998.
36 From the pages of The Kentucky Kernel a Full-page Publicity Photo and event announcement, The Temptashuns, King Records. The Kentucky Kernel, Tues., Nov. 3, 1964, Page 8." (This page, shared with the Torques', was a promotional advertisement by Cecil Jones Entertainment).

Chapter 10

37 The Kentucky Kernel, Friday, Jan. 15, 1965, p. 3.

38 The Kentucky Kernel, Thursday, Feb. 4, 1965, p. 2.

39 The Kentucky Kernel, Thursday, Feb. 4, 1965, p. 1.

40 Waller, Don, The Motown Story, Charles Scribner's Sons, New York, 1985. p. 108.

41 Aronson, Virginia, The History of Motown, Chelsea House Publications, Philadelphia PA, 2001, p. 24.

42 The Kentucky Kernel, Bulletin Board, March 31, 1965.

43 The Kentucky Kernel, Thursday, April 8, 1965, p. 5.

44 Dylan, Bob, "Like a Rolling Stone," Columbia-4-443346, SESAC, 1965.

45 Crawford, Richard, America's Musical Life, W.W. Norton & Company, Inc., 2001. p. 792.

46 The Kentucky Kernel, Thursday, Sept. 16, 1965, p. 3.

47 From the pages of The Kentucky Kernel, 1965.

Chapter 11

48 University of Kentucky yearbook, The Kentuckian, 1966, p. 250.

49 Zeh, John, "Billy Love Leaving Local Radio Scene," The Kentucky Kernel, Thursday, March 24, 1966, p. 6.

50 Bashe, Philip, Teenage Idol, Travelin' Man: The complete biography of Rick Nelson, Hyperion, New York, N.Y., 1992. p. 239.

51 Zeh, John, "Songs From The Past Offered In Show" . . . an excerpt from a review of the Little Kentucky Derby Concert, The Kentucky Kernel, Monday April 18, 1966, p. 2.

52 Billboard, June 4, 1966

53 A goodbye inspired by lyrics from "The Days of Wine and Roses" by Henry Mancini and Johnny Mercer and Cole Porter's "Ev'ry Time We Say Goodbye."

Chapter 12 Epilogue

54 Lyrics in a song from the '40s titled, "Somewhere in England," RCA-Victor B-11129, recorded by Vaughn Monroe.

55 Wilder, Thornton, Our Town, HarperCollins Publishers, Inc., New York, N.Y., 1938. p. 108, Act III.

Bibliography

The following books and magazine articles were either referenced or quoted by the author in the preceding text: Most published sources are clearly identified in the text. Others are cited by chapter in the end notes, but they represent a small part of the actual research. Interview sources are listed at the end of this Bibliography.

Billboard magazine

The Kentucky Kernel, Student Newspaper, University of Kentucky, Lexington, Ky.

WLAP Radio Survey

WVLK Radio Survey

Bashe, Philip, Teenage Idol, Travelin' Man: The complete biography of Rick Nelson, Hyperion, 1992.
Hyperion
114 Fifth Avenue
New York, N.Y. 10011

Carr, Patrick, The Illustrated History of Country Music. Garden City, New York. Doubleday & Company, Inc., 1979.

Editors of Country Music Magazine, The Comprehensive Country Music Encyclopedia, Country Music Magazine/Times Books, a Division of Random House, Inc., New York, 1994.

Crawford, Richard, America's Musical Life, W.W. Norton & Company, Inc., 2001.
W.W. Norton & Company, Inc.
500 Fifth Avenue
New York, N.Y. 10110
www.wwnorton.com

Eng, Steve, A Satisfied Mind, The Country Music Life of Porter Wagoner, Rutledge Hill Press, Nashville, Tennessee, 1992.
Rutledge Hill Press
513 Third Avenue South
Nashville, Tennessee 37210

Granata, Charles L., Sessions with Sinatra; Frank Sinatra and the Art of Recording, A Capella Books, An imprint of Chicago Review Press, Inc., 1999.
A Capella Books
814 North Franklin Street
Chicago, Illinois 60610

Guralnick, Peter and Jorgenson, Ernst, Elvis Day By Day: The Definitive Record of His Life and Music, Ballantine Books, 1999.
The Ballantine Publishing Group, a division of
Random House, Inc.
New York, N.Y.

Guralnick, Peter, Last Train to Memphis, Back Bay Books, Little, Brown and Company, Boston, New York, Toronto, London, 1994.
Guralnick, Peter, Sweet Soul Music, Rhythm and Blues and the Southern Dream of Freedom, Harper & Row, Publishers, New York, N.Y., 1986.
Harper & Row, Publishers Inc.
10 East 53rd Street
New York, N.Y. 10022
Bertrum, Alfred, Guthrie, A.B. Jr, The Blue Hen's Chick: An Autobiography, University of Nebraska Press, 1993, originally published, 1965.
Jennings, Waylon with Kaye, Lenny, Waylon, Warner Books, Inc., New York, N.Y., 1996.
Warner Books, Inc.
1271 Avenue of the Americas
New York, N.Y. 10020
Jones, Margaret, Patsy, The Life and Times of Patsy Cline, HarperCollins Publishers, Inc., New York, N.Y., 1994.
Lee, Brenda, Little Miss Dynamite, The Life and Times of Brenda Lee, Hyperion Books, 2002.
Hyperion Books Hyperion
77 West 66th St.
New York, N.Y. 10023-6298
Lehmer, Larry, The Day the Music Died; The Last Tour of Buddy Holly, The "Big Bopper" and Ritchie Valens, Schirmer Books, 1997.
Schirmer Books
1633 Broadway
New York, NY 10019
Murray, Robert K. & Brucker, Roger W., Trapped! The Story of Floyd Collins, Kentucky, 1979.
The University Press of Kentucky
663 South Limestone Street
Lexington, KY 40508
Pierce, Patricia Jobe, The Ultimate Elvis, Elvis Presley Day By Day, Simon &. Schuster, New York, New York, 1994.
Simon & Schuster
1230 Avenue of the Americas
New York, New York 10020
Rice, Russell, Kentucky Basketball's Big Blue Machine, Strode, 1976.
The Strode Publishers, Inc.
Huntsville, AL 35802
Ridington, Amber, Ph.D., Rovers, Wrestlers & Stars, 'The Quonset Auditorium.'
Folklore from the writer and Producer of this documentary presented on KET, Kentucky Education Television, 2010. 600 Cooper Drive, Lexington, KY 40502.
Schuster, Joe, "Long Live The King," EveryBody's News, Cincinnati's Free News, Arts & Entertainment Weekly, Issue # 289, March 25-31, 1994.

Selvin, Joel, Ricky Nelson; Idol for a Generation, Contemporary Books, Inc., Chicago, Illinois, 1990.
Waller, Don, The Motown Story, Charles Scribner's Sons, New York, 1985.
Ward, Terry, "Teen Landmark Vanishes," Montage . . . A journal of life in Marion County, Vol. 8, No. 2, pages 14-19, The Lebanon Enterprise, summer 1998.
Wilder, Thornton, Our Town, HarperCollins Publishers, Inc., New York, N.Y., 1938, 1965.
HarperCollins Publishers, Inc.
10 East 53rd Street
New York, NY 10022
Zeh, John, "Billy Love Leaving Local Radio Scene," The Kentucky Kernel, Thursday, March 24, 1966, Page 6.
Zeh, John, Songs From The Past Offered In Show . . . an excerpt from a review of the Little Kentucky Derby Concert, The Kentucky Kernel, Monday April 18, 1966, Page 2.

Sources of Research and Enrichment:

Collectors Choice Music, A catalog of music and a wealth of music history.
Music Business magazine.
"Singles Reviews," Record World, Vol. 19, No. 929, Page 8, March 27, 1965.
"Stubborn Kind of Fellow"/"In Mist and Rain" received a Three Star Pick Review.
Reminisce Magazine, Reiman Publications, 5400 S. 60th St., Greendale, WI
"Fond Flashbacks", a look at specific years from the past, recalling the people, places and events that made the news.
Vanity Fair Magazine, 4 Times Square, New York, N.Y.
Alexander, Paul, Boulevard of Broken Dreams: The Life, Times, and Legend of James Dean, Penguin Books USA, Inc., 1994.
Penguin Books USA, Inc.
375 Hudson Street
New York, New York 10014
Amburn, Ellis, Buddy Holly: a biography, St. Martin's Press, 1995.
St. Martin's Press
175 Fifth Avenue
New York, N.Y. 10010
Anonson, Virginia, The History of Motown, Chelsea House Publishers, 2001.
Chelsea House Publishers
Philadelphia, Pennsylvania
www.chelseahouse.com
Atkins, Chet with Bill Neely, Country Gentleman, Henry Regnery Company, 1974.

Henry Regnery Company
114 West Illinois Street
Chicago, Illinois 60610

Aquila, Richard, That Old Time Rock and Roll; A Chronicle of an Era, 1954-1963, Shirmer Books, A division of Macmillan, Inc., New York, 1989.
Macmillan, Inc.
866 Third Avenue
New York, N.Y. 10022

Bacon, Tony, 50 Years of Fender, Balafon /Miller Freeman Books, 2000.
Balafon Books
115J Cleveland Street
London, W1P 5PN England

Campbell, Glen and Carter, Tom, Rhinestone Cowboy, Villard Books, 1994.
Villard Books, a division of
Random House, Inc.
New York, N.Y.

Caraway, Robin, Newport The Sin City Years, Arcadia Publishing, Charleston, SC, 2002.
Arcadia Publishing
2 Cumberland Street
Charleston, SC 29401

Caskette, Alan, The Harmony Illustrated Encyclopedia of Country Music, Crown Publishers, Inc., New York, N.Y., 1986, 1994.
Crown Publishers, Inc.
201 East 50th Street
New York, N.Y. 10022

Clayson, Alan, Only The Lonely, Roy Orbison's Life and Legacy, St. Martin's Press, New York, N.Y., 1989.
St. Martin's Press
175 Fifth Avenue
New York, N.Y. 10010

Country: The Music and the Musicians Published for the Country Music Foundation by Abbeville Press, Inc., 1988.

Darin, Dodd, Dream Lovers (the magnificent shattered lives of Bobby Darin and Sandra Dee), Warner Books, Inc., New York, N.Y., 1994.
Warner Books, Inc.
1271 Avenue of the Americas
New York, N.Y. 10020

Dawidoff, Nicholas, In The Country of Country, People and Places in American Music, Pantheon Books, a division of Random House, Inc., New York, N.Y., 1997.
Random House, Inc.
New York, N.Y.
www.randomhouse.com

Dickerson, James, Goin' Back To Memphis; A Century of Blues, Rock 'n' Roll and Glorious Soul, Shirmer Books, New York, 1996.

Edwards, Don, Life is Like a Horse Race, the Lexington Herald-Leader Company, 1999.

Emery, Ralph with Cox, Patsi Bale, The View From Nashville, William Morrow and Company, Inc., New York, N.Y., 1998.
William Morrow and Company, Inc.
1350 Avenue of The Americas
New York, N.Y. 10019
www.williammorrow.com

Emery, Ralph with Cox, Patsi Bale, 50 Years Down a Country Road, HarperCollins Publishers Inc., 2000.
HarperCollins Publishers Inc.
10 East 53rd Street
New York, N.Y. 10022

Escott, Colin with Hawkins, Martin, Good Rockin' Tonight, Sun Records And The Birth Of Rock 'N' Roll, St. Martin's Press, New York, N. Y., 1991.
St. Martin's Press
175 Fifth Avenue
New York, N.Y. 10010

Fitzgerald, F. Scott, The Great Gatsby, Simon and Schuster Inc., New York, N.Y., 1925.
Simon and Schuster Inc.
Rockefeller Center
1230 Avenue of The Americas
New York, N.Y. 10020

Ford, Thomas W., A.B. Guthrie, Jr., Twayne Publishers, a division of G.K. Hall & Co., Boston, 1981.

Freeth, Nick and Alexander, Charles, The Electric Guitar, Courage Books, An imprint of Running Press Book Publishers, Philadelphia, Pennsylvania, 1999.
Running Press Book Publishers
125 South One Twenty-Second Street
Philadelphia, Pennsylvania, 199103-4399

Gaines, Steven, Heroes & Villains; The True Story of The Beach Boys, New American Library, 1986.
New American Library (NAL Books)
1633 Broadway
New York, New York 10019

Halprin, Lawrence, The RSVP Cycles: Creative Processes in the Human Environment, George Braziller, Inc., New York, N. Y., 1969.
George Braziller, Inc.
One Park Avenue
New York, N. Y. 1016

Jensen, Joli, The Nashville Sound: Authenticity, Commercialization, and Country Music, CMF and Vanderbilt University Press, 1998.
The Country Music Foundation Press and Vanderbilt University Press Nashville and London.
Judd, Naomi, Love Can Build a Bridge, Villard Books, a division of Random House, Inc., New York, 1993.
Jorgensen, Ernst, Elvis Presley: A Life in Music, The Complete Recording Sessions, St Martin's Griffin, 1998.
St Martin's Griffin
175 Fifth Avenue
New York, N.Y.10010
Mason, Bobbie Ann, Clear Springs, Random House, Inc., New York, N.Y., 1999.
Random House, Inc.
New York, N.Y.
www.randomhouse.com
Mason, Bobbie Ann, Elvis Presley, Penguin Putnam, Inc., New York, N.Y., 2003.
Penguin Putnam, Inc.
375 Hudson Street
New York, N.Y.
Kingsbury Paul, The Grand Ole Opry History of Country Music. New York: Villard Books, a Division of Random House, 1995.
Lewis, Thomas S.W., Empire of the Air, HarperCollins Publishers, 1991.
HarperCollins Publishers
10 East 53rd Street
New York, NY 10022
Malone, Bill, Country Music USA. Published for the American Folklore Society by The University of Texas Press, Austin and London, 1968.
McNutt, Randy, King Records of Cincinnati, Arcadia Publishing, Charleston, SC, 2002.
Arcadia Publishing
2 Cumberland Street
Charleston, SC 29401
Neely, Tim, Standard Catalog of American Records, Krause Publications, Iola, Wisconsin, 2000.
Krause Publications
700 E. State Street
Iola, WI 54990-0001
Nite, Norman E., Rock On, Harper & Row, Publishers, New York, N.Y., 1974, 1982.
Noyer, Paul Du, The Billboard Illustrated Encyclopedia of Music, Billboard Books, An imprint of Watson Guptill Publications, New York, 2003.
Oermann, Robert K., America's Music, The Roots of Country, Turner Publishing, Inc., Atlanta, Georgia, 1966.

Turner Publishing, Inc.
1050 Techwood Drive, NW
Atlanta, Georgia 30318

Pugh, Ronnie, Ernest Tubb; The Texas Troubadour, Duke University Press, Durham, London, 1996.
Contemporary Books, Inc.
180 North Michigan Avenue
Chicago, Illinois, 60601

Shestack, Melvin, The Country Music Encyclopedia, Thomas Y. Crowell Company, New York, KBO Publishers, 1974.

Smith, Gerald L., Ph.D., Black America Series, Lexington, Kentucky, Arcadia Publishing, Charleston, SC, 2002.
Arcadia Publishing
2 Cumberland Street
Charleston, SC 29401

Smith, Joe, Off The Record, an oral history of popular music, Warner Books, New York, N.Y. 1988.
Warner Books, Inc.
666 Fifth Avenue
New York N.Y. 10103

Streissguth, Michael, Eddy Arnold, Pioneer of the Nashville Sound, Schirmer Books, An Imprint of Simon & Schuster Macmillan, 1997.
Schirmer Books
1633 Broadway
New York, New York 10019

Szatmary, David P., Rockin' In Time; A Social History of Rock-And-Roll, Prentice Hall, 1987.
Prentice Hall
A Simon & Schuster Company
Englewood Cliffs, New Jersey 07632

Tracy, Steven C., Going to Cincinnati; A History of the Blues in the Queen City, University of Illinois Press, 1993.

Ward, Ed, Stokes, Geoffrey and Tucker, Ken, Rock of Ages, The Rolling Stone History of Rock and Roll, Summit Books, A Division of Simon and Schuster, Inc., 1986.
Simon and Schuster, Inc.
1230 Avenue of the Americas
New York, New York 10020

Wertheimer, Alfred, Photographs; Perry, Jr., the E. Warren and Henderson, Amy, Essays, Elvis 1956 Published on the occasion of the Smithsonian traveling exhibition Elvis at 21, Welcome Books, New York, 2009.

White, Timothy, The Nearest Faraway Place; Brian Wilson, The Beach Boys, And The Southern California Experience, Henry Holt and Company, Inc., 1994.
Henry Holt and Company, Inc.

115 West 18th Street
New York, New York 10011

Wolfe, Charles K., Tennessee Strings; The Story of Country Music in Tennessee, The University of Tennessee Press, Knoxville, 1977.
The University of Tennessee Press
Knoxville, Tenn.

Yearbooks of life at the University of Kentucky, Lexington, Kentucky depicting the times and their change in a decade of change.

1963 Kentuckian Vol. 65, 1964 Kentuckian Vol. 66, 1965 Kentuckian Vol. 67, 1966 Kentuckian Vol. 68, (Page 330). 1967 Kentuckian One and Two, '68 Kentuckian and '69 Kentuckian.

Polk's Lexington (Fayette County, Ky.) City Directory, Vol. 1954 XXXI

Polk's Lexington (Fayette County, Ky.) City Directory, Vol. 1958 XXXIV, R. L. Polk & Co., Publishers, 12th and Central Pkwy, P.O. Box 225, Cincinnati 1, Ohio (Original address of the Publisher).

Interviews:

Dugo, Mike, '60s Garage Bands, a Q&A interview, 2010.

NPR National Public Radio, All Things Considered, Remembering Grady Martin, Interview with bassist and session musician member of the A-Team Bob Moore from Nashville, Tennessee, December 10, 2001. A Celebration of the life of guitarist Grady Martin who passed away on Monday December 3, 2001 after a long illness was held in Nashville.

Author's note: I was blessed to have met Mr. Martin at RCA Studio B in Nashville in August, 1962 and another occasion while visiting a recording session in 1964 in Columbia Records' Studio (the original Owen Bradley Quonset hut on 16th Ave. South). Grady Martin was the session's lead guitarist. He had an uncommon touch with his instrument, making the difficult journey from mind to strings seem effortless.

—T.S.
Lexington
2017

Discography

People, Places, and Making the Music.

Session personnel are all members of The Temptashuns/Magnificent 7. Other musicians and singers are listed where appropriate. All recordings were produced on 45-RPM vinyl singles and packaged in plain paper slipcovers.

Lemco release of "Strawberry Man"/"Sexy Ways" was packaged in the same format as used for LP Albums in a 45-rpm size. Titles and Photograph of The Temptashuns appeared on the cover. Original liner notes, written by the author for record's release, were not included in artwork.

All sessions were recorded monaurally. Various pickup mics used were Telefunken, Neumann, Shure, and Altec. Organ was wired directly to console of recording mixer on all recordings after "Autumn Love" and "The Big B."

Mastering was done in Nashville, Tenn. at 15 i.p.s. from a monaural tape, most likely on a Scully lathe, employing a Westrex head. Liner notes, from albums recorded in the Quonset hut by other artists, note the Scully was the mastering lathe used at Columbia's Bradley Recording Studio at the time

Session notes:

Sessions 1, 2*, 5, 6, 7, 8** and 9 were recorded in Lemco Recording Studios, Lexington, Ky.

Session produced by: Cecil Jones and The Temptashuns/Magnificent 7.

Recording Engineer: Cecil Jones

Sound Technician: Cecil Jones

Studio Mix: Cecil Jones

Engineered and Mastered at Owen Bradley/Columbia Recording Studios, Nashville, Tenn. Columbia Audio Engineer: Not known

Records production: Columbia Records, Terre Haute, Ind.

** Session 2 photography: Bedford Studio, Lexington. Artwork layout and liner notes for record sleeve: Tony Stallard.*

Session 3 and 4 tracks were recorded in King Recording Studios, Cincinnati, Ohio.

*** Session 8 tracks were re-recorded in Columbia's Bradley Recording Studios, Nashville, Tenn.*

Original recordings by The Temptashuns and Magnificent 7 bands were released on 7 record labels; Lemco, Federal; a subsidiary of King Records, Dial, Sue, Symbol, Eastern, and EMI/Stateside, London (2005) and EMI (America).

Session 1 1963
Autumn Love b/w The Big 'B'

Session 2 1964
Sexy Ways b/w Strawberry Man

Session 3 1964
Pretty Ways b/w Strawberry Man

Session 4 1964
You're Gonna' Cry b/w Love Gone, Love Return

Session 5 1964
Stubborn Kind of Fellow b/w In Mist and Rain

Session 6 1966 (Private Release)
Gigi b/w Stubborn Kind of Fellow

Session 7 1966
She's Called a Woman b/w Since You've Been Gone So Long

The song, "She's Called a Woman," is included in a 27-Track Album, released in the summer of 2005 titled, Soul of Sue Records: New York City, EMI. Original recordings were remastered at Abbey Road Studios, London.

The song, "She's Called a Woman," is also included on Disc 4, Track 24, in a 4-CD boxed set album, released in 1994 titled, The Sue Records Story: New York City, EMI (America) label, EMI 7243 8 28093 2 6.

Session 8 1968
Ooh, Baby Baby b/w Never Will I (Make My Baby Cry)

Session 9 ca. 1969
Take Me On b/w Skokie Drive

About the Author

Tony Stallard is a writer-musician born in Kentucky. Raised and educated in Lexington, receiving a Bachelor of Architecture, University of Kentucky 1970. Retired, following thirty-five years an architect, Tony's Silent Pictures of creative expression in words and still-photographs, blended with music, presented now and then as Time Train, are passions handled with care.

Tony's poetry and nonfiction pieces have appeared in *Kentucky Monthly* magazine, *The Apalachicola Times* newspaper, and a comment of the month featured in *Garden & Gun* magazine.

Sadly, Tony slipped away on August 20, 2020.

Index